Class E 4-4-0 No. 157 heading a Continental boat train on the former timber viaduct

THE SOUTH EASTERN
AND
CHATHAM RAILWAY

By

O. S. NOCK
B.Sc., M.I.C.E., M.I.Mech.E., M.I.Loco.E.

LONDON:

Ian Allan Ltd

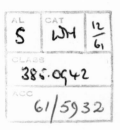
Made and printed in England by
STAPLES PRINTERS LIMITED
at their Rochester, Kent, establishment

Contents

Bibliography

History of the Southern Railway (1936), C. F. Dendy-Marshall.
Express Trains English and Foreign (1889), Foxwell and Farrer.

British Railways:
  The South Eastern (1893), J. Pearson Pattinson.
  The London Chatham & Dover (1897), J. Pearson Pattinson.

Autobiography of Samuel Smiles (1905).
The South Eastern Railway (1953), R. W. Kidner.
The London Chatham & Dover Railway (1952), R. W. Kidner.
Boat Trains and Channel Packets (1957), Rixon Bucknall.
S.E.C.R. Locomotives 1898–1923 (1947), F. Burtt.
The Gateway of England (1956), Rivers Scott.
The Locomotives of R. E. L. Maunsell (1954), O. S. Nock.
The Locomotives of the London Chatham & Dover Railway (1960), D. L. Bradley.
The Official Guide to the S.E.C.R. (1912).
The Centenary of Ashford Works (1947).
Bradshaw's Railway Manual, Shareholders Guide & Directory (1914).
Journal of the Stephenson Locomotive Society, Aug. 1958; April 1959; January 1960.

Preface

LOOKED at in the broadest sense there is romance in the beginnings, the rise and the development of any large business undertaking; but if ever there was a railway system the progress of which could be epitomized by the word romance in its most spectacular and theatrical meaning that system was the South Eastern & Chatham. Taken together, the South Eastern and the London Chatham & Dover railways had all the character of some complex, but intensely human personality. There were moments of solemnity and high endeavour, wild flights of fancy, moments of drama, and no less of high comedy, times of dire financial trouble, law suits, grievous setbacks by fire, robbery, and a cataclysm of nature in the Warren landslip of 1877. It all reads like the ingredients of a vivid saga of Victorian life in England as told by Charles Dickens. And then out of this maelstrom comes the working union of 1899, and the eventual emergence of the South Eastern & Chatham as one of the smartest, best run, and most punctual railways in the whole kingdom.

In a book of this size one cannot do more than touch upon the mere outline of the events taking place in the wild, competitive days of old. Through the kindness of Mr L. C. Johnson, Archivist of the British Transport Commission, I have been able to study the old minute books of the Boards of the South Eastern and the London Chatham & Dover railways, and from those old records, set out in the copperplate handwriting of the day, one can sense the atmosphere of many a stormy meeting, as when the Chatham neared its financial crash, or when Watkin forced the resignation of Cudworth. Samuel Smiles in his autobiography gives us no more than a glimpse of South Eastern affairs, and one would dearly like to have heard verbatim some of the orations whereby the rival colossi ruled their respective railways. One comes to feel that Forbes always had the edge on Watkin. The South Eastern Chairman was all the time dour, grim, and relentless, whereas the immense responsibility of the precarious Chatham finances rested lightly on Forbes's shoulders, and in his memorable cartoon 'Spy' catches the light touch, the impish sense of humour that enabled Forbes to ride out storm after storm, and to enjoy life to the full.

At the turn of the century the story changes from inter-railway warfare, clashes of personality and the elements of melodrama to an account of first class railway management, and I am glad to be old enough to have seen many of its results at first hand. But one's own personal observations could form no more than a drop in the ocean against so vast a subject as the S.E.C.R., and its constituents, and in addition to studying the works listed in the bibliography I have had help from a number of good friends. From the Southern Region of British Railways I have had footplate passes, and the loan of many photographs; Mr Charles E. Lee and Mr H. A. Vallance have made available to me books from their personal libraries, while the municipal authorities of Folkestone and Dover have put their local records at my disposal. I am particularly grateful to the Dover Harbour Board and to their Chief Engineer, Mr J. W. Sutton, for much information about the successive additions to the Admiralty Pier, and the building of the Marine Station. Above all there is the Curator of Historical Relics, British Transport Commission, who has in his care that priceless relic the Wainwright Class 'D' 4-4-0 No. 737 in all her original glory, and who has loaned me many historical photographs.

O. S. Nock.

20 Sion Hill,
Bath.
January 1961.

SOUTH EASTERN & CHATHAM RAILWAY

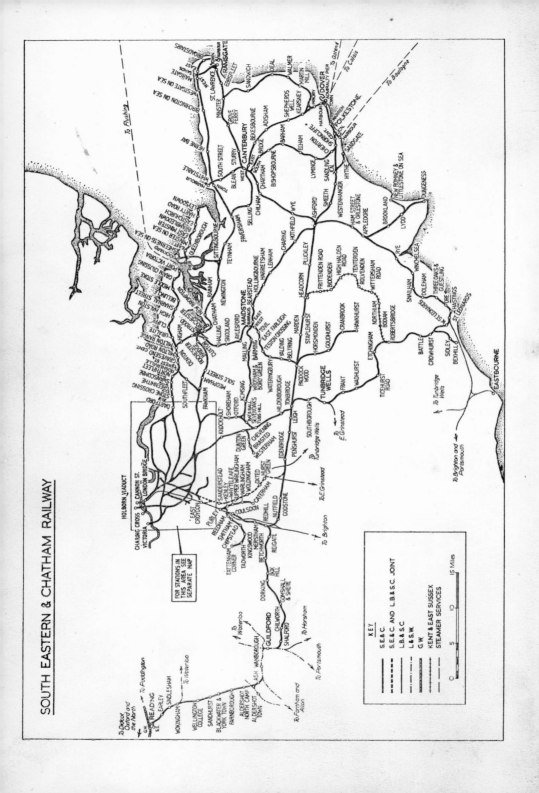

I

Pioneering in Kent

THE earlier railways of this country were for the most part notable for their directness and for their fine grading. The London & Birmingham, the Southampton, the North Midland went through regardless of the terrain, and were usually involved in engineering constructional problems that were stupendous in their day. With the South Eastern Railway, authorized as early in railway history as 1836, one might have imagined it would be the same. Dover was so obvious a goal: so naturally the railhead of all Britain, that there would have seemed every advantage in getting there by the straightest and most direct route. Two courses might have seemed obvious and equally acceptable alternatives: one, the historic route of the Dover Road, the present A2 highway, crossing the Medway at Rochester, and continuing in a veritably straight line through Faversham to Canterbury; there was also an excellent alternative via Maidstone, Ashford and Folkestone.

A railway driven down beside the very backbone of Kent in the style of a Brunel, or a Stephenson, would have been virtually impregnable. Attacks from either side would have been little more than diversions, to be swallowed up by the main enterprise once they got into financial difficulties. But there were no large business interests at the country end to join in the promotion of such a line. Down on the Straits of Dover there was no rising industrial centre like Birmingham, no great ancient trading port like Bristol. The strategic and continental interests at Dover were obvious, but there was no flourishing trade waiting to be picked up. Thus the South Eastern Railway for all its potential greatness was launched in a somewhat moderate way. There were no funds available for the building of a London terminus in the grand style of Euston, Paddington, or even of Kings Cross; and the parsimony thus engendered led the South Eastern into a quagmire from which it did not climb out for nearly seventy years!

Far from planning a station that would be worthy of its pioneer place as the gateway to the Continent, or where overseas visitors would first set foot in London, the original project made use of the tracks and stations of two local lines in South London – the London & Greenwich, and the London & Croydon. The ultimate growth of the South Eastern, both in suburban and main line travel, was utterly unforeseen. One can only suppose that in those very early days railways were so closely associated with the expanding industries and commerce of the Midlands and the North that the possibilities of similar travel developments in the green shires of Kent and Sussex were not given a second thought. There is something of the Hudson *dictum* about early South Eastern history: that as long as points A and B were connected by rail it did not matter how long and circuitous the intervening route might be.

The original line of the South Eastern, which was sanctioned by Act of Parliament in 1836, ran from London Bridge, which was then no more than the terminus of the London & Croydon Railway, via Oxted, Tonbridge, Maidstone and Ashford to Folkestone and Dover. It seemed as though the intention was to connect up as many centres of population as possible on the way down, regardless of the overall mileage. All this was in total contrast to the policy of the great trunk lines that were under construction elsewhere. The London & Birmingham, for example, narrowly by-passed Northampton; the Great Western left Wallingford and Abingdon on one flank, and Wantage on the other – quite apart from the fact that a line up the Kennet Valley instead of up the Vale of the White Horse would have placed considerably larger centres of population on the direct route.

Government intervention is often blamed for the circuitous nature of the South Eastern main line, as actually built; but if the original promoters had planned to go straight for Maidstone, or even Tonbridge instead of meandering through some of the hilliest regions of the North Downs to pass Oxted they might not have been saddled with the incubus of sharing a substantial stretch of the line with the Brighton. Scarcely a year after the authorization of the original line the South Eastern made another step towards their eventual discomfiture. The junction with the London & Croydon line was originally planned to be at Corbett's Lane, near to the site of the present North Kent East Junction, and less than a mile west of New Cross; but to save constructional costs, no doubt, the South Eastern secured authority to link up with London & Croydon at Norwood. The latter line then ran to what is now West Croydon, and the projected South Eastern Railway was to run southwards over the present route through East and South Croydon before heading into the hills for Oxted.

On the face of it this amendment was a good move, but in that same year of 1837 the Brighton Railway was authorized, from Norwood southwards, and Parliament then suggested that as the two railways would run so nearly parallel, in adjoining valleys, for a distance of twelve miles, further economies in construction and subsequent operation would be possible if the two companies shared the tracks over this distance. At the very outset the arrangement was a curious one, and provided for the line line being constructed by the Brighton company, and for the South Eastern to purchase it immediately afterwards, at cost price. The South Eastern, by this agreement, made its already roundabout main line still more so, and by the terms of the agreement was not at first allowed to stop any of its trains at the intermediate stations of the old Croydon Railway, between Croydon and New Cross.

At first the Brighton had very much the best of the deal. In common with the rest of its original main line there was no gradient steeper than 1 in 264, and while this was easy enough to maintain from Norwood through Croydon and Purley it involved some tremendously deep cuttings in the approaches to the mile-long tunnel under the crest of the Downs, at Merstham. And it was for this very section that the hapless South Eastern was induced to pay! At the southern end the point of divergence was at Redstone Hill, not far from Reigate, and was originally known as Reigate Junction. South Eastern ownership extended northwards to Stoats Nest, near Coulsdon, after which running powers were exercised over the Brighton and Croydon lines to New Cross. Reigate Junction became the familiar Redhill, and over this route, 89 miles from London Bridge to Dover, the South Eastern main line trains travelled for almost a quarter of a century.

As if to emphasize the complicated nature of the South Eastern relations with the Brighton, constructional work progressed much more rapidly between Croydon and Redhill than it did on the South Eastern proper. The line through the North Downs, despite the heavy engineering work, was opened on 12th July, 1841, whereas the first section east of Redhill was not opened until a year later. Once clear of the Brighton entanglements the South Eastern went straight enough for its ultimate objectives. The original intention of a diversion through Maidstone was dropped, and between Redhill and Ashford, indeed, the course of the railway shows a maximum divergence of no more than half a mile from a dead straight line drawn across the map between the two towns. At the eastern end, of course, the line had to swing slightly to the south of that straight line, to pass through Folkestone, but it was a fine direct route for all that.

In studying the origins of the South Eastern and comparing the country end, as one would call it, with all the complexities and entanglements in the London area one cannot fail to be struck by the many inconsistencies, which were 'built in', as it were, from the outset. Nearer London, where the pressure of local traffic might have been expected to make operating a difficult and delicate task, the company agreed to share its line with the Brighton, and to be content with no more than running powers over twelve miles of suburban territory leading to within three miles of the London terminus. Out in the Weald of Kent, the larger stations – Tonbridge, Paddock Wood and Ashford – were built new with fast lines in the centre, and separate platform roads, so that expresses could have a clear run, irrespective of any local trains that might be standing in the stations. The Engineer, Sir William Cubitt, was a strong advocate of fast running, and the line was laid out accordingly. In later years he adopted the same feature of station layout on the Great Northern, at Hatfield and Hitchin.

The line was completed to Dover in February, 1844, and by that time there were schemes for branches in all directions, covering practically the whole of Kent except the north coast between Chatham and Ramsgate. One of the most important of these projects was the North Kent loop, via Dartford and Strood. At that particular time there was no thought of crossing the Medway, as it was presumably thought good enough for a station at Strood to serve Rochester and Chatham. Instead, an extension from Strood to Maidstone was planned, which would connect with the branch running north from the main line at Paddock Wood. Hastings was to be reached by a branch from Ashford, serving Rye and Winchelsea *en route*, while there was to be a northern extension from Hastings to Battle.

The inconsistencies in layout were apparent on some of the earliest branches. A line was built on a more or less direct course from Ashford to Canterbury, and was continued to a terminus in Ramsgate; but to get to Margate one had to go into Ramsgate and then reverse direction, and it was not until the days of the Southern Railway that one could travel to Margate from Canterbury, Folkestone or Dover *without* changing direction. Again Deal was reached *not* by an extension along the coast from Dover, but by a branch from Minster Junction, near Ramsgate. The Great Western, in its earliest days, was dubbed the Great Way Round, but while the initials did not fit so neatly the same tag could be applied with even greater emphasis to some journeys one could make on the South Eastern. The mileage from London Bridge to Deal, for example, was originally 102, against the present run of 86½ via Sevenoaks and Dover. Margate by the old South Eastern route via Redhill and Ramsgate was also 102 miles from London compared with the present 74 miles. All these country branches in East Kent were open by the middle of 1847, and by that time the South Eastern management was doubtless looking forward to the establishment of a very pretty little monopoly.

Apart from his foresight in laying out the main line for really fast running there was little to tax the engineering ability of Sir William Cubitt until he came to Folkestone. Thenceforward, however, in carrying the line across the Foord gap and through the chalk cliffs he used methods that became the sensation of the day. This stretch of line is so familiar to us in these times that it is apt to be taken for granted, albeit as a place of considerable danger to the line. Indeed, recalling the colossal extent of landslips that have occurred in the Warren, more than one railway enthusiast has expressed to me his concern for the safety of the line in the Martello, Abbots Cliff and Shakespeare's Cliff Tunnels, all of which lie so near to the stretch of railway that has been so severely affected from time to time. The geological formation between Folkestone and Dover includes some abrupt changes, however, and all the ground was subjected to the most careful and exhaustive scrutiny before the line was built.

There is first a Greensand ridge, blocking in the eastern end of the Weald, and this is crossed at Westenhanger and Sandling Junction. Descending from this ridge the line comes down on a beautifully even gradient of 1 in 266, but still at high level as Folkestone is neared. To maintain the gradient, and reach the high undercliff on the eastern side a viaduct 100 ft high was necessary across the Foord gap, carrying the railway in spectacular style high above the narrow, winding streets of old Folkestone. Before reaching the chalk cliffs proper there was one more obstacle, a ridge of hard gault that outcrops the chalk, and through it was driven the Martello Tunnel. This picturesque name was taken from the watchtower of Napoleonic days that stands on the shore nearby.

Between the Martello Tunnel and Dover Harbour is less than five miles, but it was a five-mile stretch that might daunt the most fearless of engineers. The preliminary surveys showed that although two considerable headlands lay between, Abbots Cliff, and Shake-

speare's Cliff, the chalk in each of these was sound. Although quite
near to the sea such was the height of Abbots Cliff in particular that
a considerable height of solid chalk existed above the proposed
tunnels and between the line of the tunnels and the sea. Cubitt
judged that these headlands could be tunnelled with complete
safety. Between the headlands it was another matter. A ledge could
be cut in the chalk, high above the sea, except at one point, where
the Round Down Cliff jutted out as a modest promontory. This was
of very different character from Abbots Cliff and Shakespeare's Cliff,
and although of chalk seemed unstable and treacherous. Cubitt
conceived the simple, yet spectacular idea of just blasting it out of
the way.

It was at this stage that he took a step that is, so far as I am aware,
unique in the early history of railways in this country. He sought out
the chief inspector of railways of the Board of Trade, General
Pasley, and laid the whole proposition before him. This was quite
at variance with the usual state of affairs in those early days, when
the railway engineers went boldly ahead on their own account and
argued with the Government inspectors afterwards. General Pasley
was extremely helpful, not only giving general approval to Cubitt's
proposition, but, so far as the dynamiting of Round Down Cliff was
concerned, recommending that Lieut. Hutchinson, R.E., be consulted, as that officer had had valuable experience of blasting on a
large scale in removing the wreck of the old battleship *Royal
George*. The actual job of blowing up the cliff led to some of
the wildest stories in the newspapers of the day, but for a factual
description of what happened I cannot do better than quote from
The Times:

'At exactly 26 minutes past 2 o'clock a low, faint, indistinct, indes-
cribable moaning rumble was heard and immediately afterwards the
bottom of the cliff began to belly out, and then simultaneously about
500 ft in breadth of the summit began gradually, but rapidly to sink.
There was no roaring explosion, no bursting out of fire, no violent and
crushing splitting of rocks and comparatively speaking very little smoke,
for a proceeding of mighty and irresponsible force it had little or nothing
of the appearance of force.'

To commemorate the occasion the Directors of the South Eastern
Railway presented Lieutenant Hutchinson with a gold watch. It
is now in the possession of his grandson, Canon Grice-Hutchinson
of Charlton Kings, Cheltenham, and it is inscribed thus:—

Presented to
Lieut. Hutchinson R.E.
by the
Directors of the
S.E. Railway Company
in token of their appreciation
of his services
rendered in blasting

THE ROUNDOWN CLIFF
AT DOVOR

on Thursday 26th January, 1843

It is curious to note that Dover was spelt with a second 'o'. Canon
Grice-Hutchinson tells me that his grandfather was killed not very
long after the dynamiting of the Round Down Cliff, when he was
engaged on some harbour works at Holyhead, from an explosive
charge detonated accidentally. It is perhaps not generally known
also that Lieutenant Hutchinson's younger brother became one of
the Board of Trade Inspectors of railways, and it was he, as Major
General Hutchinson, who had the grim task of conducting the
enquiry into the terrible runaway train disaster at Armagh, Great
Northern Railway of Ireland. Canon Grice-Hutchinson tells me
that the presentation watch given to his grandfather in commemora-
tion of the Round Down Cliff job still goes.

That great operation took place on 26th January, 1843, and twelve
months later the trains were running through to Dover. In Shakespeare's Cliff the chalk did not seem to be quite so sound as in Abbots
Cliff, and Cubitt took the precaution of driving two single line
tunnels, and constructing the arches in Gothic shape, so as to lessen
the pressure on the crown of the arch. The distinctive shape of the
bores, clearly seen from Dover Harbour against the picturesque
outline of Shakespeare's Cliff makes this one of the most striking
tunnel entrances anywhere on the railways of Britain. From the
tunnel down the grade into Dover the line was carried on a timber
trestle viaduct built on the beach, of which the piles were driven
down deep into the solid chalk. It was not until a widening of the
line was needed, in Southern Railway days, that Cubitt's trestle
viaduct was dismantled.

At first the railway terminated some little distance short of Dover
Harbour. In 1844 the Admiralty Pier did not exist, and passengers
for the Continent had to make their own way to the quay from which

the packet boats sailed. On the French side of the Channel the railway had not yet reached Calais, and in those early years the South Eastern Railway concentrated its maritime activities upon Folkestone. At the outset it certainly seemed a most unlikely packet station. There was nothing in the way of a natural haven. On Telford's advice a simple sheltering had been provided for the local fishing fleet, and on three occasions that great civil engineer had been called into consultation with a view to its enlargement. In 1843 the plain fact remained that it was silted up, virtually useless, and heavily mortgaged to the Government.

The arrival of the South Eastern Railway at Folkestone changed everything. Accounts differ as to the precise way in which it was done, but certain it is that the railway bought the harbour at rock-bottom price, and the steeply-graded connecting line from the main line was sanctioned, for goods traffic only, in the same year, 1843. Here again is another instance of the roundabout approach to certain key points made in the early day of the line. While the heavy engineering works east of the Martello Tunnel were in progress Folkestone was the temporary terminus of the line, and the goods line to the harbour was built from this point, near the site of the present Folkestone Junction station. This meant a reversal of direction for all traffic proceeding to or from the harbour, and a change of locomotives. In view of the importance that Folkestone Harbour was to attain in the working of a large proportion of the Continental traffic one questions if a direct line from the harbour on easier gradients was contemplated at that time so that the boat trains could be run down to the pier by their own engines, as at Dover, and much time saved on the journey. On the face of it the line from Folkestone Junction to the harbour has every appearance of a hurriedly-projected afterthought.

It was all so unlike Cubitt's handling of the rest of the job. Here was a new railway being laid out in the grand manner, with quadruple tracks through the larger stations to permit of the interrupted running of fast trains, and yet at Folkestone those responsible produced one of the most inconvenient layouts imaginable, with intervening gradients that came to involve the use of *four* locomotives with the heaviest trains. It will be told in a later chapter how strenuously the South Eastern sought to extricate itself from the tangle; but what might have been easily possible in 1843 or 1844 was vetoed by local opinion in the seventies of last century.

The development of the harbour works at both Folkestone and Dover is a subject of special interest in the history of both constituents of the South Eastern & Chatham Railway, and is dealt with at length in further chapters. To complete the story of early railway work in the country districts of Kent it is necessary to move from the Straits of Dover to the Thames Estuary. The earliest part of the whole system was, of course, the Canterbury & Whitstable Railway, which was opened in May, 1830. Although this short line is of great historical interest from its very early date, and from its associations with some of the earlier railway pioneers in the persons of William James, George Stephenson, Locke, and Edward Fletcher, it always remained something of an oddity from its restricted loading gauge through Tyler's Hill Tunnel, and the exceedingly heavy gradients, that were at first worked by cable haulage. It was purchased by the South Eastern Railway in 1853, but never came into the general operating network of that company. With the construction of the London, Chatham & Dover Railway the need for it, as a means of connecting Canterbury with the coast, virtually ceased.

Nearer London a subsidiary line of far greater importance had come into the possession of the South Eastern Railway, and was being fully used for passenger and goods traffic by the year 1849. Since the construction of the Greenwich Railway in 1835 – the first railway in London – little further had been done to provide any form of railway transport on the south side of the Thames estuary between Greenwich and the Medway. It is true that the district was then largely rural, and it was served by coach services, and certain very slow river steamers. Even then, however, Gravesend was a place of some importance, and the Medway towns of Rochester and Chatham were still without any immediate prospects of railway communication. For transport of goods, moreover, the river had always provided a very slow and roundabout route, for while the distance from Gravesend to Rochester was little more than six miles as the crow flies it was a good thirty by water, sailing round the Isle of Grain. To obviate this journey the Thames & Medway Canal had been projected, and while work was commenced in 1800 the job took no less than twenty-four years to complete.

The reason for this extraordinarily protracted construction lay principally in the long tunnel through the chalk between Higham and Strood, $2\frac{1}{4}$ miles long. The tunnel was not continuous, as there was an opening near the halfway point. This was intended as a passing place for the barges. The tunnels were made 30 ft wide, of which 6 ft was taken up by the towing path. In the year 1845 a single line of railway was laid by the Canal Company between Gravesend and Strood; this was constructed along the banks in the open country, and along the towing path in the Higham and Strood tunnels. First and second class passengers only were carried, but as the second class single fare between Strood and Gravesend was a mere 6d. no one had any cause to complain.

Then, in 1846, the whole undertaking was purchased by the South Eastern Railway. They had to pay £310,000 for it, but it provided an almost ready-made route over the most difficult part of the way from New Cross to the Medway. The Canal was drained and a double line of railway laid along the former water course between Strood and Gravesend, while the westward continuation was made over the North Kent line through Dartford to the junction with the London & Croydon, and with the London & Greenwich at Corbetts Lane. The complete route from London Bridge to Strood was brought into regular operation in July, 1849. By this time the South Eastern Railway was certainly spreading its tentacles over the fair land of Kent, and only needed the construction of the link between Strood and Maidstone to complete one more step to a promising monopoly. But while Kent was the Company's own special preserve – or so it might have been thought – its management in early days was not averse to excursions further afield.

The Reading, Guildford & Reigate Railway was one of many small concerns, sponsored locally but with the ill-concealed intention of selling out to one of the larger railways before it had become too deeply involved. It linked up with the Great Western at one end, and with the Brighton, and with South Eastern at Redhill, cutting intermediately across the South Western at Guildford. Making contact with four major railways the prospect for ultimate absorption must certainly have appeared good, but it was perhaps one of the least likely of the four, the South Eastern, that took advantage of the situation. From the outset an arrangement was made whereby they worked the line, and it was purchased outright three years later, in 1852. This line has special personal associations for me. When my parents lived in Reading nearly all my earliest holiday journeys were made over this route. When we were bound for Margate or Folkestone the through trains coming off the Great Western at Reading had the special attraction of avoiding London, and with it the hazards of changing stations with the mountains of luggage our family always seemed to take.

The acquisition of the Reading line was a characteristic piece of South Eastern expansionist activity. And the branch from Ashford to Hastings was another. At one time it was proposed to put in a southern curve to the Brighton main line at Redhill, so that trains could run direct from Dover or Folkestone to Brighton without the need for reversal in Redhill station. This particular spur was never built. It was nevertheless a haphazard and inconsistent expansion on the part of the South Eastern Railway, for while new lines were built in the country, and others acquired, the most extraordinary situation was developing near London. Yet from that situation there emerged some operating developments of the most far-reaching kind which put the South Eastern and the Brighton in the forefront of signalling evolution, at a time when the great lines running north had not progressed beyond the hand signals of the old 'policemen'.

II

The Approach to London

It was not until the year 1836 that London had any railway in
full operation. Then, although many great projects were in hand,
it was nothing more than the Greenwich Railway, a short line in
itself, but one that was to assume immense importance before many
years had passed. Compared with the great industrial lines of the
north, and the trunk routes from London to Bristol, and to Birmingham that were then under construction the Greenwich line had more
than the passing appearance of a 'stunt', a speculation in which the
railway formed only a part of the whole. Why, for example, was it
necessary to build the whole line on arches? As one of its avowed
objects was to give Londoners the opportunity of a ride in the country
it would surely have been infinitely cheaper to build it at ground
level.

One feels that those arches were part of the speculation. It was
intended to equip them as dwelling houses, at a time when London
was beginning to spread rapidly. A certain Lt. Col. Landmann was
responsible for the suggestion of the arches, and he secured the job
of supervising the construction. Such a viaduct stretching for three
miles across the country was bound to create an enormous amount of
interest, and as there was then little else in the way of building
anywhere in the neighbourhood it was conspicuous for miles
around, especially from the higher ground to the south. The
Mechanics Magazine, of 12th September, 1835 has a most interesting
account:

'The London & Greenwich Railway viaduct is now fast approaching
completion and presents a very imposing appearance. It forms a highly
interesting object from the summit of Nunhead Hill, at the back of
Peckham, from which the whole range of arches, seen in nearly its entire
length, appears like the "counterfeit presentment" of a Roman aqueduct.
Nunhead Hill is decidedly the best point from which to obtain a general
view of this magnificent work, which there forms a part of the foreground
to an exquisite and comprehensive panorama of the metropolis, in its
whole enormous length from Chelsea to Greenwich, with all its "domes
and spires and pinnacles", amongst those of Westminster Abbey and St
Pauls are of course the most conspicuous.'

The opening, and early operating was accompanied by a good deal of what we should now set down as 'ballyhoo'. Regimental bands played the trains in and out of the stations; most of the traffic was derived from pure joyriding, and the cynics dubbed all those who ventured on the line 'noodles'. One critic referred to the railway as 'the new tomfoolery', and of course there was a certain ring of truth in his comment if attention is paid to the more extravagant accompaniments of travel on the line. Very few years were to pass, however, before the ballyhoo and joyriding was to change to deadly earnest, and this music-hall stunt of a railway was to provide the earliest example of severe traffic congestion.

Its western terminus, adjacent to London Bridge, was considered a highly desirable point for embarking and discharging passengers and freight. For although the immediate neighbourhood was foul in the extreme London Bridge itself provided a ready access to the City and all the commercial interests centred around it. From being an excursionists paradise the emphasis at London Bridge station quickly changed from pleasure to hard business. In May, 1839, came the Croydon Railway, and arrangements were made for the latter to share the terminus and nearly two miles of the line to the point of divergence at Corbett's Lane Junction, almost exactly marked by the one time Southwark Park station. Corbett's Lane was soon to become the same kind of embarrassment as Redhill developed into some years later. Through it everything funnelled on to the overcrowded, last 1¾ miles into London Bridge.

At the termination of the line the Croydon Railway built its own station, adjacent to and to the north of the Greenwich platforms, and the congestion was concentrated on the bottleneck between the terminus approach and Corbett's Lane. Before coming to the operating features on that remarkable stretch of line there is a good deal to be said about London Bridge station itself. Few great stations have developed in a more promiscuous way. At the very inception of the terminus there was one hitch after another. It was quite in keeping with the flair for publicity displayed by the Greenwich Railway to have a grand ceremonial entrance, and early in 1836 a classic design had been prepared that would have been a serious rival to the Doric Arch of Euston – if it had ever been built. But London Bridge was not ready for the time fixed for the opening of the railway, and for ten months the traffic was worked from a temporary terminus at Spa Road, Bermondsey. This point lies exactly one mile out of London Bridge, and a permanent station for local traffic was built there in 1843.

Apparently the Greenwich Railway was opened to London Bridge while the station was yet unfinished; but nevertheless a great banquet was held on 14th December, 1836, at which the Lord Mayor of London was present, after which his Lordship and numerous other guests made a trip down the line to Deptford. Some time before this, however, a considerable enlargement of the station had already been foreseen. The promoters of the Greenwich Railway had not considered their line as complete in itself; they had looked forward to extensions into Kent and Surrey. Thus, when first the Croydon Railway and then the South Eastern based their plans on the use of London Bridge and the tracks of the Greenwich Railway all was going as the original promoters had hoped. The allocation of platforms on the *north* side of the station to the Croydon Railway was shortsighted. Traffic on both lines developed very rapidly, and two more tracks were laid down between Corbett's Lane and the terminus in 1842.

Before that, however, at Corbett's Lane, one of the first major railway junctions in the world, difficulty was being experienced in regulating the traffic. The policemen responsible for setting the points for outward bound trains could not 'spot' the locomotives of oncoming trains early enough to be sure of setting the road correctly, and so the famous Corbett's Lane 'lighthouse', as it was called, was erected. Although its working was primitive in the extreme it can be considered the first signalbox to be erected anywhere in the world. The indications were twofold: the trains carried distinctive head codes, so that the policeman on duty could recognize them and set the route accordingly; indications were displayed from the 'lighthouse' showing which way the points were lying. Thus if by any chance the policeman had mistaken the headcode of an oncoming train and set the route wrongly the driver could see the error displayed from the 'lighthouse' and would not go careering down the wrong line.

One could criticize both the headcodes carried on the trains, and the indications from the 'lighthouse', in the light of present-day practice. Greenwich trains had no distinguishing marks, while the Croydon trains had a red ball hung out of the leading coach by the conductor. At night these trains had two white lights on the front of the engine, one above the other. This could be a negative kind of indication, for if the lamps went out, or fell off, or if the conductor forgot to hang out the red ball, or dropped it, a Croydon train could be mistaken for one bound for Greenwich. The point indications could be similarly criticized. If the points were set for the Croydon line a large red-orange disc was displayed, or a red light at night; for a Greenwich train the disc was turned on edge and a white light shown at night. Despite its shortcomings the Corbett's Lane 'lighthouse' was nevertheless an outstanding 'milestone' in railway operating practice.

When the additional tracks were put in for the Croydon trains, in 1842, they were naturally built on the south side of the line so that trains to and from Croydon could run between Corbett's Lane and London Bridge without conflicting with the Greenwich trains. This was logical enough at Corbett's Lane, but when it came to London Bridge everything had to cross everything else! The platforms for the Croydon and Greenwich trains were in reverse, as compared with the running lines outside. By that time, too, plans were well advanced for bringing in the South Eastern and the Brighton trains as well. Unless something was done about the terminus there would be utter chaos in a few years time. The first step out of the impending morass was when the Greenwich company exchanged its part of the station for the Croydon platforms, so as to avoid all the complication of crossing over. This took place in 1840, in anticipation of the opening of the Brighton line.

For some time the Greenwich trains were kept entirely separate, using one section of the station, while the other section was used jointly by the remaining three companies. It was managed by the Brighton, Croydon and Dover Joint Station Committee. Having regard to the ramifications of the Brighton and South Eastern, as compared with the Greenwich line, this may seem surprising; but by the early 'fifties' of last century traffic on the Greenwich line had developed to such an extent that the total number of trains per day was very nearly equal to that of the other three companies combined! It was then quite a fair division of the terminal premises. It is specially interesting to recall that the whole property at London Bridge belonged to the Greenwich Railway, and it was that railway which had to secure Parliamentary sanction, in 1840, to build a new station for the joint use of the Croydon, Brighton, and South Eastern Railways.

Before any steps were taken to implement the provisions of this new Act much was to happen in the near neighbourhood of London Bridge. From the outset the Greenwich Railway had 'cashed in' heavily on its position as owner of the line out to Corbett's Lane, and had charged excessive tolls for its use by the Croydon Railway. These amounted to 4½d. per passenger, and although the Board of Trade had urged a substantial reduction in the interest of the public,

the Greenwich company insisted upon its 'pound of flesh'. Far from
making any reduction they would have charged more if they had had
their own way, but 4½d. per passenger was the maximum amount
permitted by Parliament. In consequence of this imposition the
Croydon Railway and the South Eastern sought to evade it altogether
by building a terminus of their own, approached by a line that would
link up with existing tracks as near to Corbett's Lane as possible.

At first sight the place chosen for the new terminus seems an odd
one, some considerable distance to the south of London Bridge, in
an area fast developing into one huge slum. At the time, however,
the choice was not quite so odd. The Bricklayers Arms Inn on the
Old Kent Road was a recognized stopping place for coaches, where
travellers from the West End joined them, and so the joint sponsors
of the new railway station were moved to describe it as a 'grand
West End terminus'! The architect was Lewis Cubitt, who afterwards built Kings Cross, and in the imposing façade of Bricklayers
Arms, and particularly in the clock tower there are points of strong
resemblance to the Great Northern terminus. Actually the contemporary drawings of the station greatly exaggerated the height of the
façade, and made it look far grander than it really was! Naturally
there was strong opposition from the Greenwich Railway, but despite this the Bill went through and received the Royal Assent in
July, 1843. No time was lost in building either the station or the line
serving it, and on 1st May, 1844, the branch was opened to traffic.

One of the most interesting points about Bricklayers Arms is
that it was planned from the outset to deal with heavy freight traffic
in addition to passengers. There was also a large engine shed, and a
feature that was unusual at that time, namely a turntable large
enough to turn an engine and tender coupled together. Elsewhere it
was then usual to uncouple the locomotive from the tender before
turning. The connection to the Croydon line near New Cross was
made on a long curving viaduct, vividly described thus, in the Official
Guide to the London & Dover Railway, as the South Eastern was
afterwards described:

'With great lightness of appearance, and marvellous economy of
materials, it possesses prodigious strength, at a tithe of the cost of an
embankment or a brickwork arcade, and may safely vie with the most
expensive arrangements, in durability and aptitude to sustain the action
of a vast railway traffic.'

In actual fact it lasted barely ten years, and in the early eighteen-
fifties it was replaced by an ordinary embankment.

The construction of the Bricklayers Arms station, and the diverting of many Croydon and South Eastern trains into this new terminus had the effect of bringing the Greenwich Company to a more reasonable frame of mind. Thoroughly alarmed at the loss in revenue from the greatly reduced tolls collected from trains exercising running powers they sought a new agreement on charges, much to the relief of the Croydon and South Eastern Railways. Despite all the propaganda and grandiloquence heaped upon Bricklayer's Arms it never achieved the slightest degree of popularity as a passenger terminus, and by the autumn of 1846, less than three years after its first opening all regular passenger services had been withdrawn. Originally projected as a joint station, the Act gave the South Eastern the option of buying the Croydon share, after due notice had been served, and by the end of 1845 it had become the sole property of the S.E.R. As such it became one of the most important goods stations on the line.

The complete failure of the Bricklayer's Arms project, from the passenger point of view threw the emphasis back upon London Bridge, and the new station, as authorized in 1840, went ahead. As completed in 1845 the new station had nine roads inside the 'shed', of which five had platform faces. The Greenwich station had three roads, with two platform faces. The joint station had a fine frontage in the Italian palazzo style, and an imposing tower like a campanile. This building was scarcely completed when arrangements were made to lease the Greenwich line to the South Eastern, for a period of 999 years, and plans were immediately put in hand for a coordination of the working facilities. It so happened that the leasing was authorized in the year of the Railway Mania, 1845, and in the panic and recession that followed things perforce remained stagnant. In 1847, however, the South Eastern obtained Parliamentary powers to enlarge the station, and to lay down yet another pair of lines between London Bridge and Corbett's Lane. So the Italian edifice of 1844, campanile and all, was demolished to make way for a greatly enlarged but more utilitarian set of buildings that came to house the headquarter offices of the South Eastern Railway.

This great project was carried through entirely by the South Eastern Railway, and as architect the company employed one Samuel Beazley, a man of considerable distinction in his day, but one who came into the railway sphere only when near the end of his life. His station buildings at London Bridge were imposing, in the Georgian style, as compared with the more exotic flavour of the 1845 building designed by Henry Roberts, under the direction of Sir William Cubitt. The South Eastern appeared then to be very much the dominating partner at London Bridge, and a contem-

porary illustration shows the Brighton side approached by a kind
of 'tradesman's entrance', under a temporary wooden hoarding.
In the short time he was engaged in railway work Samuel Beazley
was closely associated with the South Eastern, and in addition to
London Bridge he designed most of the stations on the North Kent
line, and also the Lord Warden Hotel at Dover. It is said that the
scale of these works and the great number of bricks required for
them caused a temporary shortage, and forced up the price of bricks,
and the cost of bricklaying!

While these constructional works were in hand discussions took
place between the South Eastern and the Brighton Railways as to
the way in which the station facilities at London Bridge should be
divided between the two companies. It was apparently left to civil
engineers to work this problem out. At that time the traffic officer,
as we know him today, was scarcely contemplated and the engineer
was omnipotent in all matters concerning the running of the trains.
So we find that in the year 1848 Cubitt, for the South Eastern, and
Robert Stephenson for the Brighton, were arranging how the
platforms in the terminus should be allocated. The two engineers
settled things, but certain members of the Brighton Board, more
farseeing than others more directly concerned, criticized the arrangements as being totally inadequate to the growing needs of their
railway, and the Brighton decided to build a station of their own,
to the south of the South Eastern terminus, and as if to emphasize
the completeness of the new division it was separated by a wall.

At the time of the enlargements of London Bridge station, first
by the joint committee, then in the Beazley enlargement, and finally
in the Brighton station the high level of the original Greenwich line
involved enormous additional cost and difficulty in building. The
following quotation, from *The Illustrated London News* of July, 1858,
gives very clear appreciation of the circumstances, referring to the
group of stations as a whole, and not merely to one section of it:

'The ground appropriated for business in the building, or for trains and
travellers behind it, under the shelter of the iron roof for the five railways
concentrating at the London Bridge Station, is far less than the Great
Western occupies at Paddington for its one single line. But the evil is
unavoidable. The whole area on which the station stands is an artificial
level. Built upon arches, it is suspended in mid-air, more wonderfully
than the "hanging gardens" of Babylon, looking down from an altitude
of seventy feet upon Tooley Street, and sending forth its convoys along
an elevated route which lifts them above the chimney pots of Bermondsey. . . . Space which has to be made by building up to a height of fifty

or sixty feet from the ground must needs be economized. Every yard of surface occupied by the London Bridge Station is as completely "forced" as a strawberry at Christmas. . . . The Greenwich traffic, which seldom includes any luggage worth mentioning, is connected by two lines of rail, used alternately for "up" and "down" trains, with a narrow platform screened off from the rest of the series under a confined shed. Next, to the right, are the North Kent rails, comprising three lines – one for arrivals, another for departures, and a third spare one for empty carriages, with platforms for the "in" and "out" traffic on either side. Its neighbour group belongs to the Dover line, and presents a width of ground which, spanned by a single roof without intervening supports, was unmatched in the world until new Paddington station was built. It extends over three rails, two platforms, and a carriage road. The Brighton, Croydon, and Crystal Palace series of lines come last, chumming together under one span of roof, but sociably contriving matters so that special pairs of rails are appropriated for the arrivals and departures of the long and the short trains respectively, with platforms, carriage road, and spare rails, for "making-up" as common property.'

By the year 1850 there were six tracks extending from the terminus to Corbett's Lane. The widening of the Greenwich viaduct under the Parliamentary powers granted to the South Eastern in 1847 was carried out on the northern side of the line, so that after this work was completed the original Greenwich lines were in the centre. There was, however, a re-arrangement so far as use of the lines was concerned, and this led to a peculiar method of working on the Greenwich line east of North Kent East Junction, where the Gravesend line diverged. The Greenwich Railway proper almost certainly adopted left hand running. An engraving of 1839, showing a train on the long viaduct would seem to confirm this, though contemporary artists were not always to be relied on for their accuracy. After the completion of the widening of 1850, three out of the six tracks were allocated to the Brighton and South Eastern main line trains, and three to the Greenwich and Gravesend locals. Between London Bridge and Corbett's Lane the allocation was thus, numbering from north to south:

Number	Original Function	New Function	Direction of Running
1	New Line (1850)	Greenwich Up	Up
2	New Line (1850)	North Kent & Greenwich	Down
3	Greenwich Down	North Kent & Dover	Up
4	Greenwich Up	S.E.R. & L.B.S.C.R.	Down
5	Croydon Down	S.E.R. & L.B.S.C.R.	Up
6	Croydon Up	Croydon Local	Up

At that time only lines 4 and 5 were shared by the two companies, though that sharing must have been an embarrassment to both, especially after the Brighton opened its line to the Crystal Palace in 1854, and a great deal of additional traffic came to he handled at London Bridge. Even so the Brighton was still there on sufferance as it were, and it was not until the year 1866 that the extensive widenings to the south of the 'viaduct', consequent upon the building of the L.B.S.C.R. South London line, that Brighton and South Eastern trains ceased to use common tracks in the approach to the terminus. By that time, of course, the whole situation of the South Eastern Railway had been changed by the arrival in London of a very serious new competitor, in the form of the London, Chatham & Dover Railway. Before coming to that very anxious and exciting stage of the story, however, there are more interesting details to be mentioned about the working in and around London Bridge itself, particularly in regard to signalling.

The intensity and complication of the traffic made it inevitable to have more comprehensive arrangements than elsewhere, and several features of railway signalling practice that were to become well-nigh universal in later years were pioneered in this area. The use of semaphore signals came about almost incidentally. C. H. Gregory, afterwards Sir Charles Gregory, was engineer of the London & Croydon Railway, and in 1841, at New Cross, he installed the first semaphore to be used for railway signalling. Although it was used to control the movement of South Eastern trains it was not strictly a S.E.R. development though it was one very quickly exploited in the London Bridge area. The curious thing about this development is that Gregory himself seems to have thought nothing of it at all. He rose to great eminence in the profession, and eventually became President of the Institution of Civil Engineers. In view of the world-wide application of railway semaphore signals one turns with interest to his Presidential Address, delivered in 1858. Such an occasion is justifiably the time for an eminent man to look back and review in retrospect some of the milestones of his career, but Gregory does not even mention it!

Still more surprising is that no reference is made either to his second, and perhaps more important contribution to railway signalling, in 1843. This time the scene was Bricklayer's Arms Junction, in readiness for the opening of the line to the new 'West End' terminus. Tall semaphore signals, in the style of New Cross, were proposed, and Gregory decided to place the actuating gear for all the semaphores concerning the junction in one place. The signals were operated to the 'line-clear' position by stirrups into which the 'policeman' placed his foot; the stirrups were arranged in a single row, and to give the man a better outlook up and down the line the stirrup frame was placed on an elevated platform. This was, indeed, the father of all signal boxes; it did not merely set down a general principle, for the style of apparatus, with all signals for one particular station or junction grouped in a single assembly, was followed in detail for very many years.

The indications displayed would be considered vague and inadequate today. The old semaphores told a driver that he had to stop or proceed. It was left to his judgment as to *where* he stopped. He was expected to know the road, and if one of the tall semaphores sprouting from the roof of the signalbox indicated that he must stop then it was considered up to his judgment and sense of responsibility to stop short of the fouling point at the junction. When the Croydon Railway became absorbed into the Brighton, in 1846, Gregory had many other irons in his particular fire, and F. D. Banister became Chief Engineer of the L.B.S.C.R. Men of the Brighton were very active in those early days in developing items of signalling equipment, though once again their genius came to be applied in a pioneer sense as much for the South Eastern Railway as for their original company.

I am referring particularly now to John Saxby and John Stinson Farmer. In the year 1850, Saxby was a foreman in the locomotive works at Brighton, while Farmer was Assistant Traffic Manager of the L.B.S.C.R. Saxby became associated with manufacture of various items of signalling apparatus. The civil engineer, Banister, had designed a double semaphore, with two arms pointing in opposite directions working in the same slot in a single post. How far the two men, Saxby, and Farmer, were in consultation before they entered upon their famous partnership it is not possible to say; it is certain, however, that Saxby's interest in signalling was soon extending far beyond the mere manufacture of the 'bits and pieces' as it were, and in June, 1856, his first patent was granted to him, for 'A mode of working simultaneously the points and signals of railways at junctions to prevent accidents'. In this same year an apparatus generally in accordance with Saxby's patent was installed at Bricklayer's Arms Junction.

There is no precise information as to where this apparatus was made. Saxby was still employed in the locomotive department at Brighton, under that fearsome character John Chester Craven, and the probability is that he made the parts himself in his spare time.

In those days there was no objection raised to railway employees having other business as a side line, and it was not until 1862 that Saxby sent his letter of resignation to Craven, then saying that he felt he could no longer give proper attention to his work as a foreman in the locomotive works. The semaphore arms in the apparatus at Bricklayer's Arms Junction showed only 'stop' and 'caution'. It was not considered necessary to have the 'all right' indication, with the arms disappearing within the slot of the post, as at that time all trains were required to slow down over each and every junction.

Although it was not interlocking in the modern sense Saxby's main idea was to prevent the signals and points being out of correspondence. The signals and points were worked by combined levers, so that the moving of the levers to set the points for the branch simultaneously lowered the signal for that line, and vice versa. There was nothing to stop the man leaving the points halfway, and presumably have both signals half lowered, but it was assumed that the man's experience and sense of responsibility would guard against his doing anything so foolish. Interlocked or not, the elevated signal cabin, with the signal posts mounted in a group above the roof became a familiar feature of the British railways from its inception at Bricklayer's Arms Junction, so much so that a more elaborate box of the same general type, installed later at Stewart's Lane Junction, became the trademark of the firm of Saxby & Farmer Ltd.

So far as London Bridge was concerned two quite large cabins were built, arranged athwart the tracks and spanning several of them. Each of these boxes had three signal posts rising from the roof, and each post carried three double semaphores in the Banister style. That these signalboxes and their array of semaphores presented an imposing sight is to say the least of it, and the artist of *The Illustrated London News* of the day made the most of it, as will be seen from the accompanying picture. None of the signals worked from these boxes gave the 'all-right' indication by disappearing inside the slot in the post. In the crowded and complicated layout in the approach to London Bridge nothing less restrictive than 'caution' was displayed. To assist drivers the routes to which the semaphores referred were shown by letter codes on the face of the blades themselves. One of my younger signalling colleagues, looking at a picture of a similar box, once asked me how they managed in fog. I'm afraid I was unable to answer the question!

Before leaving these early signals reference must also be made to the lamps used. Looking at the old illustration it will be seen that there is only one lamp for each *pair* of semaphores. This is no mistake

Shakespeare's Cliff tunnel and viaduct. A reproduction of a beautiful contemporary water colour by George Childs, showing a Sharp 2-2-2 locomotive on an up train.

[British Railways

COATS OF ARMS

Above, left: South Eastern Railway
Above: London Chatham & Dover Railway
Left: S.E.C.R. Managing Committee

One of the Cudworth 'Mail' engines, S.E.R., of 1862 design.

Above: L.C.D.R. Martley 2-4-0 *Templar* of the 'Reindeer' class.

Below: S.E.R.: a Cudworth 2-4-0 as originally built, 1860 class.

[British Railways

The approach to London Bridge in the 1860s, showing the two picturesque signalboxes built by Saxby & Farmer Ltd. From a contemporary woodcut in *The Illustrated London News*.

of the artist, but a faithful representation of a most ingenius device invented by John Saxby. The one lamp casing and one burner provided for night indications of both semaphores, simultaneously and independently. Inside the lamp casing were two horizontal, circular, trays, each mounted on a vertical spindle. One of these spindles was hollow, so that the second could revolve freely inside it. These spindles were connected by bell cranks to the rodding actuating the semaphores so that they worked together – one tray revolving with the movement of one semaphore. To the trays were attached curved coloured glasses, red and green, and the revolving of the tray brought the appropriate colour between the light from the burner and the lens in the outer case. With a lens on each side of the case the indications for the up line signal were shown from one side, from the movements of the tray concerned, and the down line indications were similarly displayed from the other side.

The high level of the original Greenwich line may have been a source of difficulty and expense when the extensions to London Bridge so far discussed were being made. It was to prove an absolute godsend later, when the extension to Cannon Street and Charing Cross was projected. Otherwise a very steep rising gradient would have been required to cross the Borough High Street, and attain sufficient altitude to cross the river to the Cannon Street terminus and provide the necessary clearance for shipping. The extension, however, belongs to a later period in South Eastern history, but enough has been written so far to show the predominant position of the South Eastern Railway at London Bridge in the early days, through its lease of the Greenwich line, and its one-time control of all traffic in the approach to the terminus.

III

Dover, Folkestone and the Channel Crossing

FOR seventeen years after the construction of the railway, from 1844 to 1861, the South Eastern was alone in the field at Folkestone and Dover. At the beginning of this period it would have been difficult to decide at which of the two places conditions in the harbours were the more primitive and decayed. Folkestone has already been mentioned in Chapter I; Dover was only just emerging from a state of almost complete strangulation from shingle. And yet it was this very shingle that had been used to make the historic port of former days. The river Dour flowing down from the hills on which the Castle stands had, like all rivers, carried with it a certain amount of silt; a spit of shingle had gradually built up on the leftward bank of the river's mouth, while efforts to keep the estuary clear, together with the gradual extension of the shingle spit had resulted in the formation, over countless years, of a haven behind the shingle. But unless dredging was continuously carried out the shingle tended to encroach across the harbour mouth, and close it to shipping.

When the railway came to Dover, there was a small tidal harbour, the entrance to which was protected by short breakwaters. Constant vigilance was needed to see that the shingle, creeping always along the bank towards the south-west did not get between the breakwaters, and so impede traffic into and out of the tidal harbour. The cross-Channel steamer services were then operated by Admiralty packets, carrying mails daily to the continent, and there was a weekly over-land despatch to India and Australia. On the French side the packet station was Calais, where there was then no railway communication. The mails had always been routed via Dover, and they continued thence after the establishment of the railway; but one can under-stand the interest of the South Eastern Railway in developing a port of their own, at Folkestone. Not only was there additional revenue to be derived from the running of a cross-Channel service, but the S.E.R. steamers plied to Boulogne from which there was better communication to Paris and the south.

The enterprise of the South Eastern in those early days knew no bounds. At that time development of railways in France was not progressing so fast as it was in England, so the South Eastern Board put up capital towards the building of a line to connect Boulogne with the main line from Paris to Lille. This was the Boulogne & Amiens Railway, which was to link up with the existing line at Longueau, south of Amiens, where the present series of junctions and yards is now situated. English railway rivalry spread to France, for the London & South Western was interested in the development of the Southampton–Le Havre route to Paris. Certain members of the Paris–Le Havre Board were also associated with the Boulogne–Amiens line, and through this connection the South Western strove with might and main to delay the construction of the latter, and thus hinder the progress of the South Eastern cross-Channel business. These delaying tactics achieved no more than a partial success, for the line was opened throughout to Boulogne in 1848.

The South Eastern Railway had good reason for backing the Boulogne project. In the same year the Northern Railway of France, with which the Boulogne line connected at Longueau, extended their own line from Lille to Calais. The through route from Paris was so roundabout and so slow, however, that if one did land at Calais it was then quicker to take the coach to Boulogne and proceed thence by railway than to go the entire way by rail from Calais by the Northern of France. In the meantime the South Eastern was actively improving its facilities at Folkestone, while those at Dover remained unchanged from those existing in 1844. The railway company found good reason in allowing the transfer between trains and the Admiralty packets to remain to stay thoroughly inconvenient, while stepping up the efficiency of its own arrangements at Folkestone.

As at Dover it was the prevailing drift of the shingle that had determined the form of the harbour, as the railway company had purchased it in 1843. The drift, however, was in the opposite direction as that at Dover. The currents hereabouts caused the drift to be up-channel, and although the 'river' here was little more than a stream, coming down through the Foord gap, it had been enough to divert the drift of the shingle temporarily away from the shore, and the spit that was gradually forming acted as a natural breakwater to the anchorage behind. As at Dover conditions had to be carefully watched, or else the drift of the shingle would block up the entire entrance. The accompanying sketch maps show four stages in the development of Folkestone Harbour, under railway management, and although the final stage depicted carries the

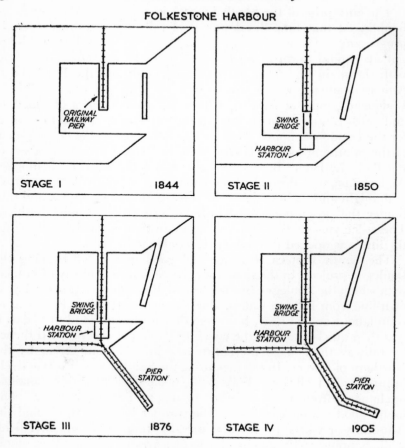

FOLKESTONE HARBOUR

story somewhat beyond the period of this chapter it forms a natural sequel.

Immediately after securing possession the S.E.R. set about construction of the railway pier – quite a short little thing jutting out into the innermost part of the existing harbour, but having the immense advantage over Dover that cross-Channel mails and goods were transferred directly from train to boat. As yet the harbour branch was not authorized for passenger traffic, and passengers were conveyed from the steamers to the Junction station by railway owned omnibuses. As in other matters at that time the South Eastern management always seemed to be two strides ahead of the situation, as it were. They anticipated developments, rather than let themselves be overtaken by them and have to improvise, and at Folkestone they began to plan some important extensions to their installation. The harbour was tidal, and yet it was evident that provision would soon have to be made for much larger ships. The quay wall on the south side of the harbour was available, but ships of the size envisaged would be able to enter the harbour only at high tide, and an ambitious scheme for improvement was put in hand, ultimately to be completed as early as 1863.

It was carried out in two stages. The first stage was planned to coincide with the opening of the Harbour Branch for passenger traffic, following the opening of the railway from Amiens to Boulogne. Following acquisition of the harbour by the S.E.R. the eastward drift of the shingle beyond the existing extent of the spit had been halted by construction of a massive stone groyne. This not only helped in keeping the harbour entrance clear for navigation, but it caused the shingle to build up to the west, to such an extent indeed that a considerable area could be reclaimed from the sea, and on it the new Harbour Station came to be built. Nature was used most effectively to save the South Eastern Railway from some heavy civil engineering work.

To reach the land in process of reclamation the railway had to be extended. Vehicular traffic passed round the western end of the harbour, but the railway pier already existed, and it was extended by means of a swing bridge. This was erected in 1847. It was one of the first of its kind anywhere in the world, and at the time of its construction considerably the largest. Over the swing bridge the railway was brought on to the spit, and the new Harbour Station was opened in 1850. The train-shed, if I may use that rather expressive American term in this instance, was at right-angles to the steamer berths, but this was only one stage in the development of the S.E.R. facilities at Folkestone. The immediate thing was to get the trains near to the steamers, and avoid the long and tiresome transfer that cross-Channel passengers continued to suffer for another eleven years at Dover. At this stage in history Folkestone was more than two strides ahead of its sister port in its transfer facilities.

Although the rise and fall of the tide at Folkestone is no less than twenty feet the harbour was in such good shape that the cross-Channel packets of the day could berth at any state of the tide, though with the far larger ships then projected this would no longer be possible. To be ready for this eventuality stage two of the harbour development was put in hand in the building of the new pier, a seaward extension from the old groyne where the largest Channel packets of the day could berth at any state of the tide.

Unfortunately the ships were ready before the pier, and rather than delay their introduction the cross-Channel services were made tidal from 1861 till the pier was completed in 1863. This was doubly unfortunate, for in that short period the South Eastern sustained the notorious accident at Staplehurst due to the ganger mistaking the day of the week, and thinking he had considerably more time to carry out a renewal job on the Beult viaduct before the passage of the Tidal boat train than was actually the case. The train came hours before the ganger expected it, and a very spectacular and destructive accident resulted. The accident received more publicity than it might otherwise have done through Mr Charles Dickens being a passenger; naturally he wrote graphically of his experience.

Curiously enough, however, it was some days before the railway authorities at London Bridge learned that the famous author was a passenger in the ill-fated train. Samuel Smiles, who was then Secretary of the Company, writes vividly of the first news they, at London Bridge, had of the accident. 'I remember one day Eborall (the General Manager) rushed into my room, which adjoined his own, and said, with frightful alarm, "I am off to Staplehurst by a special engine: I hear there is an awful accident".' After telling the well-known details Smiles continued:

'Of course, the company had to bear all the expense involved by the accident. Everything was done for the relief of the sufferers, and the people of the neighbourhood were most kind. Gallimore, the district inspector, and Benge, the foreman platelayer, were found guilty of manslaughter, and were sent to prison. But their punishment could not remedy the awful injury that had been done.

'Not long after the accident a young lady called upon Mr Eborall and claimed some damage for the injury done to her dress. It was necessary to ask for references – for it was a practice of certain persons to make trade of claiming compensation in railway accidents – he desired to know if any person was with her at the time the accident occurred. "Yes!," she said, "my mother, and Mr Charles Dickens." This was the first time we had heard that Charles Dickens was in the train.'

Meanwhile the inconvenience of railway operating on the harbour branch remained, with the reversal of direction at Folkestone Junction in the case of the boat trains. Nevertheless the Harbour Station was so much more conveniently situated for the townsfolk that they used it in preference to the junction, even though it meant changing trains. At that time there was no station on the site of the present Folkestone Central, which despite its name has always been anything but central so far as the town is concerned. Shorncliffe was the first station west of Folkestone Junction. A project that was eventually to become part of a major plan of South Eastern Railway development was the construction of the short branch line from Sandling Junction to Hythe, in 1872. On the face of it this would appear to have been one of those local connections that would serve a useful purpose in the heyday of railways, and then decline in the face of advance of road transport. This, of course, is what did happen with the Hythe branch.

It is, on the other hand, a most interesting might-have-been! Whether there were any concealed designs at the time of its original construction it is hard to say, but the extension to Sandgate in 1874 was a move of some significance. Although one railway historian has described this event as a 'development of minor importance', it needs no more than a glance at the map to see where a further extension beyond Sandgate would have taken the railway – straight to Folkestone harbour! This project came fully into the open in later years and caused a tremendous furore in the neighbourhood. But if it had been built, what a magnificent run for Continental boat trains it would have made! Unfortunately the project came too late.

The early eighteen-sixties were a time of great enterprise and great ideas on the South Eastern; with the introduction of the fine new ships on the Boulogne service in 1861–2, the inconvenience of working on the Folkestone Harbour branch was thrown into still bolder relief, and sensing local opposition to a railway on the coastal side, which was to come so vigorously into the open in after years, the South Eastern put forward tentative proposals for a line that would diverge leftwards from the main line at a point *west* of Shorncliffe, follow a falling gradient a little steeper than the 1 in 266 of the main line, and then curve round to pass under the Foord Viaduct and join the Harbour branch almost at the water's edge. It was an admirable scheme from the railway point of view, but the opposition of local property owners killed it before the South Eastern even got to the stage of promoting a Bill in Parliament. At that time in railway history there was every incentive to the South Eastern to improve the Folkestone service, for the London Chatham & Dover Railway was then in existence and entering into strong competition for the Continental traffic.

The entry of the 'Chatham' into the field of railway operation in East Kent opens another and very complicated chapter in the story; but before leaving Folkestone to follow the rather slow build-up of cross-Channel facilities at Dover some mention is deserved of the

new ships put into service on the Boulogne run in 1861–2. Built by
Samuda Brothers, these two ships, the *Victoria* and the *Albert Edward*,
must have been the finest and most handsome of any plying on the
narrow seas around Britain at that time. They were evidently designed by someone with a flair for publicity, to give the very embodi-
ment of speed; they had clipper-bows, well-raked masts and funnels,
and to give them an air of special distinction the funnel-tops were
bell-mouthed. This was a feature followed in all ships subsequently
built for the South Eastern Railway. They were paddle-driven, had
a displacement of 374 tons, and steamed at 12½ knots. These two
ships, later reinforced by a third of similar design, the *Napoleon III*,
operated the Folkestone–Boulogne service for upwards of twenty years.

It must be admitted that until the coming of the 'Chatham', the
South Eastern Railway did not seem to pay very much attention to
Dover, as a packet station. They had the mail contract, but for
reasons just discussed were lavishing far more attention on Folkestone, where their interests were not confined to the harbour or to
the Channel passage. At Folkestone the railway company had things
entirely in their own hands, at Dover there were far wider, and sometimes conflicting, interests present, and for some years railway
developments were hamstrung. After the first opening of the line in
1844 it was not long before the local rejoicings were forgotten in a
realization that things were going ahead rapidly in Folkestone while
in their own town, the premier Cinque Port, no steps were being
taken to improve the transfer facilities at the harbour that existed in
pre-railway days.

The situation was complicated. The existing harbour, such as it
was, came under the jurisdiction of the Harbour Commissioners, a
body over which the Corporation of Dover, as such, had no control.
Watching the developments at Folkestone with some anxiety the
Corporation began to make plans for a municipal pier and landing
stage between the existing harbour area and the east cliffs, on which
the Castle stands. Although this was a long way from the existing
railway station it was hoped that if good transfer facilities were installed the South Eastern Railway could be persuaded to extend their
line. It was evident at this stage that little or no opposition would
be raised by the business people and residents of Dover, rather the
reverse. Interest in port facilities at Dover, however, was far more
than a local affair, and responsibility for development did not remain
for long in the hands either of the Corporation, or of the South
Eastern Railway.

For a thousand years the Castle has been a Royal stronghold. For double that time, and far back into the mists of time, Dover has been the gateway to all England, and its very nearness to the Continent inevitably commanded special attention in planning the naval, military and commercial strategy of the whole country. For many years the Corporation was directly responsible to the Sovereign, but in the reign of King James I the responsibility was delegated to a high officer who combined the duties and titles of Constable of the Castle, and Lord Warden of the Cinque Ports. His assistants became known collectively as the Harbour Commissioners. At the time of the construction of the South Eastern Railway the great Duke of Wellington was Lord Warden, but before that he had given some considerable attention to the unsatisfactory state of the harbour, and in 1836 a Parliamentary Inquiry was set up. As usual with such procedures things moved very slowly, and although certain improvements had been made internally, no real advance could be seen by the time the railway was completed.

The independent action of the Corporation in proposing a municipal pier, and the findings of the Parliamentary Inquiry may have precipitated matters, but in fact the Admiralty decided to commence work on a long breakwater, as a first stage towards a series of piers and breakwaters that would eventually constitute a National Harbour at this most strategic of places on the English coast. This grandiose scheme had originally been put forward in the reign of Queen Elizabeth I, when the threats of invasion gave rise to much urgent thought for the national defences. But coming to the time of the South Eastern Railway it is important to appreciate that the Admiralty plans lay completely outside the area over which the Harbour Commissioners held sway. This project which began in 1847 was under national rather than local jurisdiction.

In face of this the South Eastern Railway could do nothing but sit down and await developments. From the outset it was realized that the Admiralty Pier, as the new breakwater became known, would have to be of quite exceptional strength and solidarity. It was built out from the shore at a point where the force of the waves in storm and gale conditions could be tremendous, and it was not surprising that the constructional work took many years. From the outset it was, of course, planned to be much more than a breakwater, though its value to the Harbour Commissioners in this respect was inestimable. It was planned as a landing stage for mail and packet services, and made wide enough to carry a double line of railway. Fourteen years were to elapse, however, before boat trains were allowed to run on to the pier and alongside the steamers.

In the meantime, although the South Eastern Railway was lavishing its attention upon Folkestone its management was not indifferent to the developments that would come at Dover with the completion of the Admiralty Pier, and while they could not do much to improve railway facilities, at any rate for the time being, there was definitely a need for a really first class hotel. The siting of this new edifice came about in a rather amusing and roundabout way. Prior to the coming of the railway the Harbour Commissioners were omnipotent so far as all matters on the shore was concerned, and land had to be obtained from them. The Commissioners struck a hard bargain and insisted upon the railway purchasing a stretch of the foreshore in addition! When the question came of choosing a site for the railway hotel the South Eastern sought permission to buy another piece of the Commissioners' land, but the request was refused, on the grounds that the railway already had the piece of foreshore which it had not put to any purpose so far.

This did not suit the South Eastern purpose at all, for they had hoped to build the hotel nearer to the town, where it would have been conveniently placed for both cross-Channel travellers, and ordinary as well. The story goes, however, that the Commissioners had got the whip hand over the railway in another respect. The station buildings proposed were in the same style as those at London Bridge in 1844, in the Italian style, complete with campanile. At Dover the latter tower was never built. No trouble would have arisen on that score had not a contemporary artist shown the thing in an illustration of the opening festivities! Obviously he had never been present at the ceremony, but drawn the scene in imagination, using the plans of the station as a guide. The Harbour Commissioners continually pressed the railway company to build the campanile, but it is said that honour was eventually satisfied and the account 'squared' when the S.E.R. agreed to build the hotel on the foreshore. Such was the origin of the world-famous Lord Warden Hotel, which was opened in 1851.

Until the year 1854 the mails were conveyed by Admiralty packets steaming from Dover to Calais, and to Ostend; in that year, however, the job was let out to contract, and a local firm, Messrs Jenkins & Churchward, of Dover, took on. They conducted the business under the name of the English, French & Belgian Royal Mail Company, and did the job very well; though seeing how smoothly things worked at Folkestone where trains, harbour facilities, and steamers were all under one management there were some who felt it would be better if similar arrangements could be made at Dover, It was extremely unlikely that a commercial undertaking would ever secure control of the harbour, since the Admiralty Pier was only part of a larger scheme intended to form part of the national defences, but there was a good deal to be said for having the mail contract on land and sea placed with a single company.

It is interesting to compare the traffic through Folkestone and Dover harbours while the South Eastern Railway was the only one concerned. Folkestone had a substantial lead in 1850, and although both ports increased their traffic in the ensuing ten years Dover was, by 1860, beginning to gain on its rival. The following figures relate only to the French traffic, and do not include the Ostend sailings from either port.

Year	Number of Passengers	
	Dover - Calais	Folkestone - Boulogne
1850	54,036	82,016
1860	76,318	96,652

When one looks at the South Eastern Railway position as a whole in the late 'fifties there would appear to be every sign of a solid, secure concern, that had shown considerable enterprise and skill in building up its system; that it was strongly entrenched in South-East London, had a main artery and an excellent system of branches in Kent, and was building up a most flourishing cross-Channel business at Folkestone, while holding the mail contract at Dover. And yet within a few years this carefully consolidating 'empire' was fighting for its very life. It was not a railway battle in the grand manner, with the South Eastern calmly directed, playing the part of an experienced campaigner staving off the fierce, but undisciplined attacks of a reckless young amateur; but a battle in which the older protagonist immediately began to resort to hasty and ill-judged improvisations – a state of affairs that was to last for nearly thirty years.

So far as the Channel crossing is concerned it seems incredible that having been well established at Dover for seventeen years the South Eastern should have seen a new and financially unstable railway company slip in, and within a year of its arrival in the town secure the Government contract for conveyance of the mails not only by land but also by sea! Never, surely, can a major railway company have been caught napping more completely; never can a great prize in transportation have been let slip after a series of most obvious warnings, or opportunities to avert the growing threat and turn it into a handsome advantage. It would seem that the South Eastern Board of the 'fifties was utterly blind to the ultimate dangers of the East Kent project. Not only was there an immediate reversal of their previous fortunes, but the battle with the newcomer was scarcely joined when they gathered into their midst that stormy petrel of the railway world, Sir Edward Watkin. After he had a short period as an ordinary director, the harassed South Eastern shareholders, scarcely knowing what they were doing, elected him Chairman of the Board, in 1866, and from that moment the fat was fairly in the fire.

The story of how a single-tracked local line running from Strood to Faversham, opened in 1858, and of doubtful financial stability, grew so rapidly as to secure the Continental Mail contract only four years later, and in so doing to shake the South Eastern to is very foundations, is one of the greatest dramas in British railway history. If ever a railway deserved the motto *'De l'audace, et encore de l'audace, et toujours de l'audace'* it was the East Kent – soon to become the London, Chatham & Dover. The arrival of the L.C.D.R. at Dover changed everything, so far as the cross-Channel services were concerned; but before coming to the developments that transformed Dover into one of the finest packet stations to be found anywhere we must retrace steps back to 1853 to follow the spectacular rise of the new competitor, to be followed so soon by an equally spectacular financial crash.

IV

The East Kent and the Mail Contract

WITH the gradual development of the railway network all over England it needed no more than a glance at the map of Kent in 1850 to show how inadequate the South Eastern Railway system then was for the county as a whole. It was then 102 miles by rail from London Bridge to both Margate and Deal; Rochester and Chatham were served by nothing better than a branch line station at Strood, on the western bank of the Medway, while Faversham, Sittingbourne, and the Isle of Sheppey had, as yet, no railway communication at all. In view of the developments elsewhere it is no wonder that influential people living in the Medway towns and eastwards towards Thanet began to press for some more direct means of travel. That they would have the backing of Parliament seemed reasonably sure, for at that time anything in the way of a business monopoly was considered against the public interest.

At the end of the year 1849 the question of constructing a direct line of railway from Strood to Dover was actively discussed, and on 29th January, 1850, a large meeting was held in Rochester. It was pointed out during this meeting how great the saving in distance and time would be between the towns in East Kent and London by the construction of such a line. Faversham, it was stated, stood to gain most, to the extent of 34 miles, though the saving to Margate and Ramsgate would be 27 or 28 miles, and even to Dover – primarily the goal of the South Eastern Railway – the saving in distance would be 16 miles. This was comparing distances with the original South Eastern line via Redhill, as the direct route via Sevenoaks was not constructed until 1868.

Although the idea of setting up a new line, independent of the South Eastern, was received with some enthusiasm, practical support for the new venture was not very readily forthcoming. There were no strong business interests backing it, and for some time after that Rochester meeting there existed a curious inversion of the usual order of things, in that engineers who were anxious to build the line were canvassing for financial support. At that Rochester meeting it was a certain Mr Taylor who had the role of engineer, and explained the route proposed; but he seems to have dropped out of the picture immediately, to be succeeded by Thomas Russell Crampton, the famous locomotive designer. A man of Kent by birth, born at Broadstairs in 1816, he would have had a natural interest in a railway through his very own county, but circumstances made easy his entry to this particular arena.

He left the Great Western where he had been at Swindon under Daniel Gooch, in 1844, and joined Sir John Rennie, under whom he could practice as a civil engineer while developing his very original ideas in locomotive design. While serving under Rennie he became associated with an engineer named Morris, and it was these two who essayed the task of securing financial support for the proposed East Kent Railway. From all accounts it took some doing, but eventually, with the assistance of George Burge, the engineer of St Katherine Docks and Herne Bay Pier they persuaded Lord Harris to form a company. The enterprise was shaky and timorous from the very start. Morris and Burge apparently saw the red light, and dropped out at an early stage, and watching events from their own well-established position one can well imagine that the South Eastern Board could look on with interest, but without the slightest alarm.

In retrospect, the trend of affairs in the mid-fifties of last century would appear to have been so obvious for the South Eastern: to let this unstable, reluctantly-supported local railway flounder along, get itself built, and then purchase it at rock-bottom price. Three years elapsed from that Rochester meeting before the Company secured an Act to enable them to build the line from Strood to Canterbury, and two years later authorization was received for the extension from Canterbury to Dover. Funds were low, and construction went forward very slowly, and when the line did eventually open for traffic throughout from Strood as far as Faversham, in March, 1858, it was single-tracked from end to end. It could be considered as no more than a rural extension of the North Kent line of the South Eastern, rather than the beginnings of a new and highly competitive main line, and its Act included a facilitations clause which required the South Eastern to handle East Kent traffic as expeditiously as its own between Strood and London Bridge.

One can be impressed, at this stage, by the extreme slowness of development of the East Kent project: three years to secure the Act for a line that was generally acclaimed; another five years to build $18\frac{1}{2}$ miles of line! Apart from the immediate neighbourhood of Chatham the country traversed was very easy, and the Medway viaduct, and the three tunnels through the chalk were not such as to cause undue difficulty. Although the line was built as a single-track provision was made from the outset for double line, and no widening of the Chatham and Gillingham tunnels was subsequently needed. When the line itself was ready, and the single track laid, the Company had no locomotives, and six 2-2-2s of the Small Hawthorn type had to be borrowed from the Great Northern Railway. The service provided was not exactly heroic, five trains a day in each direction, taking 50 min for the run of 18½ miles.

Despite the facilitations clause in the Act of the East Kent Railway the South Eastern put every obstruction in the way, and even went to the extent of announcing publicly that they would handle no East Kent traffic. It was at this stage that the grand strategy of the South Eastern management began to go seriously awry. If they had been helpful, and allowed the East Kent to muddle along it would seem that sooner or later the impecunious newcomer would have ground to a standstill, and its impoverished owners would have been glad enough to sell out, for whatever they could get. But the attitude of the South Eastern antagonized everyone, including Parliament, and the way was opened for the startling developments that were to follow.

To an onlooker the attitude of the South Eastern Railway in face of this threat must have been very puzzling, but at this very time Samuel Smiles, the famous biographer of the Stephensons and other eminent engineers, was appointed Secretary, and in his own autobiography he throws an interesting and amusing light upon proceedings around the South Eastern Board table. Smiles was naturally elated at getting the job so quickly after being left redundant by the amalgamation of the four northern companies which formed the North Eastern, but Robert Stephenson gave him a plain hint as to what he was in for at London Bridge, and in a letter dated 29th November, 1854, he wrote:

'My dear Sir,

'I am very glad to hear of your success, and I trust sincerely it may be permanent; but I fear you will find the South Eastern a very difficult concern to keep in train satisfactorily. More of this when I have the pleasure of seeing you.'

Smiles continues:

'As Robert Stephenson had predicted, it was not a very quiet berth in which I found myself, at the Board-room of the South Eastern Railway. The direction of the company was in a state of transition. Mr Macgregor, the former chairman, had been dispossessed of his office by a majority of the directors but no new chairman had been appointed. The ministry was without a head, and the opposition was strong. It was not so much business as speech-making, that seemed to be the work of the Board. Macgregor was often attacked, and defended himself with ability.

'There was even a third party at the Board, headed by Mr Forster, member for Berwick, who, however, like Harry o'the Wynd, often fought for his own hand. I soon found that Mr Forster was ready to trip me up about the composition of the minutes. The reason was, that he had been disappointed in not securing the election, in my place, of a fellow-member of the Reform Club, whom he had introduced and supported. I had therefore to be cautious. When my minutes were first read, he disputed their accuracy. I said that, so far as I knew, they correctly registered the decisions arrived at by the Board. "That may be," he said, "but they do not give 'the proceedings'." He appealed to the solicitor, who constantly sat at the Board. The solicitor referred to the Act, which said "minutes and proceedings". I had therefore to amend my ways, and insert not only what was determined upon, but what was proposed and discussed. All this was, of course, with a view to future proceedings, when an appeal came to be made to the shareholders.

'The majority of the Board, not having a good speaker, determined to introduce a new man for the purpose of meeting Macgregor and Forster. They found him in an able gentleman, who, however, was without a qualification. The majority gave him the qualification, and elected him to a vacant seat. He soon proved his power as a speaker, by walking into Macgregor. The latter had sent to the Register Office, and ascertained the nature of his qualification. He then rose, pounced upon the new man like a vulture, and tore him to pieces. It was exciting and amusing, but it was not business. I had never seen such a thing before. In former times, I had seen men of active habits meet round a table for the purpose of getting through their work, and pass their minutes without rising from their seats. But here were men who rose to their feet, and made elaborate and cutting speeches, without getting through any work at all. It seemed to me a fruitless waste of time.'

Smiles had scarcely settled into his position before there came the great bullion robbery. The story of this affair has been told many times and has recently been featured in a television programme. Although the details of this exciting and well-planned *coup* might provide inspiring material for any of the writers of detective fiction from Conan Doyle onwards, so far as the South Eastern Railway was concerned Smiles aptly sums up the position:

'Railway companies have neither souls nor bodies, but they have purses; and when it was found (as afterwards appeared) that a person high up in the Passenger Department was in collusion with a guard and a common thief to rob the company of the gold carried on the line for the

Left: Sir Charles Gregory, Engineer of the London and Croydon Railway; inventor of the earliest signal boxes on the S.E.R.

Right: Sir Edward Watkin, Bart., Chairman, S.E.R.

Left: Sir Francis Dent, General Manager, S.E.C.R. Managing Committee, 1911–1920

Right: R. E. L. Maunsell, Chief Mechanical Engineer, S.E.C.R. 1913–1922.

Folkestone Harbour: a very early drawing showing the first swing bridge.

Folkestone Harbour in later Victorian times, showing, amid the masts of shipping, the second swing bridge.

[Folkestone Public Library

Folkestone Harbour

South Eastern & Continental Steam Packet Company steamer *Ondine*, in service 1847–1855.

Above: L.C.D.R. paddle steamer *Empress*, introduced on the Dover–Calais service in 1887.

Below: S.E.C.R. turbine steamer *Maid of Orleans* built 1918, sunk by enemy action June, 1944.
[*British Railways*

London bullionists, it must be admitted that things had been allowed to go a great deal too far, and that a clearance of some of the incapables (to say the least of them) must soon be made.'

The plain fact was that £14,000 in gold bars had vanished into empty air, and for eighteen months there was not a clue as to how it had happened. The discovery, and subsequent confession of one of the gang, revealed that the whole thing had been facilitated by the active participation of the Assistant Superintendent in the Passenger Manager's Office at London Bridge, one Tester, who before the discovery was made had left the S.E.R. service to become General Manager of the Royal Swedish Railway. The circumstances in which, all unsuspecting, he returned to England on a visit to some friends and walked straight into the net that was prepared for him were not the least interesting part of the story. Far from continuing his distinguished post in Sweden he, like the guard of the mail train on which the robbery took place, was sentenced to fourteen years' transportation. From a case like that of Tester, and from the divisions round the Board table, it is not surprising that the South Eastern outwardly appeared hesitant and irresolute in meeting the East Kent threat.

Faced with the prospect of South Eastern obstruction at Strood once the East Kent line was built, the latter company determined to have their own line into London. Better communication with the capital had been the major argument advanced in favour of the East Kent Railway at the 1850 meeting in Rochester, but with the South Eastern management in its then state of mind the East Kent would be constrained to nothing more than a local shuttle service. At this stage luck – other than financial of course; – was on the side of the East Kent, and the thrusting out from London of two independent railways gave a clear pointer to the way the East Kent might make its entry. The accompanying map shows how this came about. The two companies were the West End of London & Crystal Palace, and the Mid Kent. The former had its 'West End terminus' on the river bank, on the site now occupied by Battersea power station; it followed the course of the present Brighton main line to Balham Junction and thence to Crystal Palace. It was the connections at the eastern end that provided the entry for the East Kent.

The Crystal Palace line connected with the main line of the Brighton railway in a triangle junction, the southern spur joining in at Norwood Junction, and the northern at Sydenham. The Crystal Palace line was worked, from its inception, by the Brighton, but the Mid-Kent, nothing more than a short branch from Lewisham to Beckenham, was worked by the South Eastern. The Mid-Kent proposed an extension through Bromley to St Mary Cray, and the Crystal Palace line was promoting an extension from its Norwood triangle to join the Mid-Kent at Beckenham. In conjunction with these proposals the East Kent put forward a scheme for a westward extension from Strood to make an end-on junction with the Mid-Kent at St Mary Cray. Naturally the South Eastern, which had a mild interest in the Mid-Kent, strongly opposed this East Kent development, which was represented as duplicating the facilities that would be provided by their own Dartford loop line, being promoted at the same time. It was at this stage that the South Eastern Board began to take the East Kent threat rather more seriously and at a meeting held in May, 1858, arrangements were made for an approach to the East Kent, without in any way compromising the directors. In the meantime the company's solicitors were instructed to continue opposing the East Kent Bill with undiminished vigour.

It is sometimes thought that it was the later advances of the Chatham line towards London that forced the South Eastern into the very expensive extension from London Bridge westwards to Cannon Street and Charing Cross. It is interesting to find therefore that at this very same Board meeting in May, 1858, before the East Kent had received authority for its westward extension from Strood, the South Eastern was actively considering the Charing Cross line, and arrangements were made for an approach to the London & South Western Railway over a proposed link with that line at Waterloo. At that stage it seemed that the South Eastern was still three strides or more ahead of its potential rival. Again, at that same meeting the chance to finance the Crays Railway, as the Mid-Kent extension was known, was laid before the Board. It was emphasized that if the South Eastern missed this chance there was a serious risk that the East Kent would take it, and thus advance their sphere of influence as far west as Bromley. A decision at this point was unfortunately postponed.

Consideration of the Charing Cross line came from a directors pledge, in 1857, to call the shareholders together and 'recommend them to promote or concur in the prosecution in next session, of such a scheme as will effectually supply access to the West End of London, and so complete the system of railway communication for Kent and the Continent.' By the late autumn of 1857, however, nothing had been done to redeem this pledge, and so Mr Eborall, the General Manager, with the active assistance of Smiles made an interesting traffic survey of the directions taken by the passengers leaving London

Bridge Station. From this it appeared that more than three-fifths of all passengers were bound for points west of Temple Bar, and as a result a proposal was laid before the Board recommending that the terminus of the proposed extension line should be at Charing Cross.

Then, in June, 1858, came a development that might have profoundly altered the whole complexion of things in Kent. In conformity with the practice of many of the early railways the South Eastern had a consulting engineer, rather than a full-time engineer of the highest standing to look after the way and works. In many cases the engineer who built the railway in the first place was retained in a consultative capacity, just as Robert Stephenson held the title of Chief Engineer to the L.N.W.R. In June, 1858, Mr Rendel having died, the South Eastern Board appointed Joseph Locke as Consulting Engineer, and in less than a month he was in a fair way to becoming charged with a vitally important task. Negotiations between the South Eastern and East Kent had reached the stage of Robert Stephenson being asked to arbitrate, and at the end of June, 1858, a very important proposal was laid before the South Eastern Board.

It was considered desirable that the South Eastern should be the proprietor of the East Kent Railway, provided that the line to Dover was completed, as authorized. First of all the East Kent was required, at its own expense, to complete the line from Strood to Canterbury, and to the satisfaction of Joseph Locke. Then, the stock capital of the two companies was to be amalgamated, and the East Kent shareholders were to receive dividends of 1 per cent less than those of the South Eastern for the first five years of amalgamation – after that period the dividends paid would be the same. Having absorbed the East Kent the South Eastern would complete the line from Canterbury to Dover at their own expense, on condition that the existing contract for the construction of the line be cancelled, and the South Eastern permitted to employ a contractor acceptable to Mr Locke.

Some of the South Eastern directors opposed the scheme of amalgamation. It was argued that when the full extent of the liabilities of the East Kent Railway was known a majority of the S.E.R. proprietors would be unwilling to accept them. The dissenters were very much in a minority, and the proposal was accepted by the South Eastern Board with a majority of eight to two. On the other side the issue was infinitely more complicated. One would have thought that the majority of the shareholders would have welcomed the merger with open arms; but throughout its history, whether as

East Kent or London, Chatham & Dover, it always seemed a case of the tail wagging the dog. Crampton himself was the contractor for the Canterbury–Dover section of the East Kent Railway, and by the terms of the proposed merger he was to be dispensed with, and someone of Locke's choice put in instead. Now as Crampton had been one of the moving spirits in the East Kent Railway from its very inception it can be well imagined how this condition of the merger went against the grain, in certain quarters, and precarious though the financial position was, even at that time, the proposal fell through.

The extent to which the East Kent Railway was short of ready money takes some believing. The slowness with which the construction of the line went forward was almost entirely due to there being nothing with which to pay the contractors. Crampton was anxious enough to get on with the job, and in October, 1858, he made an offer to the Board, that included these two significant items. He would carry on, and as payment became due for works completed he would advance the money to the company at an interest rate of 10 per cent. In the same letter he offered to lend them £10,000 for twelve months at 5 per cent to enable them to buy the land for the station and yards at Canterbury. It is no wonder that the works progressed slowly, and no wonder either that some of the South Eastern directors were unwilling that their company should take over such a tangle of liabilities.

In the meantime the Act authorizing the East Kent's westward extension from Strood to St Mary Cray was passed, and in the following year, 1859, this small, shaky but audacious concern fairly hoisted its 'battle ensign', by changing its name to the London, Chatham & Dover Railway. There could no longer be any doubts as to its ultimate intentions. With running powers over the Mid-Kent, and the Crystal Palace lines its way was now clear to the south bank of the Thames, at Battersea. The only 'fly in the ointment' was that none of the lines were yet built. As yet, the original line did not extend east of Faversham, let alone to Dover, though the single-tracked line of the Mid-Kent, from Bromley to St Mary Cray, had been working since August, 1858.

The Board agreed to Crampton's proposals and work went ahead with the important connecting link between Canterbury and Dover. Cubitt as engineer of the company, was, of course, required to keep a watchful eye on the progress of Crampton's contracts, but despite the financial arrangement that had been made in the previous autumn, things were still far from well, and in September, 1859,

Cubitt was compelled to report that the progress of the work between Canterbury and Dover was 'highly unsatisfactory'. Crampton got a sharp letter from the Board, with the warning that the directors would make a personal inspection in a month's time. Although the building of the line was financed in so unorthodox and risky a way the railway as a whole was a good one and well suited to fast running. There were curves, as through the Medway towns, and some hard gradients; but for the most part it was a fine open road on which one could go as hard as the engines of the day were capable. The final stretch from Canterbury to Dover included the long tunnel through the chalk at Lydden summit, and two more considerable tunnels at Dover itself.

With the existing liabilities, of which certain South Eastern directors were familiar enough, and the prospect of paying tolls for running powers over the lines from St Mary Cray to Battersea the desirability of coming to terms with the South Eastern before it was too late was obvious enough, and at a Board meeting on 10th November, 1859, it was reported that Lord Sondes, Chairman of the L.C.D.R., was anxious to re-open negotiations. To check any would-be speculators on the Stock Exchange it was considered essential that any such negotiations should be kept as secret and confidential as possible, and a meeting was arranged at the London Tavern on 23rd November, 1859, at which Lord Sondes, and two other L.C.D.R. directors met the Hon. James Byng, Chairman of the S.E.R., and Messrs Thomson and Rich. To the consternation of the South Eastern representatives, on the very next morning *The Times* published news of the meeting. Even though there was no reference to the subjects discussed the mere fact that there *had* been a meeting was enough to set tongues wagging, and assuming that the leakage could only have come from the Chatham side a strong protest was sent to Lord Sondes.

Although the threat of competition was serious the South Eastern could well afford to take a detached air towards the newcomer. In the year 1859 the dividend paid on the ordinary stock was 4½ per cent and at that time even the London & North Western was not paying more than 4¾ per cent. Several directors were most insistent that any approaches for amalgamation should come from the Chatham side. By all the laws of business probability the L.C.D.R. would be on its knees before long and the take-over could be made on very advantageous terms. Unfortunately the South Eastern management of the time was not merely aloof, but aggressive, and wider interests that were averse to the establishment of a one-railway monopoly in Kent took the side of the weaker of the two protagonists. The chances of agreement were lessening with every month that passed, and the stage was slowly getting set for the thirty-five years of warfare that was to bring the railways of South-Eastern England so low in public estimation.

From the mounting antagonism between the two companies we must turn for a moment to the expansion of the Chatham system itself. The line to Canterbury was at last brought into service in July, 1860, and a regular service to London operated from December of the same year. By that time the Victoria Station & Pimlico Railway had completed the bridge across the Thames at Battersea, and when the service was inaugurated the L.C.D.R. trains ran into Victoria. In so doing three separate sets of running powers were exercised: over the Mid-Kent, from St Mary Cray to Bromley; over the Crystal Palace, from Bromley to Battersea, and thence over the newly-completed bridge of the Pimlico company into Victoria. A year later the line was opened between Canterbury and Dover – at first only to the Priory station; but in November, 1861, Dover Tunnel was completed and the Harbour station was brought into service. This latter was on the site of the present Hawkesbury Street Junction, and little more than a stone's throw from the rival South Eastern terminus, situated on the beach. So, by the end of the year 1861 the venturesome newcomer was the London, Chatham & Dover Railway in fact, as well as in name.

Despite the odd way in which it had grown up the new line was already a potentially formidable competitor for the overseas mail and continental traffic at Dover. The distance from the Harbour station to Victoria was only 81 miles in comparison with the 87·5 miles to London Bridge by the South Eastern route via Redhill. At first, however, there was not a great deal in it, for what Chatham gained in distance they lost in running facilities. The heavy gradients of the route were bad enough in themselves but at the London end the meandering course via the Crystal Palace and Balham was hardly suitable for the handling of heavy main line traffic. So, in 1860 Parliamentary powers were obtained for the L.C.D.R. to construct a line of their own into the very heart of London: a two-pronged drive as it were, with terminal stations at Victoria and Ludgate Hill, and connections with the northern railways at Farringdon Street. By this means the main line to Dover would be shortened by three miles; but the saving in running time would be nearer ten minutes.

The Board was evidently thinking well ahead, for in the autumn of 1860, long before the line to Dover was complete, enquiries were being made about cross-Channel ships, and feelers put out to find out the prices at which the present holders of the seaborne mail contract might sell some of their vessels. This contract was in the hands of Messrs Jenkins & Churchward, of Dover, but the Chatham seems to have got wind of an impending Government intention to place a single contract for the conveyance of the mail from London to the French coast. In retrospect the Chatham Board are seen as nothing if not optimistic! Their line to Dover was being constructed only with the most precarious of financial backing; they were getting still more involved in London, and now they were considering the purchase of a fleet of steamships. This latter project had evidently got well beyond the stage of consideration by the December of 1860, for in that month a certain Mr Morgan was appointed Naval Architect to the Company.

A still more momentous appointment was shortly to follow. Applications were invited for the post of General Manager. Hitherto the concern had not been large enough to warrant the employment of any such person, and one gathers that the running of the railway had been largely in the hands of the engineer, Cubitt. One of the applicants for the new and most important post was F. P. Cockshott, who was then on the South Devon Railway. One pauses for a moment to reflect upon how the history of railways in Kent might have been changed had that brilliant operating officer secured the post, and gone to Victoria Street instead of to Kings Cross as he did some four years later. The Chatham Board favoured instead the application of James Staats Forbes, then Manager of the Dutch Rhenish Railway. They must have been extremely anxious to secure his services, for at a meeting on 22nd March, 1861, when he was offered the job he explained that he could not take over fully till his Rhenish agreement had expired. 'Never mind that', said the Chatham people in effect. 'Give us what time you can,' and his formal appointment was fixed as from 1st September, 1862, for a period of five years.

For a company perpetually tottering on the brink of bankruptcy Forbes was an expensive luxury from the very outset. One recalls Richard Moon's stinging protest to the Marquess of Chandos at the salary paid to William Cawkwell when he was appointed General Manager of the London & North Western, yet here was the L.C.D.R. Board giving J. S. Forbes the same salary, £1,500 per annum, for managing a rickety half-finished local line in Kent! That, however, was not all. Many years later, writing his obituary notice in *The Railway Magazine* Mr. G. A. Sekon put Forbes down as 'a past master in the art of *bunkum* . . .', and from that first interview in March,

1861, he seems to have twisted my Lords Sondes and Harris, and all the other titled and distinguished gentlemen of the Chatham Board, round his little finger. Not only did he secure an enormous salary, but it was arranged that if the net receipts increased over the net receipts on the first year's working after the completion of the line to Dover, he was to receive 1 per cent commission. There was a rider to this part of his agreement, however, namely that his commission was never to be less than £500 per annum! Forbes certainly got away to a good start as far as his personal fortune was concerned.

Although he did not take up his full-time duties with the L.C.D.R. until September, 1862, the dynamic influence of Forbes was felt almost at once. Though he feathered his own nest very successfully one cannot deny that he worked very hard and energetically, and the securing of the mail contract in 1862 was largely due to his opportunism. It would have seemed that the South Eastern was in a strong position to take on the whole job. They had a well-established route, and good steamers, but the Government route stipulated a sea passage from Dover to Calais. The South Eastern was closely allied with the Northern Railway of France, and strongly favoured Boulogne, not only because its railway ally was strongly established there, but because the port facilities were so much better. When the Government decided to place the mail contract in a single hand it was naturally offered to the South Eastern. It is easy to say that the Board was blind to all the immediate consequences in making the decision it did in refusing the contract; but the South Eastern management was always more mindful of its shareholders than its passengers, and clearly saw less profit than prestige in carrying the Government mails.

All the same the attitude of the Company seems to have been a curious one. They were then carrying the mails on land, and on consideration of this the Admiralty had permitted the extension of the railway from the Town station – on the site of the present locomotive sheds – to run on to the completed portion of the Admiralty Pier. Express trains from London carried both local and Continental passengers, and a stop was made at the Town station to set down passengers not going by boat. The latter were not in the ordinary way permitted to make use of the station on the pier. One cannot imagine anyone really wanting to, for it was a primitive thing, very much exposed to the weather, and reached only by a walk across the cobble-stones on the seaward side of the Lord Warden Hotel. Although so well established alongside the boats the South Eastern refused the contract.

With characteristic audacity the Chatham leapt into the breach, making an arrangement with Messrs Jenkins & Churchward for the sea passage, and the Continental service began in July, 1862. Even then facilities at Dover were not complete, and at a Board meeting held on the 18th of that month a resolution was passed drawing the attention of Messrs Cubitt & Crampton to the fact that no objection remained to the immediate completion of the 'tramway' from Dover Harbour station to the pier, and it was expected they would make every exertion to get it completed quickly. It was not quite so easy as all that. There were local restrictions to be surmounted, and while the South Eastern, without the contract, continued running on to the pier, it was not until 1864 that the L.C.D.R. trains were able to do the same.

In view of the approaching completion of the L.C.D.R. to Dover, the South Eastern sought to improve their own facilities at Folkestone by construction of a direct line to the Harbour, avoiding the need for reversal at Folkestone Junction, and the difficulties associated with the severe gradients of the Harbour branch. But, as told in Chapter III, this proposal came to nought, and before the year 1862 was out negotiations were in hand for a pooling arrangement with the Chatham over Continental traffic. On Saturday 31st January, 1863, Lord Harris, Sir Cusack Roney, and Charles J. Hilton met three South Eastern directors at the Westminster Palace Hotel, and agreed on a provisional system of pooling traffics, but it was not until 2½ years later, on 7th September, 1865, that the final agreement was concluded, an agreement that was to prove a godsend to the Chatham and a millstone round the neck of the South Eastern.

The agreement included traffic to the Continent from all stations in a six-mile radius of Charing Cross via Dover, Folkestone and any other port that might be used along the coast anywhere between Ramsgate and Hastings. Not only Continental but inland traffic to Dover and Folkestone from the same prescribed area in London was included. This latter part of the agreement was to lead to a lengthy lawsuit with heavy damages awarded in favour of Chatham. But to revert to the actual agreement, there was established a common fund into which the traffic receipts from both companies was to be paid, and the fund was to be divided on a sliding scale, as follows:

Year	Percentage to S.E.R.	Percentage to L.C.D.R.
1863	68	32
1864	66	34
1865	65	35
1866	64	36
1867	61	39
1868	59	41
1869	56	44
1870	54	46
1871	52	48
1872	50	50

After 1872 both companies were to continue to receive 50 per cent. How the South Eastern directors were ever persuaded to sign such an agreement defies the imagination. They had two ports, instead of one; the Chatham did not serve Folkestone at all, yet they would receive a goodly proportion of the South Eastern receipts, both from inland and Continental traffic. 'The art of bunkum' was being practised to good effect from the Chatham side.

V

The London Competition and the Crash

THE Metropolitan extensions of the London, Chatham & Dover Railway, authorized in 1860, can be considered in three sections:

(a) Penge to Herne Hill;
(b) Herne Hill through Ludgate Hill to Farringdon Street on the Metropolitan;
(c) Herne Hill to Battersea.

The company displayed considerable skill in getting other railways to invest in its projects, and there is no doubt that the policy of establishing good running connections with as many other trunk lines as possible in London was entirely sound. Quite apart from the railway politics of mid-Victorian times these connections came to prove invaluable for the handling of through north-south traffic in two world wars. Lord Sondes, and the Chatham Board of 1859–60 indeed planned better than they knew, and it is ironical that a group of lines that was to prove of such immense strategic value was at first nothing but a financial millstone around the necks of those who projected it.

The Great Northern and the London & South Western both invested heavily in the London extensions of the Chatham, in return for nothing more than running powers. The latter company obtained, at a mere fraction of their total cost, two lines driving into the heart of London districts where the potential business was enormous. While the South Eastern had advanced no further into the capital than London Bridge the Chatham crossed the river and established a station actually in the City, at Ludgate Hill. For many years after its construction the northward continuation to join the Metropolitan, at Farringdon Street, probably brought in little revenue; but that connection was the bait that brought in the big Great Northern investment, just as the connections between Longhedge and Clapham Junction brought in the South Western. The western extension from Herne Hill was the first of the new lines to be constructed, and the

completion and opening took place simultaneously with the opening
of the new section of Victoria station.

The so-called 'Chatham-side' of Victoria arose from congestion in
the original station of the Victoria Station & Pimlico Railway, used
at first by the Brighton, the Chatham and the Great Western.
Then the V.S.P. built the separate station on the east side of the
Brighton station, and the Chatham people, with their usual skill in
getting others to share the cost, arranged with the Great Western to
become joint lessees of the new section. The Great Western must
have got mighty little out of it. Victoria had no more than a service
of local trains. From time to time sporadic attempts were made to
run Great Western express services from the Midlands into Victoria,
but they could never have been profitable. The new section at Victoria
and the direct Chatham line as far as Herne Hill were opened in

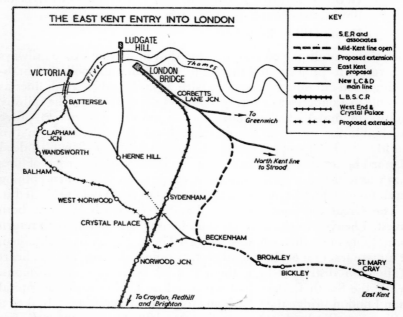

August, 1862, though having crossed the Thames the line descended
steeply to Stewarts Lane, and then climbed again to reach the eleva-
tion of a line on arches, continuing thus through Clapham and
Brixton to Herne Hill. The 'direct line' was completed in July,
1863, by the opening of the section through the Penge Tunnel, and
from that date Chatham trains ceased to use the old roundabout
route over the West End of London & Crystal Palace Railway.

The northward connection from Herne Hill did not go ahead so rapidly. No difficulty was experienced in getting through to the Elephant & Castle; but in crossing the river the project was held up for a time by the Corporation of London. Because of its proximity to the new Blackfriars road bridge, it was insisted that the railway bridge should have the same number of arches; and as the Corporation apparently could not make up its mind as to the design of the road bridge the L.C.D.R. bridge was also held up! Delays or not, the whole extension work of the Chatham was going ahead rapidly enough to awaken the South Eastern to their own position in South London, and to put a new sense of urgency into the protracted deliberations over the westward extension from London Bridge. Things might have gone ahead more rapidly, but the South Eastern Board was actively encouraging support from the South Western in what promised to be a very expensive piece of construction, and the running connection at Waterloo was an important part of the scheme. The line was promoted by a separate company, the Charing Cross Railway. It was authorized in 1863, and in considera-tion of the heavy engineering work involved was completed in remarkably quick time.

As an operating proposition it proved a nightmare for many years. Anxious to counter the thrust into the City by their Chatham rivals the South Eastern included in their great scheme a second terminus north of the river. For the City business-man Cannon Street was superbly sited, no more than a few minutes walk from the Bank of England; but for very many years the South Eastern per-sisted in the practice of making nearly all their trains call at Cannon Street on the way from London Bridge to Charing Cross. The result was that every train had to reverse direction, be re-engined, and cross the path of every other train at the junction immediately south of the Cannon Street river bridge. This practice persisted right down to the year 1914, even with some Continental boat expresses, which, starting from Charing Cross, called at Cannon Street to pick up mail traffic.

It is difficult today to imagine the 'London' into which the Chatham and the South Eastern cut when the Metropolitan extensions were built, now nearly a hundred years ago. Southwark, renowned as it might have been for its ancient and picturesque galleried inns, was a most unsavoury district. The old houses had been allowed to degener-ate into a shocking state of dilapidation, and many were overrun with vermin. The district immediately north of the river was not very much better. The Strand was then no more than the largest of a number of old streets lined with tall and picturesque old houses. The establishment of the new railway terminus at Charing Cross, the building of the fine hotel was the first step towards the opening out and modernizing of the whole area, and many of the older properties in these days which might have scheduled as buildings of historical interest and restored to a state of good repair were swept ruthlessly away. The South Eastern Board evidently had an eye to the preservation of some relics, for they voted a sum of £1,600 for the erection of a replica of the Eleanor Cross in the forecourt of Charing Cross Station, and the architect got a sharp rebuke when it was discovered that the sum allocated had been exceeded by £200!

The Chatham line, in particular, was saddled with the reputation of being a great destroyer of old houses, and it was largely in consequence of this that the railway which could least afford it was more or less forced to run the first workmen's trains, at what we should now consider fantastically low fares. These trains ran in each direction between Victoria and Ludgate Hill, and were known as the 'Workmen's Penny Trains.' Great care was taken to check the *bona fides* of the passengers using these trains. Each prospective passenger had to apply for a weekly season ticket, price one shilling, not later than the Thursday of the previous week; then he was required to give the name and address of his employer, and in return the shilling ticket authorized him to travel once a day in each direction between any two stations on the route. Passengers were not allowed to vary their journeys from day to day. If a man specified, for example, Elephant & Castle to North Stockwell he was not allowed any variation during the week. No luggage was allowed, other than tool bags up to a maximum weight of 28 lb.

The South Eastern managed to get the Charing Cross Railway completed before the Chatham was able to open its line to Ludgate Hill – in fact the S.E.R. won this particular race by nearly a year. By this time it must have been evident that a battle royal was on with the Chatham, and some of the more wide-awake of the South Eastern shareholders began to feel that a greater vigour and strength of leadership was needed from the Board. On the Chatham side, Forbes, as General Manager, was going great guns, but under the Chairmanship of the Hon. James Byng the South Eastern was pursuing a course more 'dignified and stately' – to use Sir W. S. Gilbert's phrase from *Iolanthe* – than the circumstances warranted. In October, 1864, a group of shareholders resident in Manchester under the leadership of Mr John Stuart urged upon Byng the need for a change in the direction of the company's affairs and suggested bringing in Edward

Watkin, who at that time was Member of Parliament for Hythe.

Manchester men who were railway shareholders would be familiar enough with the activities of Edward Watkin at that time, in his persistent endeavours to sell the Manchester, Sheffield & Lincolnshire to one of the larger companies on highly advantageous terms. Wakin himself had, of course, the most grandiose ideas on railway empire building, and had visions of a line from Manchester to the northern shores of France (via the Channel Tunnel) and eventually under one management – his management. The Manchester group suggested that someone on the Board might be persuaded to retire, so that a seat could be found for Watkin. At first this suggestion got a rebuff, and John Stuart was reminded that the wishes of all shareholders had to be taken into account in the election of directors, not only the desires of a relatively small group. It was always said that Watkin was the stormy petrel of the railway world, and even at this first suggestion of his inclusion a first class row blew up around the South Eastern Board table.

Apparently, after the text of a letter to be sent to Stuart had been agreed upon by the full Board, one of the directors had suggested to Samuel Smiles, the Secretary, that a certain phrase be left out. At the next meeting when the omission was discovered the strongest exception was taken to this irregularity. The wrangle went on for more than a month, but by dint of not a little back-stage lobbying the resignation of a certain Mr Whatman was secured, and Watkin was elected in his place on 19th January, 1865. Less than two months later he became Deputy Chairman, and in March, 1866, he succeeded Byng as Chairman. A new vigour was instilled into the conduct of South Eastern affairs with a vengeance, but unfortunately for the travelling public Watkin combined with his vigour a pugnacious, aggressive, uncompromising nature that seemed to revel in fighting to get his own way.

Before Watkin joined the Board the South Eastern had become involved in two elaborate projects in competition with the northern and western connections of the Chatham. These became known as the Charing Cross Northern and the Charing Cross Western Railways. The first was intended, primarily, to link up with the London & North Western, though connections with the Midland and Great Northern were also envisaged as a future development. The western extension was to run via South Kensington and Hammersmith. This latter scheme was put forward before the authorization of the Metropolitan District Railway. In that same year, 1864, a Joint Parliamentary Committee, considering a number of schemes for establishing railway communication in and across London decided in favour of an underground line, and by 1868 the first section of the District Railway, between South Kensington and Westminster, was opened for traffic. This killed the 'Charing Cross Western' Scheme stone dead, but the northern proposal went much further.

By March, 1864, negotiations between the South Eastern and the London & North Western had reached the stage of definite financial proposals being made, and agreed on both sides. No difficulty was anticipated in raising the necessary capital. The two major companies decided that the shares should be made available to their own shareholders with a guaranteed dividend of 5 per cent. The South Eastern stated that they were prepared to work the line, if they were asked. To judge from the cordial tone of the correspondence that passed between the two secretaries, Samuel Smiles for the South Eastern, and Charles Edward Stewart for the North Western, all was set fair. There was a mild hitch in November, 1864, when the Charing Cross Northern applied to the South Eastern for payment of costs in prosecuting their bill. It was explained that they had no funds of their own; but the South Eastern politely but firmly declined. A year later all seemed settled, though for one reason or another the scheme still hung fire. Then came the financial crisis of 1866 which affected so many businesses throughout the country, and in 1868 the whole project was abandoned.

Instead, connecting services with the South Western and the North Western were inaugurated by rather more roundabout routes. When the Charing Cross Railway was built Waterloo terminus was a modest affair with no more than four platform roads, and the middle road between Nos. 2 and 3 platforms was extended through the back wall of the station building and over a single-line viaduct to join the new South Eastern line. This connection was put in at the time the Charing Cross Railway was built, and from the year 1866 a service was worked between London Bridge and Kensington, travelling into and out of Cannon Street, via Waterloo, Clapham Junction and so to Addison Road. An even more circuitous journey was worked from Cannon Street to Euston, via Waterloo, the West London line, and Willesden. While these services might have had some value for intermediate traffic, as internal London services they were very poor in comparison with the Chatham route through Ludgate Hill.

The South Eastern had countered the onward rush of the Chatham fairly well in other directions, and in anticipation of the increased

Spey, one of the L.C.D.R. 'Small Scotchmen': 0-4-2 type, by Martley, built Neilson & Co. 1866.

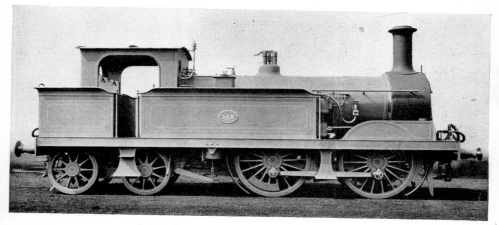

S.E.R. One of James Stirling's 'Q' class 0-4-4s.
[*British Railways*

Albion, one of the 'Large Scotchmen', built Neilsons, 1873.
[*F. Moore*

Above: The Dover Club Train, S.E.R., passing Tonbridge. Note the old-type signalbox and the track ballasting.

Below: A down goods passing Grove Park, hauled by a standard Stirling 0-6-0. Note the tarpaulin wagons, with high semi-circular ends.

[*L.G.R.P. Nos. 21978 and 21251*]

Above: L.C.D.R. Continental Boat Express near Bickley, hauled by 2-4-0 locomotive No. 54, of the 'Europa' class.

[*L.G.R.P. No. 21259*

Below: S.E.R. Ladywell station on the Mid-Kent line, with a Cudworth 2-4-0 arriving on a City-bound train.

[*British Railways*

James Staats Forbes.

A cartoon by 'Spy' published in *Vanity Fair* of 22nd February, 1900, entitled simply 'L.C.D.R.'.

[*British Railways*

competition for the main line traffic, had pushed ahead the big project of the Tonbridge direct line. In May, 1862, Parliamentary authorization was obtained for the fine new main line from St Johns to Tunbridge – as it was then spelt. Although the grading was much heavier than on the old line via Redhill it saved 13 miles on the journey to Folkestone and Dover, and the saving in time was considerably greater than the reduced distance would imply. The complications and delays on the line used jointly with the Brighton were eliminated, and fast straightforward running could be made with the express trains. As a piece of civil engineering the new line can rank with the best in the country. The track alignment is relatively straight, and the long tunnels at Polhill and Sevenoaks were splendidly constructed. There are also two shorter tunnels, south of Grove Park and between Chelsfield and Knockholt (originally called Halstead).

Although it is a digression from the London competition the South Eastern Board had good reason at that time to exercise particular care and scrutiny where tunnel construction was concerned, for no more than a month before the Bill authorizing the Tonbridge direct line passed through Parliament they had received an alarming report concerning the condition of the Wadhurst Tunnel, on the Hastings line. The section between Tunbridge Wells and Robertsbridge had been in operation since 1851 and now, after less than eleven years service, it was reported that Wadhurst Tunnel was in danger of caving in! The original specification had called for four rings of brickwork and cement in lining the tunnel; but the contractors had skimped things, and put in only one ring. The railway engineers had evidently not been alive to what was going on in the dark recesses of the tunnel, and the contractors, Messrs Warton & Warden, had, to use a modern colloquialism, 'got away with it'. The directors appointed John Hawkshaw and T. E. Harrison to make a thorough inspection. Apparently it was a long drawn out process for it was not until October, 1862, that the relining of the tunnel was authorized by the Board.

The consequences of that original negligence and the way it was subsequently made good are still with us today. To cut the expense of relining to a minimum some of the new lining was put *inside* the original profile, thus reducing the clearance between the tunnel walls and the trains. In Southern Railway days this led to the necessity of special narrow stock, and more recently still to strictures in the design of the diesel-electric multiple unit trains now used on the Hastings service. Without this restriction in clearance the 'Schools' class 4-4-0 locomotives might never have been designed; in this respect the restriction may well be regarded as a blessing in disguise, for the annals of British steam locomotive performance are immeasurably the richer for the inclusion of the many magnificent runs made by the 'Schools'. What may have happened originally at Wadhurst, no such troubles were allowed to develop in the long tunnels on the Tonbridge direct line, and the new line was opened throughout in April, 1868. Although principally concerned with through traffic this line did open up a new district of great beauty that became highly favoured as an outer-residential area for London people.

With the opening of the Tonbridge direct line the South Eastern and the Chatham were now equipped, on equal terms, for the thirty years slogging match. Of course the South Eastern was far better placed financially. It is perhaps unfair to Edward Watkin to recall that the dividend on the ordinary shares began to fall from the very moment that he joined the Board. It is unfortunate that his arrival coincided with the general slump of the middle 'sixties' of last century. But even in the very worst year, 1867, the South Eastern *did* pay a dividend of $2\frac{1}{2}$ per cent, and despite all the heavy expenditure on the Charing Cross railway and the Tonbridge direct line the position, so far as shareholders were concerned, was improved in the succeeding three years. Then came the Franco–Prussian War of 1870, which brought a wave of prosperity to Britain, and with a remarkable upsurge of traffic receipts the South Eastern was back into the 5–6 per cent dividend range, by 1871.

Although spreading its tentacles so widely and working its new services with economy and skill the L.C.D.R. was soon to reap the whirlwind of its previous financial operations. The troubles that came to beset the Chatham are sometimes attributed to the running of unremunerative services. This is not the case, for in 1865 the working expenses of the line amounted to only 66 per cent, while in the really bad slump year the expenses rose only slightly to 70 per cent. Although there was always a vast amount of cheese-paring to save money, which rendered the company unpopular with the travelling public, there was never a time when the working expenses exceeded the amount received in fares and freight charges. The circumstances of the financial crash are unconnected with the running of the railway as a transportation concern, so it is best to tell the tale and to get it over as soon as possible. The most significant point is that the emergency gave J. S. Forbes the opportunity to secure almost complete control.

From the outset the Chatham had been financed largely by its contractors, and the rates of interest they managed to extort from the Board, suggested that they were prepared to 'cash in' on a big scale. Although the Chatham must have been paying an enormous amount in interest on loans this was just acceptable so long as the contractors were prepared to play. The financing of the Metropolitan extensions was much helped by the investments of the Great Northern and the London & South Western, and the soundness of those extensions from the railway point of view was hardly in doubt, otherwise the hard-headed Board of the Great Northern would not have supported it. In May, 1866, the oncoming slump was signalized by the failure of several banking houses; Messrs Peto, Betts & Company, the main contractors to the L.C.D.R. went bankrupt, and instead of obtaining further loans, albeit at something approaching a money-lender's rate, the Chatham could not meet certain debentures that fell due on the 30th June. A month later J. S. Forbes and Mr Johnson, the Secretary, were appointed Receivers in Chancery.

During the proceedings of the Committee of Investigation that was set up many questionable transactions were revealed. Little if anything had been paid in dividends, and the only people who had got anything out of it were the contractors, who had not only been paid for the work, but had subsequently been paid high rates of interest for their financing operations. Of course there was a great deal of outspoken comment on the findings of the Committee. Lord Sondes the Chairman of the Company, resigned, and Sir Morton Peto, the principal contractor, as a Member of Parliament, found it necessary to call a meeting of his constituents to explain his own part in the collapse. The extraordinary thing is that the railway continued to run. It was expected at the time that either the Brighton or the South Eastern would step in and pick up the bits at rock-bottom prices; but one can quite understand the hesitancy with which any well-established and profitable concern looked towards such a collection of liabilities. There was a natural feeling that even the Committee of Investigation had not uncovered the full extent of the troubles.

So the luckless Chatham was left to flounder in the morass of its own making. Lord Harris succeeded Lord Sondes as Chairman, but litigation dragged on for some years. There were two Arrangements Acts, one in 1867 and another in 1869, and under the provisions of the second one things were finally settled in February, 1870. By then circumstances were almost ripe for J. S. Forbes to assume the supreme command, and in 1873 he became Chairman &

Managing Director. While all the trouble had been in progress the pattern of train services in the London area had been gradually extended, and while investors and the public in general had been shaken by the Chatham collapse other railways showed no disinclination to co-operate with the unfortunate company in the running of trains. It is extraordinary to recall how many new services were inaugurated during the critical years between the 'failure' of June, 1866, and the settlement of 1870.

In the January of the 'collapse' year, 1866, many of the Chatham local services on the City line were extended through to Farringdon Street, while Great Northern trains began working through to Ludgate Hill. This latter service must have been an early success, as from August, 1866, it was extended at both ends, and operated between Hatfield and Herne Hill. At a still later date this service, instead of terminating at Herne Hill, turned westward at Loughborough Junction and ran to Victoria. Some trains were worked by the G.N.R. and some by the L.C.D.R., and locomotives of the latter worked northwards to New Barnet, Enfield, or Finsbury Park. In 1869, trains of both the Midland and the London & South Western Railways began working to Ludgate Hill. The Midland eventually ran to Victoria, with L.C.D.R. trains working reciprocally to Hendon, while the South Western began a service in April, 1866, from Kingston, via Clapham Junction, Longhedge, Brixton and Loughborough Junction.

The South Western was evidently bent on fully extracting its 'pound of flesh' for the investment it had made in the L.C.D.R. extensions in London, for at various times it ran to Ludgate Hill by three different routes. A second one was from Richmond via Hammersmith, Addison Road, the West London Extension Line, Longhedge and Brixton. The third was from Wimbledon via Merton, Tooting, Tulse Hill and Herne Hill. The eastward spur from the L.C.D.R. line at Snow Hill, connecting with the City Widened Lines of the Metropolitan in the direction of Moorgate, rather than of Kings Cross, was part of the Chatham policy of putting connecting spurs in every conceivable direction, whether there was any traffic or not. An extraordinary number of the L.C.D.R. trains terminated at Moorgate, though as the late G. A. Sekon once remarked, it was surprising anyone used them over the City section. Between Moorgate and Ludgate Hill it was much quicker to walk! Yet Forbes agreed with the Metropolitan that there should be *eighty* L.C.D.R. trains a day running into Moorgate.

Apart from the congestion and the chronic unpunctuality what a feast for the eyes of a railway enthusiast Ludgate Hill station must have been in the early 'seventies, with Great Northern, London & South Western, and Midland trains all passing through in addition to those of the owning company! Those first days were perhaps the most colourful, for although the Midland had not then adopted its famous 'red', the Chatham engines were gaily painted in green, with brown underframes, and the South Western trains were hauled by the handsome little Beattie 2-4-0 tanks, then resplendent in a rich red-brown, with much brilliant lining-out, and a profusion of polished brass and copper work. The Chatham engines were the famous 0-4-2 tanks, the 'Scotchmen', built by Neilsons, carrying Scottish names, and designed by Archibald Sturrock of the Great Northern. Having mentioned individual locomotives it is now time to turn from the ebb and flow of railway politics, for at least one chapter, for a look at some of the early engines and trains.

VI

Early Locomotives and Trains

THE curiously roundabout and cumbersome way in which the South Eastern Railway first began to operate a public service has already been mentioned. Its locomotive affairs were equally complicated, for in 1842 its twenty-six locomotives were pooled with those of the Croydon Railway. From the outset Benjamin Cubitt was Locomotive Superintendent; he was a son of William Cubitt, the civil engineer who had built the line, and like the great majority of early locomotive engineers he had, perforce, to take stock designs from one or other of the many locomotive manufacturers of the day. Unlike the Great Western before Gooch came on the scene, the South Eastern purchased wisely, and the twenty-six engines contributed to the pool were mostly 2-2-2 singles of Sharp Roberts design, with 5 ft 6 in. diameter driving wheels.

There is a beautiful coloured plate of one of them, from an F. Moore oil-painting, in Dendy Marshall's *History of the Southern Railway*. They were gracious, handsome little things in dark green, with red-brown underframes. Both chimney and dome stood on a square pedestal; the chimneys were bell-mouthed, with a deep copper top, while the huge, brass, urn-like dome had the square pedestal also of polished brass. Nearly all of them were named. One found the inevitable *Samson* and *Goliath*, but the majority were much more original, including sonorous Saxon titles like *Eadbald*, *Ethelbert* and *Egbert*; invaders of the Kentish shores like *Hengist*, *Horsa* and *Caesar*, with *Shakespeare* and *King Lear* to add a pleasing literary flavour. The giants *Gog* and *Magog* were somewhat incongruous on a couple of little Bury 0-4-0s, and later there came the notorious *White Horse of Kent*. The locomotive affairs of the Joint Committee were controlled by the South Eastern superintendent, and in 1845 Benjamin Cubitt was replaced by James I'Anson Cudworth. Cudworth was responsible only for the South Eastern line, whereas Benjamin Cubitt took in the Brighton and the Croydon Railways as well.

Cudworth was no more than 28 years of age when he got the job. His early experience had been obtained in North Eastern England,

70

and it was perhaps only natural that he should have come under the influence of the Stephenson school of engine designing. For a period of nearly 10 years South Eastern locomotive practice pursued a wavering and uncertain course, introducing engines of the Stephenson long-boilered type, and a number of Crampton's. The *White Horse of Kent* was a 2-2-2, with all wheels ahead of the firebox. She was put forward as a typical example of the best standard-gauge practice at the time of the Royal Commission on Railway Gauges, in 1845, but unfortunately for her sponsors Daniel Gooch had made a number of test runs on her over the South Eastern line, and she provided him with some first-rate ammunition. The driving wheels were flangeless, and because of the large amount of overhanging weight at the rear end she developed a most alarming yawing action at any speed. Gooch said she was definitely unsafe, and David Joy in his diaries writes that 'she signalized herself by going off the road several times and killing a man or two.'

Despite this experience, however, Cudworth persisted with the long boiler type for several years. The *White Horse of Kent* was converted into a 2-4-0, and the very first engines built at Ashford Works, in 1853–4, were of the same general type, specially for the heavily-graded Hastings line. In the meantime, as if the long-boilered engines were not enough trouble, the South Eastern invested in some 4-2-0 Cramptons, built by Tulk & Ley, of the Lowca Ironworks, Whitehaven in 1847. The precise history of these engines is a little obscure, but the rather astonishing fact must be noted that four 4-2-0 long-boilered 'Stephensons', built by Bury, Curtis & Kennedy, were *rebuilt*, as Cramptons in order to improve their riding. By the year 1855 Cudworth was nearing the end of his experimental days. His career is indeed almost the exact opposite to that of some other distinguished locomotive engineers one could name, who began with simple, straightforward designs and then launched out, with little success, into the 'fancy stuff'. Cudworth, after years of experimenting with long-boilered types, and Cramptons, turned to simplicity, and produced some first rate designs.

Two large classes, which between them mustered 159 locomotives, became the mainstay of the South Eastern main line traffic outside the London suburban area. These were the 0-6-0 goods, of which the first were built at Ashford in 1855, and the 2-4-0. The 0-6-0s had double frames, very tall bell-mouthed chimney, large polished brass domes on which were mounted Salter-type safety valves, and a second safety valve column over the firebox. Technically they were small engines, with cylinders no larger than 16 in. by 24 in., but they ren-

dered some 40 years of good service on the line. Many of them were
rebuilt twice, once in Cudworth's day, and again by Stirling. There
were fifty-three of these engines, all built at Ashford, and construction
of them continued down to 1876, the year of Cudworth's departure.

The 2-4-0 design of 1857, with 6 ft coupled wheels and 16 in.
by 24 in. cylinders, was quite an outstanding success, and eventually no fewer than 116 locomotives of this class were at work. The
earlier examples had Cudworth's coal-burning firebox, a piece of
original and pioneer design that might have been developed further
had not the extremely simple alternative of the brick-arch been
invented elsewhere. The Cudworth 2-4-0s were very long-lived
engines. Like the 0-6-0s construction of them continued, to an unchanged design, from 1857 to 1875. The first six came from Wilson's
of Leeds, a further 42 came from other contractors, while no fewer
than 68 were built at Ashford. James Stirling rebuilt many of them,
putting on his own 'straightback' type of boiler, but still they received
no cabs. In their later days they were maids of all work on the
South Eastern, working locals, main line expresses, and on their
lesser duties no one ever seemed to take them to a turntable. Much of
their work was done tender first. As rebuilt by James Stirling they
were still distinguished by the broad polished brass band over the
driving wheel splashers.

As an engine designer Cudworth will be best remembered by the
7 ft 2-2-2 singles he built for the Continental expresses. These latter
trains were of two kinds, the Continental Mail Expresses, which ran
to the Admiralty Pier at Dover, and the 'Tidals', which ran to
Folkestone. Even after the latter service had become a regular one,
consequent upon the extension of the harbour facilities at Folkestone,
the service continued to be known as the 'Tidal' among railwaymen,
so much so that the name was used officially on the train describer
instruments used in the signal boxes at Cannon Street, and the
junctions between that station and London Bridge. In view of their
duties on these crack trains the Cudworth 2-2-2 singles of 1861 were
always known as the 'Mails'. Very good work they did on these trains
for over 20 years, with one slight intermission that will be mentioned
later.

The 'singles' worked the boat trains from Cannon Street, and the
duty of haulage over the short journey between there and Charing
Cross was performed by any kind of engine that happened to be
available. Very frequently Cudworth 2-4-0s were used, more often
than not travelling tender first. On the main line run the 2-2-2
'Mails' did excellent work. Some of the booked intermediate timings

were remarkably sharp for the period 1870–80, including such spurts as Tonbridge to Ashford, 26½ miles in 29 minutes, pass to pass. It was quite usual for the Continental Mails, and the Tidals to be run at the maximum permitted speed of 60 m.p.h. for most of the distance between Paddock Wood and Headcorn, though in the days of the Cudworth engines the loads were not unduly heavy – about 100 tons.

The intermission in their 20 years of continuous service arose out of the strained relations that developed between Cudworth and Sir Edward Watkin. Apparently Cudworth was not disposed to toe the Watkin line, and the latter, in almost complete secrecy, persuaded John Ramsbottom to design some 2-4-0 passenger engines for the South Eastern. The great North Western engineer had then retired from his labours at Crewe, and was in private practice as a consultant. Watkin, who was frequently in Manchester on M.S.L. business, not only commissioned Ramsbottom to design the locomotives, but without a word to his own locomotive superintendent placed orders for ten of them with Sharp, Stewart & Company, and ten with the Avonside Engine Company, of Bristol. When Cudworth got to hear about this little transaction he was furious; so were certain members of the Board, and it fired off the powder-train that led to the period when Watkin's relations with a majority of the directors were very strained, as told in the next chapter. Cudworth resigned, but in the light of the Chairman's action his departure was tantamount to a dismissal. No engineer worth his salt would have stayed in face of such an insult.

At the time it could be considered as nothing but very rough justice for a man who had provided the South Eastern Railway with a stud of such excellent engines. But he did not have to wait very long for his just reward. The new engines, reputedly designed by Ramsbottom, bore a striking resemblance to the famous 'Precedent' Class of the North Western. The wheelbase was exactly the same, the cylinders were of the same dimensions, and the boilers and fireboxes were of generally the same proportions; had they performed like the celebrated North Western 'Jumbos' they would have been acclaimed on all hands. They arrived on the South Eastern during the brief period when Sir Edward Watkin's son was locomotive superintendent, and were sometimes known as the 'Watkin's', in consequence; but the men nicknamed them the 'Ironclads', why, no one seems to know.

By their leading dimensions these engines were the most powerful express passenger class on the line, and naturally they were put on to the Continental Mails, and the Tidals. Equally quickly they were taken off and relegated to less important duties, and the Cudworth 'singles' took up their old duties again. Why the 'Ironclads' should have failed so completely is a mystery shrouded in the mists of time. It is probable that through some relatively minor defect in the valve setting they were sluggish in running. One can well imagine that after A. M. Watkin's resignation had been forced by the rival faction on the Board nobody particularly minded if deficiencies were found in the so-called 'Watkin' engines, and no trouble was taken to cure them of their defects. Anyway, the Cudworth 'singles' enjoyed another 8 years on the Continental expresses, until James Stirling's 4-4-0 'Mail' engines took the road, in 1884. One would like to think Cudworth himself derived great enjoyment from this episode!

The South Eastern Railway was just emerging from its experimental days in locomotive design when the 'Chatham' came into existence, and for the first few years the locomotive affairs of the latter company were very much in keeping with the chaotic state of its finances, and general conduct of affairs. At first Joseph Cubitt acted as locomotive superintendent, and he in turn called in Crampton. Between the two of them they made a pretty mess of it! The first six locomotives were built by R. & W. Hawthorn, 'by agreement' with the East Kent Railway. There appears to have been no question of a straightforward 'order'; one can infer that some arrangement of extended credit was made, for it is most unlikely that the railway company had any money to pay for them. These engines, which were 4-4-0 saddle tanks, were designed by Crampton; they were a hopeless failure. No later than March, 1858, Cubitt was reporting to the Board that the first five had all failed and were out of traffic. The sixth, which, with becoming modesty on the part of the designer, was named *Crampton*, had not then been delivered.

The Board was so concerned at this inglorious start to the Chatham story of locomotive 'practice and performance' that Daniel Gooch was called in as adviser, and in a very short time he had condemned the Cramptons out of hand. This must have been a painful duty for Gooch, as Crampton had been one of his most valued assistants at Swindon in earlier days. Gooch went a good deal further. Having had bitter experience on the Great Western of what can happen when men who are primarily civil engineers dabble in locomotive design, he recommended the appointment of a proper locomotive superintendent. Gooch was no doubt consulted as to a suitable man, for the choice fell upon William Martley, a man trained in the Forth Street Works, Newcastle, an establishment owned by Gooch's brother, Tom. At the time of his appointment he was District Locomotive Superintendent of the South Wales Division of the Great Western. However, the introduction came to be made, the choice of Martley could not have been a happier one. It was one of the most fortuitous appointments the Chatham Board ever made.

Martley must have been a delightful character. He seems to have accepted the fantastic conditions under which the railway was being managed as a challenge to his skill, and to have set about his problems with a zest and good humour that proved the sheet anchor of the whole concern. If mechanical engineering affairs had been handled with less resolution, and less ingenuity in improvisation the London, Chatham & Dover Railway must surely have collapsed physically as well as financially. The full story of how things were kept going would be fascinating not only to locomotive enthusiasts, but to practical engineers in any branch of the profession. Knowing a little of what was going on we can smile at a minute recorded at the Board Meeting of 2nd February, 1861:

'The subject of the detention of the first train from Canterbury this day having been discussed,

'Resolved, that Mr Martley be desired to report the cause of such detention.'

At the time of Martley's appointment the Chatham had no proper locomotive shops, and it was not until nearly a year later that any steps were taken to establish anything of the kind. Then in March, 1861, at the same Board Meeting that appointed J. S. Forbes as General Manager, it was agreed to purchase the Longhedge Farm, near Battersea, for the sum of £1,609 16s., as the site for the new locomotive shops. The Chatham, running true to form, of course, had no money to pay for it; some form of deferred payment was arranged, but the company defaulted on this, as in everything else financially, and at the time of the crash the vendors of the farm were threatening to seize the machinery that had been installed in the works. It was amid alarms of this kind that the fine engine-building traditions of Longhedge Works were gradually built up, though it was naturally some years after its establishment that the first new locomotive was built there.

With the six Crampton locomotives of 1858 next to useless Joseph Cubitt had had to collect engines where and when he could, preferably at rock bottom price, so that when Martley took over he found, among others, two Hawthorn 2-2-2s that had been intended for use in the Crimea; one 0-6-0 goods purchased second- or third-hand from Brotherhood, the Chippenham contractor; one 0-4-0 'wing' tank from Hawthorns; and six Hawthorn 2-2-2s, on loan from the Great Northern. Martley continued the process after his arrival and the collection of miscellaneous motive power was reinforced by four inside-framed 4-4-0s, again from Hawthorn, that had been built for a defaulting South American railway; three ancient 2-2-0s from the London & North Western, and two Sharp Stewart 0-4-2s. How Martley secured these two engines makes interesting reading.

Apparently he was making periodic visits to the locomotive building firms to see if they had anything cheap, for immediate delivery, and in this particular case it happened that Sharp, Stewarts were building a series of 0-4-2 tender engines, of Patrick Stirling's design, for the Glasgow & South Western Railway. Strangely enough, delivery to the latter company was not urgently needed, and the builders, probably with the idea of getting their money earlier, suggested to Martley that the 'Sou'West' might come to an arrangement. They did, and so two Stirling 0-4-2s arrived on the Chatham in August, 1861. By this transaction Martley got two excellent new engines, but whether Sharp, Stewart got paid for them, or the Glasgow & South Western Board got their 'consideration' is a moot point!

In distinguishing his engines Martley followed the practice he had grown up with on the Great Western, of using no numbers at all, only names; and the names he chose reflect his own personality and keen sense of humour. Who but Martley, for example, in circumstances prevailing on the Chatham, would have named express engines *Flirt*, and *Frolic*! The two Sirling 0-4-2s were named *Brigand* and *Corsair*, ostensibly after two of Gooch's broad-gauge engines on the Great Western with which Martley had been associated in earlier days; but one suspects that after the nature of the man there was an allusion to the methods he himself had used in 'lifting' them out of the Glasgow & South Western fold. Ahrons, in a characteristic piece of writing, denies that there was any connection between these names and the enormously inflated fares extorted from first and second class passengers in the trains hauled by these locomotives!

Other Chatham names ranged from the heavy classical, and mythological to the heights of whim, fantasy and wild nature, so that one finds *Ajax*, and *Vulcan*, alongside *Sylph*, *Ianthe*, *Gadfly* and above all *Calypso*. But perhaps the most amusing titles of all were bestowed in 1873 on two 0-6-0 goods engines obtained in characteristic circumstances. By that time Martley was getting a good deal of 'law and order' into Chatham locomotive affairs, but in this case Sharp, Stewart & Company were left with a couple of incomplete 0-6-0s on their hands. They had been ordered by the standard-gauge Pembroke & Tenby Railway, but when that line came into the broad-gauge fold the order was cancelled, and the builders immediately began to look round for a likely purchaser. So they offered them to the Chatham, and eventually Martley took them, unfinished and without tenders, for a knock-down price that was all to the liking of the Chatham Board. And these two engines he named *Huz* and *Buz*!

The full history of the Chatham locomotive has so fully and recently been told by Mr D. L. Bradley that no detailed reference is needed to it here. It is, indeed, so involved and concerns so many different classes of locomotive that many chapters of the present book would be needed. But Martley's own engines deserve a special mention, and foremost among these stand the series of 2-4-0 express passenger locomotives put on the road between 1862 and 1873. The first four had names signalizing the beginnings of a new era in Chatham locomotive affairs: *Dawn, Alert, Herald* and *Pioneer;* Martley's sense of humour transcended even this auspicious occasion, and the fifth of this first class was the delightful *Frolic*. Then, as if to pull himself back to realities, came *Vigilant*. There was nothing frivolous about the engines themselves. They all survived to carry the initials 'S.E.& C.R.' on their tenders, and *Dawn*, which was not scrapped until 1907, ran a million-and-a-quarter miles in her life of 45 years.

In March, 1869, all Martley's hard work at Longhedge reached a new point of triumph when the first locomotive to be built entirely in the company's works took the road. A vast amount of rebuilding had been done there, but no new work. Indeed such had been the shortage of funds during the construction of the new 2-4-0s, and so frequently had work been stopped, that Martley once remarked it was an enigma to him how they ever got finished. And so the first engine from Longhedge Works was duly named *Enigma*. The other two of this class were the *Mermaid* and *Lothair*. The choice of the name *Enigma* recalls the Ramsbottom 2-2-2 *Problem* on the North Western. The latter engine was the first to have the Giffard injector, and the 'problem' was to get the injector to work.

The 'Enigmas' were the forerunners of the very celebrated 'Europa' Class of 1873, designed specially for the Continental Mail expresses, and the increased traffic overseas following the end of the Franco–Prussian War. More funds were available by then, and the engines were needed urgently, so tenders were invited for them from ten different manufacturers, and Bradley records that the prices asked varied from £2,930 to £3,650. Sharp Stewart's were successful at the lower figure, and it is pleasant to be able to add that all four engines were paid for in full within two months of their being received at Longhedge. These four engines were named *Europa*, *Asia*, *Africa* and *America*. Authorization for two more engines of the same class was given for construction at Longhedge, but because of financial troubles work went ahead so slowly that they were not completed until two years after Martley's death – till 1876, in fact. It was intended that these two engines should have been named *India* and *Ethiopia*, but the names were never carried.

The London suburban tank engines of the Chatham should not be placed in any way behind Martley's main line 2-4-0s, either for distinction or working efficiency; for although many of the trains were chronically delayed, and the stock hauled was wretched both in appointments and dirtiness, that was not the fault of the locomotives. The introduction of the Metropolitan services in 1866, necessitating the use of condensing apparatus, brought urgently to the fore the need for new and powerful engines. Martley can have had little time to work out a design of his own, and so he based the specification on which tenders were invited on Archibald Sturrock's very successful 0-4-2 well tank engines introduced in 1865 for the Metropolitan traffic of the Great Northern. These latter engines had been built by Avonside, but Neilson's secured the L.C.D. contract, and thereby hangs a protracted and dismal tale.

I should say at once that there was nothing whatever the matter with the engines themselves. They were every bit as good as their Great Northern counterparts, and the length of service rendered by them, varying from 38 to 42 years is testimony in itself. At the time they were ordered, Chatham finances were just descending to their very lowest ebb, and although the contract price was £2,400 per engine Neilson's agreed to the payments being spread over 7 years providing the price was raised to £3,350. Desperately short of ready cash the Chatham agreed to this very large increase, and even then the builders had to threaten court action before they received final payments. Apart from all this, the 'Scotchmen', as they were known, were handsome, beautifully kept engines. Apart from the shape of the chimneys and the position of the dome immediately behind the chimney they were very similar to Sturrock's engine. They all had Scottish names, of islands off the West Coast, and well-known rivers. Here again Martley showed his interesting taste in nomenclature, for some of the larger and better-known islands such as Skye and Mull were omitted and others like *Iona*, *Jura* and *Ulva* were included.

There were fourteen of the first batch of 'Scotchmen', all delivered in 1866, and they took the place of the 'Rose' Class 2-4-0 tank engines in the London suburban area. The latter class inaugurated the 'Workmens Penny Trains' in 1865, referred to in Chapter V, running between Ludgate Hill and Victoria. They left at 4.55 a.m. from either end, called at all stations, took roughly an hour on the journey, and were composed of the worst stock the Chatham could find. Then, in 1873, when the Chatham was in a better state financially, six more 0-4-2 well tanks were ordered from Neilson's, similar to the original batch, but with larger cylinders, 17 in. by 24 in. against 16 in. by 22 in. In these engines the similarity to Great Northern practice was heightened by the use of domeless boilers, and a handsomely-shaped safety valve casing quite in the style of Patrick Stirling. The 'large Scotchmen' on the L.C.D. were just as much the counterparts of the Stirling 0-4-2s of 1868, as the earlier 'Scotchmen' had been of Sturrock's Great Northern design; but although the later engines were also built in Scotland the names bestowed on them were *Albion, Thanet, Erin, Cambria, Mona* and *Scotia*. The first named was quite recently concerned in a most amusing photographic mix-up. From a certain historical source I had arranged to have a picture of the famous G.W. Atlantic No. 171; imagine, then, my surprise when the L.C.D. 0-4-2 well tank turned up instead.

With the death of William Martley a great period in Chatham locomotive history came to an end. It is unfortunate that much of his skill as an engineer was expended in making freak designs serviceable, in repairing engines when he must have been wondering whether the money would be forthcoming to pay the weekly wage bill at Longhedge. Yet he won through, and his 2-4-0 express locomotives were daily entrusted with some of the fastest running south of the Thames. The 'Europa' Class, in particular, earned a great reputation on the Continental mail trains, and were used on that service for some considerable time after the Kirtley 4-4-0s were running. This is no discredit to the latter engines which were designed particularly for the heavy seaside trains to Ramsgate and Margate. The Continental Mails were lighter, and the 'Europas' could handle them comfortably.

VII

Watkin versus Forbes

OUT of the tangled skein of affairs left after the financial collapse of the London, Chatham & Dover Railway, Forbes climbed into a position that made him a virtual dictator. From the year 1873 he held the title of Chairman & Managing Director, and his rapid ascent to supreme power in a time of crisis was typical of his whole life. A senior executive officer, seeing the way things were going in the early 'sixties, might well have been pardoned for seeking the earliest chance of ending his contract and getting out. Not so Forbes, however! He stayed in the thick of it, and his motto might well have been 'I'm all right, Jack', for no one else salvaged anything out of the wreck. And while he took the Chatham firmly by the hand, to lead it on a chimerical, will-o'the-wisp course for 25 years, during which time not a penny was paid in dividends on the Arbitration Ordinary Stock, the leadership of the South Eastern was no less high-handed though more profitable to the proprietors.

The year 1873 was notable also for a highly significant change in the management of the South Eastern Railway. In that year the General Manager, C. W. Eborall, died, and one can detect the hand of Watkin in what subsequently transpired. At a meeting held on New Year's Eve at the close of that year the Board decided to abolish the office of General Manager altogether, and it was arranged that the Chairman, Watkin himself, should take most of the duties. Although not styled as such Watkin had the power of a managing director as well as being Chairman of the Board, so that he and Forbes were on precisely similar terms. It is hard to resist the suggestion that Watkin took the idea from Forbes's appointment earlier in the year, and that the death of Eborall gave him his chance to seize executive as well as directorial power.

The period of unrestricted competition, squabbles, and expensive lawsuits between the two companies lasted for the full 21 years in which Watkin and Forbes were the respective Chairmen. Many economies were practised in running the railways, with the result that the rolling stock was poor, much of the fixed equipment was antiquated, and punctuality was shocking. The public got a pretty

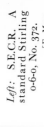

Left: S.E.C.R. A standard Stirling 0-6-0, No. 372.
[*F. Moor*

Below: S.E.C.R., late L.C.D.R. 0-6-0 goods engine No. 588; formerly No. 129, 'Adrian' class, built by J. Fowler & Co., named *Vespasian*, rebuilt 1890, scrapped 1909.
[*British Railways*

Top: South Eastern main line bogie third built just before the working union with the L.C. & D. at the end of the 1890s.

[*British Railways*

Above: Brake first of the 1921 'Continental' stock. These coaches, which had a small saloon compartment with armchairs, in addition to the normal compartments, were unusual in having a gangway at one end only.

[*G. M. Kichenside*

Below: A family saloon of 1900. One of these vehicles survives on the Longmoor Military Railway.

[*L.P.C.*

The roof disaster at Charing Cross, December, 1905.
[*The Railway Magazine*

View from the Avenue theatre, which was damaged by the crash.
[*Radio Times Hulton Picture Library*

Above: Hythe station, Kent, showing an up train for Sandling hauled by a Cudworth 2-4-0, as rebuilt by J. Stirling.

[*British Railways*

Below: Dungeness: a Stirling Class 'B' 4-4-0 with branch train standing near to the lighthouse.

[*F. Moore*

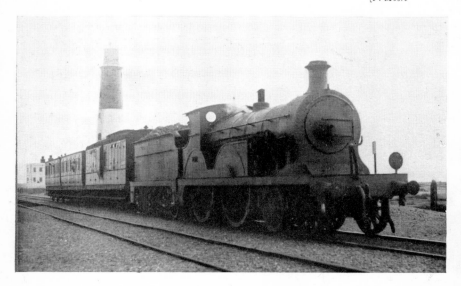

raw deal from both railways, save in the running of the crack express passenger trains; but on the South Eastern Watkin, despite all, managed to maintain quite a good dividend for the ordinary shareholders. The lowest S.E.R. dividend during the 1873–94 period was 3¾ per cent, but for most of the time the shareholders were receiving between 4½ and 6 per cent. Forbes had but one iron in the fire; admittedly there were times when that 'iron' was almost too hot to hold, but Watkins's other interests were many. Having gone to such lengths to secure his election to the Board some of the South Eastern shareholders became rather dubious of where this action would eventually lead.

Watkin's association with so many other railways, and his grand strategy of trying to establish a continuous chain of railway communication from Manchester to the French coast under his management, savoured a little too strongly of the Mania days to be widely accepted. The phaeton career of George Hudson, and the ruin in which so many investors were involved would be a personal memory to many thinking men and women in the 'seventies, and the collapse of the Chatham, on their very doorstep as it were, provided an even more immediate object lesson. Watkin, as Member of Parliament for Hythe, was well known in Kent, and in the political arena he was sure to have as many deadly enemies as he had friends. The Manchester, Sheffield & Lincolnshire, and even the Metropolitan were little more than names to many men and women of Kent; but here, on their own shores was Watkin sponsoring what to many was a fantastic project in 1875, the Channel Tunnel.

The extent to which the people of Kent had become suspicious, and critical, of railway development was never shown more clearly than over the ambitious Folkestone scheme of 1875–6. This was the second, and final attempt of the South Eastern Railway to retrieve some of the loss in efficiency in operation arising from the original, ill-judged siting of the Harbour Branch, and to achieve something approaching parity with Dover and the Chatham. Now that the shortened main line, via Sevenoaks, was in operation there was everything to be gained by improvement at Folkestone. It might have seemed that the South Eastern was in a strong position. Sir Edward Watkin, in addition to the prestige and influence he had gathered as a railway director, was a Member of Parliament for Hythe, and as such would be well qualified to further the cause of the new development. The branch line from Sandling Junction to Hythe had recently been completed to Sandgate, and the extension to Folkestone Harbour looked a logical and natural continuation.

Before any detailed plans were drawn up this new proposal seemed to be clear of nearly all the objections raised to the South Eastern schemes of 1861, in that there would be little interference with property. The more southerly of the two earlier proposals had involved a line at the foot of the cliffs, below the Leas, that would have been reminiscent of the famous stretch of the Great Western between Dawlish and Teignmouth. Those responsible for drawing up details of the 1875 scheme sought to eliminate the opposition that the earlier scheme had encountered by carrying the line in tunnel under the Leas cliffs, but some surface line could not be avoided at the eastern end where the line of the cliffs fell back and the broad level beach west of the existing harbour installations occurred. This level stretch was ideal from the railway point of view, as it provided space for sidings, locomotive facilities and so on. Unfortunately it lay beneath cliffs that constituted a part of the fashionable Leas promenade, and strange though it may seem at this distance in time it was upon this point that the whole admirable project failed.

There was a good deal more to it than a battle over amenities. In Victorian England generally there were no particular scruples about cutting up the countryside, destroying pleasant prospects and demolishing historic buildings, if there was a chance of fat dividends to follow; but in Kent the story of railway promotion was largely one of bitter disillusionment. The spectacle of the Chatham debacle was still vividly in everyone's mind, and although the South Eastern had managed to keep solvent, and had continued to pay a dividend on its ordinary shares the public at large was generally suspicious of anything that involved heavy expenditure. Moreover Sir Edward Watkin was not by any means a popular figure in the district. By many he was regarded as much more likely to support Parliamentary business that was likely to feather his own nest, as a railway director, than measures calculated to benefit his constituents. With a section of the local populace there was an almost immediate reaction to any project with which Sir Edward was connected: 'Where's the catch in it?'

From the very outset the 1875 scheme had the implacable opposition of the Earl of Radnor. As the largest landowner in the district he wielded immense influence, while the lawyer who sponsored the scheme, one Richard Hart, seems to have antagonized his fellow solicitors in Folkestone, and made easier their massing on the opposite side. The opposition lost no time in plastering their objection, in the form of posters, all over the town. So sustained, indeed, was this campaign that Sir Edward Watkin felt it desirable to try and get the feelings of the ordinary people. If local opposition was really so strong there would be little chance of getting a Bill through Parliament. So Richard Hart prevailed upon the Mayor of Folkestone to call a public meeting. This brought a fresh crop of posters in opposition, and when the meeting actually did take place, on 3rd February, 1876, it was boycotted by the principal opponents of the scheme.

At the meeting the arguments advanced in favour were reasonable enough. While Folkestone was developing as a watering place it was highly desirable that commerical prosperity should be developed concurrently. The South Eastern Railway was prepared to spend such a sum as would put Folkestone on complete party with Dover as a port, and this offer should not be refused. Watkin himself referred to the influx of visitors to Hythe and Sandgate since the building of the branch line from Sandling, and met the criticism that smoke from the trains would ruin the amenities, by the facile remark that they would agree to the inclusion of a clause in the Bill prividing that coal should not be used while passing between Folkestone and Sandgate. Unfortunately Hart, in the course of his ordinary business, had been incautious enough to remark concerning a mortgage on a house on the Leas, 'I'll have nothing to do with it. We shall have a new line soon, and when the engines are puffing and smoking under your noses, you'll soon see what will become of the value of your West End houses'!

That this remark got placarded around the town shows something of the antagonism, and suspicion that the advocates of the scheme gathered round themselves. There were remarks that Sir Edward Watkin was quite prepared to spend £300,000 of the South Eastern shareholders money to fill his own pocket and ruin the town, and following the relatively small meeting of 3rd February, which was generally favourable, more posters appeared saying that the meeting was quite unrepresentative, and at varying stages in a long diatribe its proceedings were apostrophized as 'bunkum' and 'bosh'. Sir Edward Watkin, in the most restrained and temperate language, had appealed to Lord Radnor, asking why he did not make some move to meet them, instead of causing his agents to plaster the hoardings. Whether or not Lord Radnor was behind the poster campaign we are not to know; the bills lost some of their force, and increased the curiosity surrounding them by being signed '*Pro Bono Publico*'.

The only response on the hoardings that was the least bit favourable was a poster with this wording:

'That whereas the Company, through their Chairman, Sir Edward Watkin, Member of Parliament for Folkestone, have given their solemn "guarantee not to interfere with the Lower Sandgate Road as a drive, nor with the Bathing Ground, nor bring the railway between the road and the sea", they are requested to keep their promise.'

It was signed 'No Surrender.'

Today we can study the maps and realize that a great opportunity was lost. Having regard to the primitive state of Dover harbour at that time it might even have influenced subsequent development there. While no doubt the grand project of the National Harbour and Naval Base would have gone ahead, the South Eastern & Chatham Railway might have built the Marine station at Folkestone instead of Dover, and been tempted to close the troublesome and expensive line through the Warren, and beneath the famous White Cliffs. It is one of those fascinating 'might-have-beens', upon which one can gossip for pages. In fact the project was killed stone dead by the opposing faction in Folkestone, though 8 years later, when the Chatham had some proposals for a line into the town it is amusing to see how local opinion rallied to the support of the 'efficiently managed' South Eastern Railway! At that time in history 'management' of the S.E.R. meant just one man, Sir Edward Watkin.

In South London the L.C.D., in 1875, strengthened its hold on a piece of territory where it was competing with the Brighton rather than the South Eastern, namely at the Crystal Palace. Thirteen years earlier the Crystal Palace & South London Junction Railway had been incorporated, as a separate undertaking. From a junction with the South London line of the L.B.S.C. at Cow Lane, near Peckham Rye, this line turned southwards to climb through Honor Oak, Lordship Lane and Upper Sydenham to reach a high level terminus right on the hill adjacent to the Crystal Palace. For the crowds who flocked to the events held there, from Test Matches to Football Association Cup Finals, the high level station was a much more attractive proposition than the Brighton station on the old West End of London & Crystal Palace line. In anticipation of the traffic to come the new terminus was laid out in the most grandiose manner. Its entrance façade and general layout were more than a faint prototype of the present Dover Marine! The difference was that the Crystal Palace was much loftier inside, and was a far grander and more imposing station than anything on the L.C.D. itself.

At first trains ran to it only from Victoria, but in 1871 the eastern spur from Cambria Junction to Loughborough Junction was put in, and from that time through trains were run from the City stations of

the L.C.D. direct to Crystal Palace High Level. The line was purchased by the L.C.D. on 1st July, 1875, and a lavish service of trains
provided to both Victoria and Ludgate Hill. It was a strenuous line
to work; from the point of divergence from the Brighton line at
Cow Lane the gradient was 1 in 78 for practically the whole way to
the Crystal Palace. Nevertheless the London tank engines of the
L.C.D., from Martley's 'Scotchmen', to the efficient 0-4-4s of
Kirtley's design, coped with it remarkably well.

For all the wasteful, senseless competition between the Chatham
and the South Eastern, stimulated by the personal rivalries of the
two Chairmen, there were some events strangely at variance with this
policy of perpetual enmity. The first of these events took place in
January, 1877, when there was a serious landslip in the Folkestone
Warren, near the eastern end of the Martello Tunnel. A storm washed
away the foot of the cliff, bringing down some 60,000 cubic yards of
chalk, killing three men, and completely blocking the line. The
moment the news of this disaster reached Chatham headquarters at
Victoria, Forbes immediately, and without any conditions, offered
the use of the whole L.C.D.R. line to the South Eastern. He is quoted
as saying: 'You cannot get with the mails to Dover, we are partners
in the mails and other business to Dover, take them over our railway.'
For two months the Dover traffic of the S.E.R. was conveyed via
Beckenham and thence over the L.C.D.R. throughout.

Subsequent events showed that Forbes was not *quite* so single-
minded as he chose to appear over the affair, for in 1884 he used the
L.C.D.R. action of 1877 as a strong argument to back his scheme for
a branch to Folkestone! More of this, however, in a later stage of
this chapter. In 1878 came the completion of the important spur
line at Metropolitan Junction between the Charing Cross line of the
South Eastern and the City line of the Chatham. By this facility the
South Eastern could run through to the Metropolitan line at Farringdon Street, and to the Great Northern and Midland Railways by
the junction at Kings Cross. There was a mild piece of awkwardness
in this development, for the Chatham, although granting running
powers, would not permit passengers in the South Eastern trains to
use their stations. The S.E.R. trains were accordingly non-stop from
London Bridge to Farringdon Street, on paper at any rate. In fact
they were probably delayed as much as all other traffic passing over
that crowded section.

For a time Watkin was on the Board of the Great Eastern Railway,
and it was then that he saw the chance of a more immediate fulfilment
of his dream of a continuous line from Manchester to the South

Coast than by the southward extension of the M.S.L.R. He joined the Board of the East London Railway, and was soon elected Chairman, and when this line was opened for traffic in 1876, linking the Great Eastern, at Liverpool Street, with both the Brighton and the South Eastern at New Cross, another section of the rapidly growing 'Watkin empire' was consolidated. At first the train service over the East London line was worked exclusively by the Brighton, but the South Eastern began a service between Addiscombe Road and Liverpool Street in April, 1880. Meanwhile Forbes could not look on and let the South Eastern have the merest particle of a traffic without striving to participate, and when arrangements were made, in 1882, for the line to be leased in perpetuity the Chatham succeeded in getting a share, though it had no physical connection with it. The other lessees were the Great Eastern, South Eastern, Brighton, Metropolitan and Metropolitan District.

While Forbes was establishing himself more firmly than ever as a virtual dictator in all matters of Chatham affairs, Watkin in using somewhat high-handed methods ran into serious trouble with the South Eastern Board in the years 1876–8. First of all he sacked J. I. Cudworth, whose fine engines were referred to in the previous chapter. He took this step without any knowledge, let alone agreement, of the Board, but when the matter came up he explained his action away by saying that the public safety required someone who would display more energy and zeal in the discharge of his duties. Watkin might have got away with this, even though Cudworth's successor was his own son, A. M. Watkin. But far from requiring, in his own son, what he had demanded from Cudworth he raised no objection to the new 'locomotive superintendent' standing for Parliament, and getting elected as Member for Grimsby. The Board, however, thought otherwise, and young Watkin was 'sent packing' almost as soon as he arrived.

The fat was now fairly in the fire around the South Eastern Board table, and for over a year it was touch and go whether Sir Edward would not follow his son. Dissatisfaction with the train service given to the public led to many letters in the Press; some contained personal attacks on Watkin himself, and in reply to all this he was moved in 1878 to write to *The Times* surely the most extraordinary letter ever written for publication by an English railway chairman:

'I have been entirely superseded in the executive management. All my recommendations for improvement have been ignored. During nearly the whole of the year a locomotive committee – upon which Mr Nathaniel Buckley has been appointed chairman and Mr Mellor principal member –

have managed or, I must say, mismanaged, without interference of any kind from me, the whole locomotive department. Some time ago, too, a traffic committee with Mr Rawson as chairman, was appointed, with whose labours I have in no matter interfered. I say, therefore, that it is to the inexperienced operations of these gentlemen who have now had their own way for about a year, that all the mismanagement which the company is suffering from is due.'

One can only add by way of immediate comment that it was during this period of 'mismanagement' that the services of James Stirling, as locomotive superintendent, were secured. He was appointed in July, 1878, on the recommendation of the locomotive committee.

The adroitness with which Sir Edward Watkin rode out the storm was typical of his skill in manoeuvre and debate. The report of the directors for the half-year July–December 1878, naturally took the strongest exception to Sir Edward's letter to *The Times*, and when the time came for the report to be presented to the shareholders, on 1st February, 1879, Watkin, as Chairman, refused to recommend the adoption of the report, and delegated the job to the deputy chairman. This reflected faithfully enough the disagreements that had persisted around the Board table throughout the previous year when there had been usually a majority of 8 : 4 against Sir Edward. At the meeting of shareholders no sooner had the adoption of the report been moved than the chairman himself rose and moved its rejection! Despite everything, the financial results of the company were the best for many years; a dividend of 6 per cent was recommended, and the meeting carried Sir Edward's amendment. Subsequent proceedings, including a poll on the subject of the election of directors, ended in a triumphant vote of confidence in Sir Edward Watkin, so that he was established more firmly than ever in the supreme command of affairs.

While the Chatham was recovering, very slowly, from its financial burdens, and the South Eastern was in the throes of internal strife, plans for the amalgamation of the two companies were being actively discussed. Things even got to the stage, in 1877, of the terms being agreed by both sides. But the terms were agreed too late to permit of a Bill being presented to Parliament that session, and when the matter was raised almost a year later the sharp divisions among the South Eastern directors were becoming common knowledge, and there seems no doubt that Forbes felt he could get better terms by waiting a little longer. To the astonishment of the South Eastern directors therefore, the Chatham proprietors turned the whole business down flat. So the competition blazed away once more, and the Chatham in 1880 by securing an Act to extend their line from Maidstone onwards to Ashford drove another prong into the heart of South Eastern country. Originally it was proposed to have a separate station in Ashford, but afterwards the L.C.D.R. obtained authority to use the South Eastern station, and were granted running powers over about half a mile of the South Eastern main line.

At the time it was built this line, through a deeply rural countryside, could have brought scant returns to the Chatham company. The most one could hope for was revenue from local traffic, for Ashford, fast becoming a 'railway town', was predominantly South Eastern in sentiment and its people were not likely to take the slower route of the Chatham to London. In the present century this 'wild-cat' scheme of Forbes became invaluable as part of an alternative boat train route, and was also used for certain through expresses of an intermediate character serving Maidstone, Ashford, and towns beyond on the old South Eastern line. Again, while the Chatham and the South Eastern were sparring over other things they cooperated in joint ownership of the Dover and Deal line, which was opened in 1881. The Chatham had received authorization for this line in 1862 but then had no funds to go ahead. The joint project with the South Eastern was agreed in 1874, but 7 years were to elapse before the job was finished.

If there was agreement between the two companies at Deal it was far otherwise at Folkestone. For some time the South Eastern had realized they had received very much the worst of it over the Continental agreement of 1865, and in 1884 when the Chatham promoted a Bill for constructing a line from Kearsney, near Dover, to Folkestone to join up with the South Eastern there, the smouldering fires of resentment blazed instantly. For once, too, the people of Folkestone and the South Eastern were very much of one mind. A pamphlet was printed, of which I have seen a copy, slanging J. S. Forbes right and left. He was referred to as the 'Chairman and Don Quixote of the London, Chatham & Dover Railway'; references were made to 'his gallant attempts to show that fiction was fact, and that the exuberant fancies of his teeming brain were realities,' and the new railway was apostrophized as 'the latest chimera of ruinous speculation.'

Certainly the arguments put forward in its favour strike one as largely specious. Forbes referred to the risk of interruption of communication between Folkestone and Dover due to recurrence of landslips in the Warren. That was certainly a good point, but when he went on to say that a direct line from Folkestone to Chatham and Canterbury would benefit the town and lower rates and fares he was practising his well-known art of *bunkum*. Still farther into the realms of fantasy was his assertion that there were many people who would prefer to travel from Folkestone to Victoria, Ludgate Hill or Holborn Viaduct, to arriving at Charing Cross, or Cannon Street, even though the journey would have to be made via Kearsney, Canterbury and Chatham.

The Folkestone pamphleteer asked why this scheme was being put forward, and put forward the following explanation: 'Just as the late Emperor Napoleon, when he found domestic calamities threatening him, tried to divert the attention of his subjects to foreign matters by stirring up European disputes, so Mr Forbes harassed by the internal difficulties that afflict his harassed company is compelled ever to be seeking repose by arousing some topic of external distraction.' The writer of the pamphlet went on to suggest that before any citizens were misled by the grandiose prospects associated with this short line they ought to ask one of the L.C.D.R. shareholders what he thought about it. Such a one, the pamphlet writer went on, 'would tell of the distress and misery of hundreds of impoverished investors who put faith in the promises of the Chatham company, of whose honesty and fair dealing Mr Forbes has now the courage publicly to vaunt. He would tell that this bitter cry of the outcast capitalist is only kept down by the reckless promotion of unremunerative new lines; thereby deluding his ordinary shareholders with the vain will-o'the-wisp hope that the bright day of dividends foredoomed never to arrive, is at last approaching . . .'

Despite all that Forbes could think up in support of the Kearsney–Folkestone project it was a forlorn hope for another reason, quite apart from the determination of the Folkestone people to have nothing to do with Forbes. In 1881 the South Eastern Railway had obtained powers to construct a line of their own from Folkestone to Canterbury. This followed the Elham valley, and to make doubly sure of countering the latest L.C.D.R. threat work on this line was pushed ahead. It was opened in 1889, and provided a very pleasant run, leaving the main line at Cheriton Junction, and running through a delightfully rural countryside. In the early years of this century, when staying at Folkestone with my parents, I travelled over it several times on expeditions to Canterbury, Ramsgate and Margate.

The 'common purse' agreement between the South Eastern and the L.C.D.R. for continental traffic, and to ordinary traffic into Folkestone and Dover had been a mounting source of grievance to the

South Eastern, and the growth of the town of Folkestone and its westward development evidently prompted Watkin to try and evade it. In western residential districts of Folkestone two new stations, one named 'Radnor Park', and another 'Cheriton Arch' were opened, while a fine new station was built immediately to the east of the existing Shorncliffe station, and named 'Shorncliffe Camp'. This latter had four running lines between the platforms, as in the older stations at Ashford, Paddock Wood, and Tonbridge. The South Eastern argued that these three stations, Radnor Park, Shorncliffe Camp and Cheriton Arch, were not 'Folkestone', and therefore lay outside the common purse agreement. The station now known as Folkestone Junction was then called plain 'Folkestone', and in the South Eastern view this station and the harbour were the only ones coming within the agreement. To strengthen their point the S.E.R. charged cheaper fares from Shorncliffe Camp than from Folkestone, and forthwith ceased to make any payments to the L.C.D.R. for Shorncliffe traffic.

In the meantime the popularity of the new stations grew. Residents in the new part of Folkestone would not make the journey down to the depths of the valley and up to the station on the far side when they had an excellent service provided for them on their doorsteps. Two years elapsed, and then the Chatham brought an action against the South Eastern, claiming £70,000 as the sum due under the 1865 agreement. Proceedings began in the Court of Chancery, in November, 1887, and in due course judgment was given in favour of the Chatham. The South Eastern promptly took the case to the Court of Appeal where it was dismissed, in November, 1888, but the Chatham, convinced that justice was on their side, took it to the House of Lords, and after a prolonged and very expensive litigation judgment was finally given in favour of the Chatham, and that company was awarded a sum of £85,000. It was a crushing defeat for the South Eastern, and the costs are said to have amounted to a quarter of a million pounds.

At the time of the uproar over the L.C.D.R. Kearsney–Folkestone project it was said that the Chatham only managed to pay the small dividend on its arbitration preference shares by the unearned income it received from the South Eastern traffic through Folkestone, and just about this time it must be admitted that in the matter of hard cash the South Eastern seemed to be losing round after round to its rival. How the South Eastern Board came to be persuaded to embark on the Chatham Central scheme passes comprehension. For some reason, lost forever in the mists of time, they decided that they must have a station of their own in the heart of Chatham. Strood, on the western bank of the Medway was evidently considered not good enough. Whether it was hoped to divert some of the main Chatham–London traffic to their own line, via Gravesend we are not to know, but in fact a large and expensive viaduct was built across the Medway, cheek by jowl with the L.C.D.R. viaduct, and a branch line from Strood constructed cutting into the lower part of Chatham and establishing there a terminus that was anything but central, despite its name. This line was opened in March, 1892, and represented virtually Sir Edward Watkin's last throw.

The old L.C.D.R. viaduct over the Medway was an extraordinary affair. The deck consisted of transverse timbers attached to the *under-side* of the main girders, and on the this deck longitudinal timbers were mounted to carry the rails. Although the old South Eastern station in Rochester has long since been closed the present main line is carried over the Medway on the South Eastern viaduct, and this slewing of the line enabled the curves at Rochester Bridge Junction to be eased.

'The Railway King', as he was often called, was then 73 years of age, and after nigh 40 years of the most strenuous and aggressive railway life his health was at last beginning to fail. He was then a director of eleven railways, including one in the U.S.A. At one time also, he was president of the Grand Trunk Railway, of Canada, and a director of both the Great Western, and the Great Eastern. In *The Railway Magazine*, G. A. Sekon once commented: 'Luckily for the shareholders of these three latter concerns, they failed to appraise the Railway King at his own worth, and consequently he left them.' The shareholders of the South Eastern, who had backed him in the troubles of 1878–9 were, by the year 1893, in open revolt, and when the time came for his retirement to be announced in 1894, not only from the South Eastern, but from all other lines with which he was connected, the stocks concerned were sharply advanced in price on the London Stock Exchange. This was enough to show how his administration was regarded in the City. Thus he went, in 1894, leaving his great rival James Staats Forbes still in the field.

VIII

Engineering Progress

In the last 20 years of their independent existences both the London, Chatham & Dover and the South Eastern were served by some very able engineers. Francis Brady on the S.E., Mills, and G. B. Roche, on the Chatham, had a tremendous task to keep the way and works in good order during times of financial stringency, and there was not on either railway an accident that could be attributed to faulty permanent way. At times the best expresses of the L.C.D. did some quite fast running, with considerably higher maximum speeds than the traveller of those days could experience on the South Eastern, or the Brighton. The long gradients east of Faversham, descending in both directions from Ensden Tunnel, and no less the descent from Lydden Tunnel to Canterbury, were favourite racing stretches. At the same time the ballasting was not finished off very tidily, and the general appearance was sometimes contrasted unfavourably with that of the South Eastern.

On the latter line, despite the smart, well-kept appearance of the permanent way, there was an overall speed limit of 60 m.p.h. over the whole railway. This was no reflection upon the locomotives, and in after years James Stirling complained that he could not get any real running, even downhill, due to this restriction. It was probably enforced for the twofold reason of minimizing wear and tear on the rolling stock, and thus reducing maintenance charges, and because the South Eastern used a great deal of shingle from the Dungeness beaches for its ballast. Shingle was a cheap and serviceable material, but with it difficulty was found in later years in getting a really solid packing such as is necessary on a road carrying fast and heavy traffic. South Eastern practice in using shingle ballast was carried on into Southern Railway days and was partly to blame for the serious accident at Sevenoaks in 1927. By that time much higher speeds were permitted, with much heavier locomotives.

Before coming to the locomotives and carriage stock of the 1878–98 period mention must be made of some important new lines, all on the Chatham system, brought into use between 1886 and 1894. Whatever criticisms might be levelled at the Chatham for much of its poverty-stricken passenger rolling stock, and for the 'wild-cat' nature of some of Forbes's competitive schemes, one must admit that no parsimony was shown in improving the line in the London area to facilitate the handling of the massive suburban traffic that was building up. Two sections of the main line were widened to provide four running roads, from Penge to Kent House, in 1886, and from Shortlands to Bickley, in 1894. In addition, the opening of the Catford loop line in 1892 provided a useful alternative route. It is said that this latter was pushed ahead because Forbes had a haunting fear of Penge Tunnel caving in. Perhaps it was the experience of the South Eastern in the Folkestone Warren that alarmed him.

The largest project in the London area was the new bridge over the Thames at Blackfriars and the new City terminal station, St Pauls, opened in 1886. Use of running powers over the Chatham line by so many companies had led to hopeless congestion over the original Blackfriars bridge and through Ludgate Hill, and the new bridge had space for no fewer than seven tracks abreast. St Pauls station, partly a terminus, contained also a pair of through lines which connected with the old line north of Ludgate Hill. The bottleneck was thus reduced to a relatively short length between this new junction and the north end of Snow Hill Tunnel where the L.C.D. line debouched to make a triangle junction with the City Widened Lines of the Metropolitan Railway.

At the opposite end of both the rival railways important developments were on hand at both Dover and Folkestone. At Dover the Admiralty Pier, on which constructional work began in 1847, was finished in 1871. The boats of both the rival companies were using the pier from 1864 onwards, the South Eastern trains using the inshore section and the Chatham stopping abreast of the landing stage used by their own steamers. From the time of completion of the pier steamers used also to berth on the outer side of the pier, as shown in some of the illustrations, though one would imagine this was a facility only to be used in the calmest of weather. At the landward end of the pier the Chatham and the South Eastern tracks were quite independent and there were no points whereby trains could run from one to the other. The single tracks over the cobblestones remained the only railway access to the pier until the time came for building the present Marine Station.

In the anxious years following the end of the Crimean War, when the political activities of the Emperor Napoleon III seemed to contain serious and incalculable risks for this country, plans were drawn up for a great National Harbour at Dover. As a preliminary a powerfully armed fort was built on the Admiralty Pier. But nothing had been done when the Franco–Prussian War broke out in 1870; and its swift course and catastrophic end for France brought a general lessening of international tension, for a while. Thus, the idea of a National Harbour hung fire, but in the meantime the Dover Harbour Board, anxious to develop the commercial activities of the port, went rapidly ahead with a scheme of its own. The outcome was the construction of the Prince of Wales Pier, as an eastern breakwater to enclose the large commerical harbour envisaged. This work began in 1892, but it was still in progress in 1898 and by that time a far more extensive plan for the development of Dover was under consideration by the Government of the day. The fulfilment of this project belongs to a later period in the story, and at the turn of the century facilities for handling the continental traffic at Dover were unchanged from those of 1871.

Had one of the most spectacular of Watkin's projects come to fruition the need for any substantial development of harbour facilities either at Dover or Folkestone would have almost disappeared. This project was the Channel Tunnel. In 1875 Watkin induced the South Eastern Board to make a grant of £20,000 towards the exploratory trials, on condition that the L.C.D. contributed the same amount. The Chatham Board of that period agreed, but for one reason or another the project lay dormant. France was convulsed in the aftermath of the Franco–Prussian War, but in 1882 the South Eastern & Channel Company was incorporated. Some trial borings were made on the seashore, near to the western end of Shakespeare's Cliff Tunnel, and it was here that a chance discovery led to a development of far more immediate value to both the South Eastern and the Chatham railways than any prospective Channel Tunnel.

One of the trial borings near Shakespeare's Cliff Tunnel struck a seam of coal. Until then the existence of a Kentish coalfield had not been suspected, but a sinking was made on the spot and for some little time the Shakespeare Colliery was worked. It was not a success, but the proven existence of the seam led to investigations elsewhere in the near neighbourhood with the result that four first-class coal producing collieries have been developed in Kent: Betteshanger and Tilmanstone, inland from Deal; Snowdown, alongside the Chatham main line near Shepherd's Well, and Chislet. These ultimately produced a good locomotive coal, used on top link express passenger workings from Dover and Ramsgate sheds. In physical and combustion characteristics it is similar to soft Welsh coal, needing a thick fire-bed, and to be well burned through at the start of a run. Today it is strange to realize that these four collieries are the only practical outcome of the oft-revived project of a Channel Tunnel.

From locomotive fuel it is an easy step to the locomotives themselves, and it is interesting to compare the practices of Stirling on the South Eastern, and Kirtley on the Chatham. Both men were of famous families of locomotive engineers, and both put on the road machines that could compare with the very best of their day. There was much of the family tradition about Stirling's work on the South Eastern. His first engines, of 1878–9, were in the direct line of descent from his brother's earliest work on the Glasgow & South Western Railway. James Stirling had succeeded Patrick in the chair at Kilmarnock in 1866, but although continuing the cult of the domeless boiler and details of construction he had broken away from his brother's addiction to the single-wheeler for express work in the remarkable 'No. 6 Class' 4-4-0s, of which the first was built at Kilmarnock in 1873. As these engines were the direct progenitors of the famous South Eastern 'F' Class they deserve a special mention. Ahrons referred to them as 'probably the most celebrated express engines that ever ran on the Glasgow & South Western'. As one of the earliest inside-cylinder 4-4-0 designs they created much interest at the time, and their splendid work on the road confirmed Stirling's confidence in the general principles on which he had worked.

When he came south, in 1878, he left a stud of fine engines in Scotland, for in addition to these 4-4-0s, twenty-two in all, there were classes of 0-4-2 mixed traffic engines, a 2-4-0 'intermediate', a 6 ft 7 in. 2-4-0 express design, a 0-4-4 tank, and a 0-6-0 goods class. On the South Eastern three of these designs were very closely followed, the 4-4-0, the 0-4-4 tank, and the 0-6-0; but the 0-4-2, as a type favoured in Scotland and on the Great Northern for fast goods and intermediate passenger work did not materialize, and in its place James Stirling put on the road an excellent class of 6 ft 4-4-0s. The first two new classes to go into service on the South Eastern were virtually of Glasgow & South Western design. The 0-6-0 goods came first, and except that the safety valves were placed on the rearmost ring of the boiler instead of over the firebox they were very similar to the Kilmarnock 'black goods' of 1877. The 6 ft 4-4-0s, the first of which was built at Ashford in 1879, had the deep running plate valence of the G.&S.W. 'No. 6' class 4-4-0s, and originally the three-piece built up chimneys in addition. They were excellent engines, and at first they were used on the more heavily graded routes of the South Eastern, to Hastings for example, and on some of the Ramsgate trains.

It is, of course, the celebrated 'F' Class that claims most of our attention on the South Eastern. Fortunately, through the recordings of Mr J. Pearson Pattinson, their performance on the road is well documented, and the logs of a number of runs are included in the next chapter. Here, we can look a little more closely at the design itself. One could not, by any stretch of the imagination, call them handsome engines. Seen broadside on, the short wheelbase of the bogie detracted from their appearance, while from any forward position the prominence of the smokebox wings tended to give a rugged, squat look to the engine as a whole. The large sandboxes mounted on the leading coupled-wheel splasher, and the exposed safety valves gave the design as a whole an austere, functional look that was inevitably contrasted with the grace and elegance of Patrick Stirling's work on the Great Northern. Yet for all that James Stirling's stud on the South Eastern had a character and individualism that was all their own.

Stirling achieved a high degree of standardization of the locomotive stock during his 20 years at Ashford, and in December, 1898, when the Managing Committee for the Chatham and the South Eastern Railways was formed, no fewer than 384 out of a total locomotive Stock of 459 were of Stirling's standard designs. More than this: of that 384, no less that 323 were of three classes only, namely:

'O'	Class 0-6-0 goods	.	.	.	.	.	117
'F'	Class 4-4-0 express passenger	.	.	.	88
'Q'	Class 0-4-4 passenger tank	.	.	.	118

The remaining Stirling engines of the S.E. 1898 stock consisted of:

'A'	Class 6 ft 4-4-0 passenger	.	.	.	12
'R'	Class 0-6-0 shunting tank	.	.	.	25
'B'	Class 4-4-0 express passenger	.	.	24

In addition to the above, five more 'O' Class goods engines, and five more of the new 'B' Class 4-4-0s were built after the fusion of the S.E. and L.C.D. stocks.

The two tank engine designs were familiar and long lived machines. To many travellers the 'R' Class were perhaps best known for their work with the boat trains on the Folkestone Harbour branch, and they must have been among the very last engines on the Southern to retain the Stirling domeless boilers. They were used also for the passenger services on the Elham Valley line. The 0-4-4 tanks bore the brunt of the London suburban service for many years. They were splendid engines, having the standard 18 in. by 26 in. cylinders used on all Stirling's South Eastern designs except the 4-4-0s of Classes 'F' and 'B'. Twelve of them were fitted with condensing apparatus, and shorter chimneys, for working the through trains to the Great Northern line, via Ludgate Hill, and the City Widened Lines of the Metropolitan. They would have made an interesting contrast to Patrick Stirling's 0-4-4 suburban tanks of the Great Northern, but I have never seen a photograph of the combination, side by side, at one or other of the northern suburban termini. James Stirling's last locomotive design, the fine 'B' Class 4-4-0 of 1898, belongs so essentially to S.E.C. days that reference to it can be conveniently left until later.

Although the Chatham and the South Eastern companies covered a roughly equal tract of country, and were in competition at so many different points, the Chatham was in reality a much smaller concern than its rival, and at the time of fusion the total locomotive stock was no more than 215. It was a far more heterogenous collection than the South Eastern stud, and the way in which older engines had been patched up and rebuilt many times reflected the financial stringency that had persisted throughout Chatham history. William Kirtley's policy was in any case different from that of Stirling. The latter introduced his three main classes the 'O', the 'Q' and the 'F' in 1878, 1881 and 1883 respectively and made no changes to any of them thereafter. Kirtley, on the other hand, in 1874–7 introduced 0-4-4 T, 0-6-0 and 4-4-0 designs, but followed these with successive improvements and enlargements as further batches were required. Thus at the time of fusion there were four varieties of 0-4-4 tank; three of 0-6-0 goods and four of express passenger 4-4-0, all of Kirtley's design. Including a class of ten 0-6-0 tanks, the Kirtleys totalled only 125 out of the entire L.C.D. stock.

At the time of Kirtley's appointment, in March, 1874, the Chatham had 124 locomotives, and it is astonishing to realize that 89 of these were still in service when he retired 24 years later. It was indeed a time of making-do and mending! There were among the engines he inherited, some excellent machines – particularly the various classes of Martley 2-4-0, with their whimsical and often humorous names. Whatever the activities of J. S. Forbes happened to be at the moment, however the financial structure of the company may have creaked and groaned, William Martley never seems to have lost his sense of humour. How else, at such a time, could express locomotives have been named *Bluebell*, *Dawn* and *Frolic*, not to mention *Mermaid* and *Lothair*! The last Martley design, the 'Europa' Class of 1873, are fit to rank with the most famous 2-4-0s that have ever run in this country, and a fine example of their work appears in full tabular form in the next chapter.

Here we are concerned with Kirtley's engines. Considering how precarious the financial affairs of the Chatham continued to remain right up to the time of fusion, it is astonishing that such a splendid tradition of locomotive designing and construction was built up at Longhedge Works. In whatever other directions the Chatham might have to skimp and starve, there was no skimping things either in the repair or maintenance standards of the locomotive stock. It is especially important to note the development of L.C.D. practice in Kirtley's years, because after the fusion it was the Chatham section of the partnership that came to exercise the greatest influence on future locomotive design. While the South Eastern engines were of a highly distinctive appearance, comparable only with those of the Glasgow & South Western, the Chatham engines were of more orthodox outline, albeit pleasing to the eye and always beautifully kept. It is, however, significant of the regard in which Kirtley's engines were held by his fellow locomotive engineers, that in Pettigrew's classic work *A Manual of Locomotive Engineering*, two of the five designs chosen for illustration on large folding plates, reproducing the working drawings, were from the London, Chatham & Dover Railway.

The products of Longhedge Works were characterized by their simplicity of design. On the largest passenger 4-4-os and goods o-6-os the cylinders were 18 in. by 26 in. and the slide valves were placed between the cylinders, permitting of a direct drive Stephenson's link motion. Screw-reverse was used in L.C.D. days. During the whole of his tenure of office Kirtley had to contend with conditions of austerity that are strongly reminiscent of British Railways since 1948. Because of the financial stringencies always prevailing attempts had to be made to keep maintenance costs at a low level; and to guard against the incidence of hot boxes Kirtley designed his engines with large working clearances in the motion, and without adjustable driving-box wedges. In consequence, and like some present-day locomotives one could name they soon became very noisy and harsh in their action. After the fusion South Eastern who had to work them on occasions dubbed them the 'clatterbangs'. The South Eastern engines on the other hand, ran with the quietness of a sewing machine; having produced a first class basic design Stirling relied on the craftsmanship of his men, whether in the works at Ashford, or at the sheds, to keep the locomotives going at concert pitch.

Kirtley could take no such line. Much more detailed consideration had to be given to each part of the engine at the design stage.

Engineers brought up on the Chatham had no sinecure of an existence, and the way in which the older engines were kept going is a
lasting tribute to the way they did their job. The experience of those
long, difficult years was built into successive products of Longhedge
Works, culminating in the 'M3' 4-4-0s. They were far from large
engines, even at the time of their first introduction in 1891; but
observers like Mr Pattinson, who knew them in their prime, considered they were generally better than the Stirling 'F' Class on the
South Eastern. The latter engines were somewhat hamstrung by the
prevalence of the 60 m.p.h. limit over the entire South Eastern line.
The Chatham had no such restriction, and the free-running of the
'M3' Class probably gave the impression that they were better
engines altogether. After the link-up, when the designing experience
and skill of Longhedge was combined with the craftmanship of
Ashford there came a series of locomotives, for all grades of service,
that for strength, longevity, and handsome appearance have proved
second to none.

Even in the last years of the nineteenth century coaching stock
was not the strongest suit of either the Chatham or the South
Eastern Railways. In his classic series of articles in *The Railway Magazine* the late E. L. Ahrons made merry over their deficiencies, over
the odd shapes and sizes of a normal South Eastern rake, over the
rigorous standard of accommodation and general dilapidation of the
Chatham varieties. In descriptions of certain excellent locomotive
performances on the latter line Ahrons gives the load in dog-boxes
rather than coaches, for that is what most of the Chatham four-
wheelers more closely resembled. Except on the Continental expresses four-wheelers remained the rule rather than the exception,
and third class passengers were automatically excluded from the
majority of the best trains. Moreover, the companies not being
regulated by law as to what they charged for other than third class
accommodation fixed the level of their second and first class fares
considerably above those of the great lines of the north, though
naturally the Chatham was at one with both the South Eastern and
the Brighton in its high second and first class fares.

Nowadays it can well be wondered how the passengers of those
times were ever persuaded to pay such fares for facilities that were
poor in comfort and booked speed, and which were usually capped
by chronically unpunctual running. Generally speaking, the travel
habit had not yet taken a hold on the people of this country. There
was no such thing as holidays with pay, and such families as did
enjoy the luxury of a seaside holiday made for the nearest watering

place. Those who used the Chatham, the Brighton, and the South Eastern had little knowledge of what was being done elsewhere. Professor Foxwell, referring to the fine service provided by the Cheshire Lines between Liverpool and Manchester, commented: 'This swarm of rapid trains have to cut their way through a maze of murky junctions, but they are punctual as chronometers. The cultured Londoner must drop many a tear when he sees such a high standard of performance daily maintained in the rude provincial air.'

The South Eastern simply *asked* for trouble and delays in the way it worked the traffic west of London Bridge. Why the fantastic practice of making all trains for Charing Cross call at Cannon Street on the way was persisted in for so long baffles the imagination! As long ago as 1889 Foxwell remarked: 'The delays will never cease until trains are worked *separately* for Charing Cross and Cannon Street, so that this crossing on the level may be put an end to.' But it was not until the present century that the old practice was abandoned, and even then one finds duplicate portions of Continental mails 'dropping in' at Cannon Street, to collect additional traffic. Strangely enough it was the railway races to the north that began to open the eyes of the people living south of the Thames to the shortcomings of their own railways. The 'races', both in 1888 and 1895, received a good deal of publicity in the newspapers of the day, and realization began to come. The South Eastern management was alive enough to the troubles on the Charing Cross line, and was engaged in some most expensive widening works. As the whole line was either on arches or on viaducts over the Thames it was a tremendous task. But as Foxwell pointed out, much of this expense could have been avoided by a complete recasting of the train service.

In the late autumn of 1888, when the excitement of the Edinburgh 'race' had died down, *The Pall Mall Gazette* took up the question of South Eastern working. An article that appeared in November gives such a vivid impression of the conditions then prevailing that it is worth quoting in full:

'The South Eastern Railway, although most favourably placed with respect to the number and situation of its London termini, is at the other end of the scale in regard to its accesses to the same. Railway experts from the Continent or America marvel that the delays are not greater. Sir Myles Fenton, the general manager of the company, has had a great deal of experience in working crowded lines in London and Lancashire. He organized the opening of the Metropolitan Railway, and was associated with that company for seventeen years. For some years he also worked the Metropolitan, and altogether he has had a railway record of forty-three years. There is no piece of traffic which required so much care, and is attended with so many difficulties, as the working of that part of the South Eastern's system which lies between London Bridge and Cannon Street and Charing Cross. A plan of the line at once shows the natural obstacles in the way of expeditious working. Trains from London Bridge to Charing Cross cannot get in without crossing the path of outgoing trains from Cannon Street, so that there is a constant crossing and re-crossing, which all means delay. Every down train from Charing Cross crosses two up lines to get on to the down line. The space in the stations is so limited that empty as well as loaded trains must be immediately despatched, and in consequence of the shortness of the line at the south side of Cannon Street bridge, an empty from Charing Cross which is being sent down to Rotherhithe Road, where they are stacked, may completely block Cannon Street station. It often happens that there are trains standing at every signal for some distance down the road, a delay with one necessarily affecting all the others, both up and down.

'Under these difficult conditions no fewer than 850 loaded trains are daily taken into and sent out of Cannon Street and Charing Cross stations. Continental expresses, seaside trains, the locals, and the others which make up this total, have all to pass through the narrow neck outside Cannon Street. Other companies can shunt their local traffic – as the northern and other lines do – and the Brighton has completed its duties when London Bridge is reached, but the South Eastern must get over the river at two points with the bulk of its traffic. The distance is so small that the delays, which are inevitable under existing conditions, irritate the public and the company gets the reputation for unpunctuality. "None the less," the general manager remarks, "up to London Bridge we can compare with any other company in the matter of punctuality". The services are also affected by delays on the line between Redhill and London, which are crowded with trains of the Brighton Company, frequently causing a dislocation of the South Eastern trains, especially during the most important hours of the day. Difficult, however, as it is under normal conditions, the working of the traffic becomes appalling when fog comes down. On the most favoured roads trains are impeded under such circumstances, but here, when the signals and trains are hid from view, there is an inevitable collapse of the ordinary service. The trains have to be hand-signalled in and out without any regard to the timetable.

'The remedy for the evil is not hid from the directors and their staff, but it means money, and that to a very large amount – how much it would be rash to say. What they are doing is to proceed by degrees, and as a first step they have widened Charing Cross bridge, and have nearly completed the same operation at Cannon Street. They have, further, acquired the land for the purpose of broadening the viaduct between London Bridge and Charing Cross, which carries at present three lines; they have obtained land in order to extend London Bridge station, and have begun the work; they have also purchased some of the land for widening

Charing Cross station. When the extensions are made at London Bridge, instead of one down road for the main line traffic there will be two, which is the minimum of other companies. The doubling of the bridge at Cannon Street will give ten instead of five lines into that station; and the Charing Cross bridge now furnishes six instead of three. This addition has been in practical use for some months, and already the extra facilities have proved advantageous, although its full value will not be realized until the whole scheme of extension has been completed.'

So far as passenger comforts were concerned the South Eastern management seemed to work upon the hope that the rougher they made things for the third class passenger the better was the chance that he would transfer to a superior class and pay the vastly higher fares. It was small comfort to the occupants of the dog-boxes to see the Hastings 'drawing-room car' train sail by, with its plutocratic passengers reclining in luxurious armchairs each decked with a spotless white antimacassar, or to be ruthlessly side tracked to allow a 'Continental Mail' – first and second class only – to go ahead. Whatever the moral justification for them, however, the American Car trains were a remarkable innovation on a railway not famed for its amenities, though the experiment, in 1892, could probably be put down as just another Watkin stunt.

The beautiful cars included in the Hastings train were built by the Gilbert Car Manufacturing Company of Troy, New York, and were shipped to England in sections. They were assembled at Ashford, and fitted with standard South Eastern bogies including Mansell pattern wooden wheel-centres. The cars themselves were relatively short, measuring 51 ft 3½ in. long, but they were decorated internally in the most extravagantly Victorian taste and seated no more than twenty-four passengers apiece: seventeen in the main saloon, and seven in the adjoining smoking lounge. The small amount of accommodation for smokers at that time is interesting! The train consisted of six of these cars, with a standard South Eastern four-wheeled brake van at each end. It was put into service on the Hastings run, in strong competition with the Brighton. The accommodation was first class only, though, strangely enough, no additional charge was made for the luxury of travel in such a train. Despite this rather surprising concession on the part of the usually-grasping South Eastern management, the train was not well patronized and was soon taken off. The later 'parlour-car' trains, introduced in 1897, carried first, second and *third* class passengers, and belong, not merely to the post-Watkin era on the South Eastern, but more correctly to the early days of the Managing Committee.

Despite the somewhat chaotic ideas of timetable planning and the general traffic strategy practised by both companies, the Chatham and the South Eastern enjoyed a very satisfactory record of safety in working. James Stirling, in company with his brother and many other eminent engineers of the day at first adopted the simple, rather than the automatic vacuum brake. On the Chatham it is astonishing to recall that right down to the year 1884 express locomotives were being built with nothing more than handbrakes! The last two engines of the 'M2' Class of 4-4-0s were the first to have power brakes, and sure enough the Chatham, at variance with South Eastern in most things, decided to adopt the Westinghouse brake. The absence of any trouble through collisions up till that time is perhaps a reflection of the moderate speeds run.

Reference was made in Chapter II to the early adoption of semaphore signalling and interlocking on the South Eastern Railway. The new stations at Charing Cross and Cannon Street were, from the outset, equipped by Saxby & Farmer Limited, with signalboxes mounted athwart the tracks and each carrying a great array of signal masts on the roof of the box. At Cannon Street, when the station was first opened, the box had four masts above it and no fewer than twenty-four semaphore arms, all immediately above the box. There were no other signals until one reached the fearsome junction that caused all the delays in crossing over immediately south of the river. Looking at old photographs of those signalboxes and remembering that the London fogs of Victorian days were probably worse than anything in living memory – bar the great 'smog' of November, 1954 – one wonders how things were managed in fog. In this respect Foxwell is again worth quoting.

'Another good word may be thrown in for these unpopular companies, and that is to praise them for the plucky way in which they carry on their traffic during *fogs*. When an English railway is hard pressed it rises to the occasion and shows the stuff it is made of, and we are never so proud of our southern lines as during dense weather. Thus in the early weeks of last January (1889), when for 8 or 9 consecutive days the fog was so thick at times that a pedestrian could not see the curb of the pavement on which he walked, it was a truly English experience to stand on the platform of such a station as Norwood Junction, and hear the Brighton expresses thunder through with not so much as half the length of a single carriage visible at once. The pluck and endurance exhibited by obscure *employees* whenever "fogging" is the order of the day are beyond words;

an unappreciative public is whirled up to its office snug and warm, and prefers to expend its admiration on those scarlet-coated heroes who are lucky enough to receive a scratch in the Soudan and a paragraph in the London papers.'

Where signalling is concerned the record of the Chatham is outstanding among all the railways of this country. J. S. Forbes, purveyor of 'bunkum' though he may have been, took a keen interest in the operating side of the railway, and he had scarcely been appointed to the general managership before he was investigating telegraph communication from end to end of the line. A year later a certain Mr Rudall was appointed Electrical Superintendent, and it was he who brought in W. R. Sykes, as a maintenance man. Sykes became closely associated with all matters concerning the running of the trains, and it was in 1874 that he produced his great invention of the 'Lock and Block' system of working. At first Forbes was horrified by the suggestion that this new idea should be tried on one of the busiest sections in the London area. He felt that so great an innovation should be installed on some quiet country branch, where the snags could be found and eliminated. But all the inspecting officers of the Board of Trade, the Colonels Rich, Tyler and Yolland, and Major-General Hutchinson were so taken with the idea, and so insistent, that it was installed at three boxes in the busiest London area, namely Shepherd's Lane, Brixton, and Canterbury Road Junction. The patent was granted to Sykes in February, 1875.

At that time the simplest form of block working relied for its safety upon the signalmen carrying out the rules. There were no positive means to ensure that the jobs were done in the correct order, and on very busy lines a signalman might make a false step. With Sykes 'lock and block' it was essential that each step was correctly carried out. One could say that the signals were interlocked with the train. Electrical interlocking was provided so that a signalman could not accept a train from the previous box along the line until the preceeding train was clear of the section ahead, and was proved clear by passing over an electrical treadle. While the safety afforded by 'lock and block' was fully recognized one can quite imagine that the expense of installation was a thing that an impoverished line like the Chatham could not undertake lightly. Then came the Sittingbourne accident of 1878, when through a signalman's error a heavily-laden 'cheap fast' from Ramsgate came up at full speed, while shunting was in progress on the main line. The Board of Trade

Inspector called particular attention to the absence of a continuous brake on the express, but Forbes realized that 'lock and block' would have prevented the accident, and to the great credit of the Chatham Board a decision was taken to equip the whole line forthwith.

Sykes himself left the railway service to devote his whole attention to manufacture the apparatus needed for the 'lock and block' system. The development of this business, from the original workshop in an arch under the line at Nunhead, is a romance in itself, but it is not part of the present story. The semaphore signals and interlocking frames on the Chatham were made by Stevens & Sons, the original patentees of the lattice iron type of signal post, and of the very simplest form of interlocking, by tappet. The Stevens form of semaphore and spectacle is easily recognized by the curious shape of the glasses: roughly triangular, with the apex of the triangle pointing towards the pivot-point of the spectacle. The same design was standard on the North British. In its later years the South Eastern was more varied in its signalling equipment, installing semaphores and interlocking frames of Evans O'Donnell type, in addition to the later products of Saxby & Farmer. Taken all round both railways approached the time of fusion well equipped, save on the very sore subject of passenger rolling stock!

IX

Locomotive Performance : 1890-96

IN view of the odium heaped upon both the South Eastern and the Chatham railways, for the sloth and unpunctuality of their passenger services it will probably come as something of a surprise to many enthusiasts of the present day to learn of the crack express trains run just prior to the merger of 1899. In addition to the boat trains the South Eastern was running non-stop between Cannon Street and St Leonards, and in strong competition with the Chatham there were trains running non-stop between New Cross and Canterbury. In the year 1894 Mr J. Pearson Pattinson logged a number of runs on the best trains, and in general the timekeeping on these lengthy non-stop runs was very good. Many of the runs tabulated in this chapter are extracted from his recordings, and so far as the South Eastern is concerned they relate almost entirely to the earlier 4-4-0 locomotives of James Stirling's design, the 'F' Class, and show these engines in a most favourable guise.

The South Eastern Railway, despite the smart and well-kept appearance of its permanent way – in such contrast to the ragged uneven surfacing of the Brighton – had an overall speed limit of 60 m.p.h. Thus, in addition to the hard slogging needed on the severe gradients between New Cross and Tonbridge, and on the Hastings line, Mr Stirling could not get any *real* running even downhill. In consideration of these handicaps, schedules such as the following clearly required excellent locomotive work.

Section	Distance Miles	Booked time min.	Speed m.p.h.
Cannon St.–Dover . . .	75½	96	47·1
Cannon St.–Folkestone . .	69¾	91	46·0
New Cross–Canterbury . .	65½	81	48·5
Sandling Jc.–Cannon St. . .	64¼	84	46·0
Cannon St.–West St. Leonards .	59½	88	40·6

At first sight it is surprising to find that the fastest runs on the S.E.R. were made to and from Canterbury, seeing that this journey involved a heavy slack in each direction at Ashford; but on the service to Ramsgate and Margate there was the incentive of competition with the Chatham. To Hastings the South Eastern had such a natural advantage over the Brighton that it bordered on a monopoly. Before coming to the runs themselves I should mention that in the tables compiled from Mr Pattinson's records the average speeds quoted have been worked out from the chainages supplied to him by the S.E.R. and by the L.C.D.R. managements.

Taking the South Eastern first, Table I concerns three runs on the main line, with loads rising from 170 to 280 tons. Before discussing the actual performances, however, the locomotives themselves deserve a rather more detailed reference. Stirling's 'F' Class 4-4-0s, the 'Mails' as they were sometimes known, were splendid engines. In view of the restriction upon maximum speed it is perhaps a little surprising that the coupled wheels were as large as 7 ft. The boiler and firebox were not large, with a total heating surface of no more than 985 sq ft and a grate area of 16·5 sq ft. The working pressure was only 160 lb per sq in. Yet they steamed well, and supplied the relatively large cylinders – 19 in. dia by 26 in. stroke, without difficulty.

In relation to their size the demands made on these engines were severe. The South Eastern was noted for its heavy loads, and the climbing on these journeys from New Cross up to Knockholt summit was extraordinarily good. Over this section the average speed on the three runs was 35·8, 34·5 and 32·8 m.p.h. With 4-4-0 loco-motives having 19 in. by 26 in. cylinders, and a grate area of only $16\frac{3}{4}$ sq ft, this climbing must have involved heavy pounding. Down the grade towards Tonbridge the speeds quoted in the table suggest that the 60 m.p.h. limit was well exceeded on Run No. 1, and all three trains must have taken the Tonbridge curve pretty smartly to make the averages subsequently recorded on to Paddock Wood. The official limit at Tonbridge was, I believe, 20 m.p.h. It will be seen, however, that speeds were no more than moderate on the fast stretch east of Tonbridge. The average speeds between Staplehurst and Headcorn give a very good idea of the maximum run over the level sections of the line, and here engine No. 2, which was doing the fastest work hereabouts, averaged no more than 57·5 m.p.h. This was not through any inability of the 'F' Class to run. When engine No. 240 was sent to France for the Paris Exhibition of 1889 she made some runs on the P.L.M. main line and reached a maximum speed of 79 m.p.h. On the third run in Table I a portion was slipped at Ashford, reducing the load to about 200 tons, and with this relief the climbing to Westenhanger was the fastest of all. There was not one check of any kind on any of these journeys.

Turning to Table II, the work of engine No. 130 on the New Cross–Canterbury non-stop with loads of 165 and 230 tons respectively can truly be described as magnificent. The uphill averages from St Johns to Halstead (Knockholt) were 40·8 and 33·5 m.p.h., and both trains were running at, or only just below the limit speed from Paddock Wood to Pluckley. The average speeds over this stretch of 15·6 miles were 59 and 57·8 m.p.h. respectively, while on the first run the average speed from the start to passing Pluckley was all but 50 m.p.h. Operating arrangements were not so good on the branch and signal checks were frequent and severe. Coming up on the corresponding evening train, admittedly on an easier schedule, the work was again very good. The gradients on the branch are awkward rather than severe, the worst stretch being from Chilham, with about 4 miles rising at such grades as 1 in 220, 1 in 176, and 1 in 200. On the fast running section of the main line from Ashford to Tonbridge nothing particular was done, but once again the hard uphill work from Tonbridge to Halstead was excellent, particularly in the average of 39·7 m.p.h. from Dunton Green to the summit on the second run, with a load of 220 tons. In this direction both trains arrived at New Cross several minutes ahead of time.

The South Eastern runs with the Stirling 4-4-0 locomotives are fitly rounded off with some excellent performances on the Hastings line. I have chosen a journey on the up morning express for detailed tabulation, but in addition to this Mr Pattinson published complete speed recorder diagrams of two other runs, and the uphill speeds from Spa Road to Halstead, on the one hand, and from St Leonards to Frant on the other, make most interesting reading. To appreciate these to the full they must be studied in conjunction with the gradient profile, reproduced herewith, and the accompanying table of speeds had been prepared to show this. On the up journey, north of Tonbridge, the engine was going splendidly up the stiff bank to Sevenoaks, and on the 1 in 122 gradient speed was settling down to a minimum of 32 m.p.h. when there came a check by adverse signals, to 18 m.p.h. at Weald Signal Box. From this the engine recovered smartly to a sustained 31 m.p.h. through Sevenoaks Tunnel. With a load of 'equal to 14', roughly 190 tons, this was good work.

It is always interesting to study locomotive work such as this in the light of more recent practice, and the speeds run on the journey just described may be compared with those on a journey of my own made in 1938 with a 'Schools' Class engine and 380 tons behind the tender. Up the heavy grade to Crowhurst the 'School' varied between 29 and 34 m.p.h., against 30 to 36 by the old Stirling 4-4-0. Then over the favourable stretch to Etchingham the 'School' ran at 65 to 74 m.p.h. where the Stirling was restricted to 60 m.p.h. and did not, in fact, exceed 57; while going up Wadhurst, where the Stirling engine registered an absolute minimum of 32 m.p.h. the 'School', despite the much higher initial speed, fell to 28½. The old Stirling engine was evidently doing some really splendid work.

S.E.R.: 8.50 a.m. HASTINGS–CANNON STREET

Load: 14 vehicles
Engine: 'F' Class 4-4-0

Location	Speed m.p.h.
Max. before Crowhurst bank . . .	36½
Min. on 1 in 100 bank . . .	30
Battle station	52
Robertsbridge, max. . . .	57
Etchingham station	50
Ticehurst Road	37
Min. before Wadhurst . . .	32
Max. between Wadhurst and Frant . .	55
Slack through Tunbridge Wells . .	33
Max. descending to Tonbridge . .	51
Tonbridge Junction	39
Max. after Tonbridge . . .	44
Weald Box signal check . . .	18
Sevenoaks Tunnel sustained . .	31
Dunton Green	55
Knockholt Tunnel min. . . .	37½
Max. descending to New Cross . .	55

Total time Hastings to Cannon St. . .	98½ min.
Booked time	95 min.
Net time, allowing for two signal delays .	91½ min.

In recent years a good deal of agitation has come from the citizens and various business interests in Hastings for a 90 minutes service to London. The log detailed in Table V, on the 3.50 p.m. down from Cannon Street, shows an actual time of 87 minutes 22 seconds to West St Leonards. The schedule was then 96 minutes to Hastings, with intermediate stops at West St Leonards, and Warrior Square, and this service was provided at a time when speeds were restricted to an overall maximum of 60 m.p.h. On the down run tabulated engine No. 91 kept time to West St Leonards despite three signal checks, and her net time of 83 minutes showed an average speed of 43·2 m.p.h. over this difficult route.

After winding round the Borough Market and London Bridge curves the engine got away very smartly to New Cross, making a faster time to this latter point than on any of the Dover runs in Table I; but the check at Grove Park came right on the bank, and thus wiped out all impetus for climbing the 1 in 120 gradient to Elmstead Woods tunnel. Despite this speed recovered well, and the times between Chislehurst and Halstead summit were faster than the Dover runs, though not up to the standard of engine No. 130, with much the same load, on the Canterbury non-stop, in Table II. The train was checked again onwards to Sevenoaks, and in view of the double slack at Tunbridge Junction no very fast running was made down the bank past Hildenborough. The engine climbed well up the heavy grade to Tunbridge Wells, on gradients mostly around 1 in 90 and 1 in 100, and after that the day was won.

Before leaving the South Eastern reference must be made to the splendid running made during last century on the Dartford line. At that time there was an up express leaving Gravesend at 10.18 p.m. that ran non-stop to London Bridge, and in Table VI are shown details of two excellent little runs, the interest of which is enhanced by the types of locomotive employed. On the first of these runs the engine was an old Cudworth 2-4-0, rebuilt by Stirling, while the second train was hauled by a standard Stirling 0-4-4 tank, with 5 ft 6 in. coupled wheels. The schedule time for this run was 33 minutes, and both engines brought their trains into London Bridge on time. The gradients are mostly undulating on fairly easy gradients. From the average speeds it would seem that both engines barely topped 50 m.p.h. at any point though the work was quite adequate for the job.

In turning to the London, Chatham & Dover it is rather curious to find earlier and more recent writers alike emphasizing the difficulty of the road, not only in respect of the gradients, but also of the curves. One would not quarrel with any such statements about the gradients, but there are not any difficulties over curves. It is true that the line is severely curved from Strood, through Rochester and Chatham to Gillingham, and nowadays there is a slack through Canterbury; but the L.C.D.R. trains used to gallop along freely enough between Beckenham and the approaches to Strood, and in the old days no slackening other than for gradients took place between Gillingham and the outskirts of Dover. Again, while the South Eastern had a line maximum of 60 m.p.h., the Chatham trains frequently exceeded 70 on the down grades, and when there was particular need for hurry the drivers had no inhibitions and ran up nearly 80 m.p.h. at times.

The records made by Mr J. P. Pattinson are most comprehensive so far as the Chatham line are concerned, and while in the ordinary way comparisons between locomotive work on different railways can be invidious and unconvincing, the early chapters of this book inevitably tend to stir up, and revel in the old rivalries between the South Eastern, and the Chatham, and there is no doubt that Mr Pattinson comes down heavily on the side of the Chatham. Fine though the uphill work of the Stirling 4-4-os undoubtedly was, it is eclipsed by that of Kirtley 'M3' 4-4-os of the Chatham. Most of the South Eastern banks could to some extent be rushed; but the Chatham had the task of starting cold up the heavy ascent from Dover to Lydden Tunnel, and Sole Street bank was commenced from the severe slack at Rochester and Strood. This restriction, like that at Tonbridge on the South Eastern, was more often than not interpreted liberally; and so one could not put down Rochester as a serious handicap. Detailed records on Sole Street bank, by Mr Pattinson, are practically non-existent, however, because at that time there were no mileposts west of Strood! Apparently the art of recording train speeds from the rail joints was not practised.

Locomotive work on the Chatham system is represented by four tables, the first two showing typical runs on the boat expresses, and the last two on the Kent Coast trains to and from Margate. It was a feature of L.C.D.R. working for nearly all express trains, even including the Continental Mails, to call at Herne Hill so as to provide connections from both the City and the West End of London. The exception so far as the tabulated runs are concerned is the 5.13 p.m. down business men's express, which ran non-stop from St Pauls to Westgate. Taking the boat trains first, Table VII gives details of three runs, all with the 'M3' Class 4-4-0 locomotives. The first was made on the sharply timed down Night Mail, while Nos. 2 and 3 were on the popular 11 a.m. day service from Victoria.

From the start at Herne Hill the climbing is continuously at 1 in 101 up to Sydenham Hill, and for small 4-4-0 locomotives the attained speeds were remarkable, particularly on Run No. 3, conveying a load of 215 tons. One would scarcely guess either, from the average speeds sustained that the section between Shortlands and Bickley contains 1½ miles rising at 1 in 95. To Strood the honours rest with engine No. 13 (Run No. 2), and with such a load as 200 tons the average speed of 49 m.p.h. from the start to this point was indeed excellent. None of the three drivers showed any trace of over-caution round the Rochester curves, and the locomotives must have been pounded hard to produce average speeds varying between 42 and 50 m.p.h. between Rochester and Chatham before tackling the $1\frac{1}{2}$ miles up at 1 in 132 through the tunnels to Gillingham, or New Brompton as it was then named.

Once up to the level road the running on all three trips was quite undistinguished to Faversham, with the more heavily loaded engines gradually falling behind. But over the hilly road from Faversham to Dover there was some grand work on all three trips. Between Faversham and Ensden Tunnel the gradient is 1 in 110–100 for 4 miles, and here engine No. 25 averaged all but 50 m.p.h., while No. 17 with the 215 ton sustained the remarkable minimum speed of 32 m.p.h. In his records Mr Pattinson does not give the milepost timings on the Night Mail, presumably because the run was made in darkness, but the average speeds shown in the table are enough to provide a good assessment of the performance. Speeds were moderate down to Canterbury, and then again the climbing to Shepherd's Well was extremely fine. In consideration of the 215 ton load it was No. 17 that stole the show here, with a minimum speed of 36 m.p.h. after $3\frac{1}{4}$ miles at 1 in 110–132.

The return runs on the 5.45 p.m. from Dover Harbour to Herne Hill were all made with loads of 200 tons, or more, and the hill climbing was again beyond praise. One has only to mention the gradients: 1 in 100–132 continuously from the start to Shepherd's Well; 1 in 132 for 4 miles up to Ensden Tunnel, and the 5 miles of Sole Street bank, practically continuous at 1 in 100. In face of such obstacles the speeds are really rather amazing from small 4-4-0 locomotives having cylinders 18 in. by 26 in.; a grate area of no more than 17 sq ft and a boiler pressure of 150 lb per sq in. It is evident also that there was no shortage of steam after these climbs, as witness the fast running of No. 20 down to Canterbury, and at Farningham Road. This train was allowed 96 minutes from Dover Harbour to Herne Hill, and with such loads it is not surprising to find there was very little time in hand.

Next comes the 5.13 p.m. from St Paul's, in later years known as 'The City Fast Train.' The loads conveyed on this were much less, but the logs included in Table IX have an added interest in that they feature the work of the earlier Kirtley 4-4-0s of the 'M2' Class and one example from the 'Enigma' Class of 2-4-0. The line is level to Camberwell, after which it rises sharply at 1 in 150–102 to join the main line at Herne Hill. On all three runs the starts were extremely

Above: Dover Priory station and locomotive yard.

Below: Ramsgate Harbour station, a view taken immediately after the grouping.   [*L.G.R.P. No.* 8899

Above: The Admiralty Pier, Dover, in pre-amalgamation days, showing an L.C.D.R. paddle steamer alongside and the S.E.R. boat train ready to leave behind an 'F' class Stirling 4-4-0.

Below: The Admiralty Pier, looking inshore, with an S.E.R. boat train just arrived and steamers berthed on both sides of the pier.
[*Dover Harbour Board*

Above: The Admiralty Pier at the time when the extension was under construction, showing Wainwright class 'D' 4-4-0s No. 730 (*left*), and No. 726 (*in foreground*) waiting to back down on to boat expresses.

Below: Reclamation work for Dover Marine Station nearly complete. Note the old signalbox in the foreground and the steamer berthed on the outward extension of the pier.

[*Dover Harbour Board*

CHARING CROSS AFTER RECONSTRUCTION

Above: Platforms 3 and 4 looking outward with boat expresses for Dover and
Folkestone loading up.

Below: Continental express preparing to leave, headed by 'E' class 4-4-0 No. 165.

[*British Railways*

smart, after which all three trains were involved in a succession of signal checks. The cessation of these checks after Sydenham Hill suggests that the slower train ahead was switched on to the slow road over the quadruple-tracked section between Penge and Beckenham Junction, for after that the City express was able to get away in good style. The uphill speeds run from Shortlands to St Mary Cray were excellent, but as on the boat trains very moderate work was done after New Brompton.

There is a heavy slack at Faversham for trains taking the Margate line, and some good running followed over the level stretch to Herne Bay. The $1\frac{1}{2}$ miles of 1 in 110 climbing immediately after the latter station is followed by a corresponding descent, and all three engines sustained a good pace thereafter. Schedule time for the 72·5-mile run from St Paul's to Westgate was 90 minutes, so that although the little 2-4-0 did not keep strict time her lateness was due entirely to the signal checks. In passing I should add that the 'M2' Class 4-4-0s had $17\frac{1}{2}$ in. by 26 in. cylinders, a grate area of $16\frac{1}{2}$ sq ft and 140 lb boiler pressure. The 'Enigma' Class engine No. 52, as rebuilt by Kirtley, had 17 in. by 24 in. cylinders, 6 ft 6 in. coupled wheels, a grate area of $16\frac{1}{4}$ sq ft and 150 lb boiler pressure. *Enigma* herself differed from the other two engines of the class *Mermaid* and *Lothair*, in having coupled wheels only 6 ft diameter.

The last two runs, detailed in Table X, contrast the work of an 'M3' 4-4-0 with one of the celebrated 'Europa' Class 2-4-0s, hauling a tremendous load, for such a small engine, of 230 tons. On the 6.15 p.m. Sunday train from Margate engine No. 191 made an excellent run, with a net gain of $3\frac{1}{2}$ minutes on schedule. On this run the driver must have taken his engine round the Rochester curves 'on one wheel' to get a good run at Sole Street bank. The minimum speed was $33\frac{1}{2}$ m.p.h., but this appears to have left the engine somewhat breathless judging from the slowness of the recovery downhill to Fawkham. The 2-4-0 *Asia*, starting from Westgate, had to make a special stop at Faversham, and from Sittingbourne her times as tabulated were roughly 7 minutes behind those of No. 191.

The subsequent running was astonishingly good. Despite the much heavier load, *Asia* ran neck and neck with the 'M3' as far as Strood – apparently taking the Rochester curves at little less than 50 m.p.h.! It was not surprising to see her fall behind to the tune of more than a minute on Sole Street bank, but from being $8\frac{1}{2}$ minutes behind at Fawkham she gained upon the 4-4-0 engine by a full minute between there and Dulwich, and her net time of $89\frac{3}{4}$ minutes represents a most admirable piece of work. Locomotive performance

on the best Chatham trains showed generally a very high standard
of hill climbing, and while the downhill running was usually fast at
Farningham Road, at Faversham travelling westwards, and at
Canterbury, it seemed traditional to take things quite easily between
Chatham and Faversham.

No mention of locomotive running on the L.C.D.R. would be
complete without reference to the two special runs made in June,
1896, on the occasion of the Grand Prix races in Paris, to convey
members of the Jockey Club. The 'M3' Class engine No. 16 was used
on both the outward and the return runs, and although the load was
light in comparison with the usual boat train standards on the
L.C.D.R. it was almost exactly the same as that of the West Coast
flyer, on the last night of the Aberdeen race of 1895, namely 70
tons. On the outward journey the 78½ miles from Victoria to Dover
Pier were covered in 81 minutes 56 seconds, and on the return
journey the time was 82 minutes 33 seconds. Mr J. Pearson Pattinson
makes the comment: 'Few finer performances have been done anywhere, and none to equal them in the South of England.' The Chatham may have been the butt of the music-hall comedians, it may have
been a nightmare to its shareholders, and the catspaw of J. S. Forbes,
but there was certainly no deficiency in the performance of its
express locomotives.

TABLE I

S.E.R.: CANNON ST.–DOVER

	Run No.	1			2			3		
	Engine No.	210			2			156		
	Load 'coaches'	'13½'			'15'			'20'		
	Load tons, approx.	170			200			280		
Dist. Miles		Actual m. s.		Av. speed m.p.h.	Actual m. s.		Av. speed m.p.h.	Actual m. s.		Av. speed m.p.h.
0·0	CANNON ST.	0	00		0	00		0	00	
0·7	LONDON BRIDGE	1	40		1	48		1	40	
1·6	Spa Road	3	23	32·9	3	30	33·1	3	23	32·9
3·7	New Cross	6	24	42·1	6	23	44·1	6	20	43·1
7·8	Grove Park	12	54	37·5	12	46	38·2	12	59	36·5
10·1	Chislehurst	17	16	32·3	17	35	28·3	18	05	27·7
12·7	Orpington	21	23	39·4	21	59	36·9	22	41	35·3
14·1	Chelsfield	23	35	38·9	24	18	37·0	25	04	35·8
15·4	Halstead*	25	58	32·8	26	43	32·3	27	44	29·3
19·3	Dunton Green	30	48	49·1	31	41	47·8	33	06	40·4
20·9	Sevenoaks	32	31	59·4	33	28	57·0	34	55	56·1
25·8	Hildenborough	38	00	53·6	39	16	50·7	40	46	50·2
28·4	TUNBRIDGE JUNC†	40	28	63·0	41	54	58·9	43	28	57·7
33·7	Paddock Wood	46	29	53·0	47	51	53·7	49	33	52·3
38·2	Marden	51	28	54·8	52	39	56·9	54	23	56·8
40·7	Staplehurst	54	16	53·6	55	27	53·6	57	13	53·2
44·0	Headcorn	57	47	54·8	58	53	57·5	60	47	55·9
49·3	Pluckley	63	45	53·1	64	52	52·9	67	04	50·6
54·9	ASHFORD	70	01	53·5	71	17	52·2	73	43	50·4
59·2	Smeeth	74	45	54·3	76	07	53·5	78	30	54·0
63·0	Westenhanger	79	18	49·3	80	45	48·5	83	00	49·8
64·2	Sandling	81	05	—	82	21	47·5	84	33	48·8
68·2	Shorncliffe				86	27	57·7	88	27	60·8
68·8	Radnor Park‡				87	14	51·7	89	09	57·7
69·7	FOLKESTONE‖				88	24	—	90	02	60·8
75·4	DOVER							96	14	—
	Schedule time. min.	82			91			96		

Note: All engines are Stirling Class "F" 4-4-0s

* Halstead now Knockholt
† Tunbridge Junction now Tonbridge
‡ Radnor Park now Folkestone Central
‖ Folkestone now Folkestone Junction

TABLE II

S.E.R.: 1.38 p.m. NEW CROSS–CANTERBURY

Run No. Engine No. Load coaches Load, tons approx.		1 130 '12½' 165		2 130 '17' 230	
Dist. Miles		Actual m. s.	Av. speed m.p.h.	Actual m. s.	Av. speed m.p.h.
0·0	NEW CROSS . .	0 00	—	0 00	—
0·65	St. Johns . . .	1 42	—	1 58	—
4·1	Grove Park . . .	6 55	43·3	8 36	34·0
6·4	Chislehurst . . .	10 53	35·6	13 01	31·8
9·0	Orpington . . .	14 11	46·0	17 09	36·5
10·4	Chelsfield . . .	16 05	44·8	19 25	37·8
11·7	Halstead . . .	17 59	40·8	21 52	31·8
15·6	Dunton Green . .	22 23	52·2	26 51	47·7
17·2	Sevenoaks . . .	24 21	57·1	28 31	61·7
22·1	Hildenborough .	30 09	50·6	33 46	55·8
24·7	TUNBRIDGE JUNC .	32 59	55·4	36 20	61·0
30·0	Paddock Wood .	39 01	52·7	42 23	52·6
34·5	Marden . . .	43 34	60·0	46 58	59·4
37·0	Staplehurst . . .	46 09	58·1	49 34	57·7
40·3	Headcorn . . .	49 25	61·7	52 55	60·0
45·6	Pluckley . . .	54 53 sigs	57·8	58 38 sigs	55·6
51·2	ASHFORD . . .	62 23 sigs	36·8	65 57	37·6
55·4	Wye	70 38 sig. stop	31·3	72 23	40·2
60·2	Chilham . . .	83 36	21·8	77 48 sigs	52·7
62·2	Chartham . . .	85 57	51·2	81 03 sigs	36·9
65·4	CANTERBURY . . .	89 48		86 01	
Schedule time min. . .		82		82	
Net time min.		77¾		81¼	

TABLE III

S.E.R.; 7.50 p.m. CANTERBURY–NEW CROSS

Run No. Engine No. Load, coaches Load, tons approx.			1 130 '12½' 165			2 130 '16½' 220	
Dist. Miles		Actual m. s.		Av. speed m.p.h.	Actual m. s.		Av. speed m.p.h.
0·0	CANTERBURY . .	0	00	—	0	00	—
3·2	Chartham . . .	6	06	—	5	55	—
5·2	Chilham . . .	9	22	36·9	8	54	40·2
10·0	Wye	15	59	42·3	15	11	44·3
					sigs		
14·2	ASHFORD . . .	21	48	—	21	15	—
19·8	Pluckley . . .	29	09	37·3	28	24	38·3
25·1	Headcorn . . .	34	49	56·1	34	03	56·4
28·4	Staplehurst . .	38	27	55·0	37	29	59·0
30·9	Marden . . .	41	30	49·3	40	28	50·2
35·4	Paddock Wood .	46	26	54·6	45	36	53·5
40·7	TUNBRIDGE JUNC .	52	41	50·8	52	12	48·1
43·3	Hildenborough .	56	27	41·5	56	06	39·8
48·2	Sevenoaks . .	63	57	39·2	64	52	33·7
49·8	Dunton Green .	65	42	53·7	66	44	50·3
53·7	Halstead . . .	71	40	39·8	72	43	39·7
55·0	Chelsfield . .	73	14	49·8	74	13	52·1
56·4	Orpington . .	74	49	54·1	75	44	56·8
59·0	Chislehurst . .	77	30	56·3	78	25	56·3
61·3	Grove Park . .	79	56	57·9	80	48	59·1
64·75	St. Johns . .	83	50	51·8	84	28	55·1
65·4	NEW CROSS . .	85	06		85	28	
Scheduled time min. . .		89			89		

TABLE IV

S.E.R.: 8.48 a.m. ST. LEONARDS–CANNON ST.

Load: Equal to 15; approx. 200 tons full
Engine: Stirling 'F' class 4-4-0; No. 79

Dist. Miles		Actual m. s.	Av. speed m.p.h.
0·0	ST. LEONARDS . .	0 00	
1·0	West St. Leonards .	2 20	—
6·2	Battle . . .	12 03	32·0
12·1	Robertsbridge . .	19 00	50·8
14·3	Etchingham . .	21 31	52·7
17·9	Ticehurst Road .	26 46	41·3
22·4	Wadhurst . . .	35 22	31·5
25·1	Frant . . .	38 52	46·3
27·4	TUNBRIDGE WELLS .	42 00	44·2
28·8	Southborough* .	44 24	35·0
32·3	TUNBRIDGE JUNC .	48 47	46·6
		sigs	
34·8	Hildenborough .	53 40	32·0
39·7	Sevenoaks . .	65 37	24·6
41·2	Dunton Green . .	67 32	46·9
45·2	Halstead . .	73 20	36·3
46·5	Chelsfield . .	74 58	47·7
47·9	Orpington . .	76 27	57·1
50·4	Chislehurst . .	79 06	56·7
52·8	Grove Park . .	81 55	50·2
56·8	NEW CROSS . .	87 04	47·3
		sigs	
58·9	Spa Road . . .	89 55	
60·0	LONDON BRIDGE .	92 23	
		sig stop	
60·6	CANNON STREET .	97 05	

Schedule time min. . .	97	
Net time min. . . .	89¼	

* Now High Brooms

TABLE V
S.E.R.: 3.50 p.m. CANNON ST.–WEST ST. LEONARDS
Load: Equal to 12; approx 160 tons full
Engine: Stirling 'F' class 4-4-0 No. 91

Dist. Miles		Actual m. s.	Av. speed m.p.h.
0·0	CANNON ST.	0 00	—
0·7	LONDON BRIDGE	1 29	—
1·6	Spa Road	3 03	34·6
3·7	New Cross	5 56	43·6
		sigs.	
7·8	Grove Park	14 22	29·2
10·1	Chislehurst	19 00	29·8
12·7	Orpington	22 48	41·1
14·1	Chelsfield	24 46	42·7
15·4	Halstead	26 56	36·1
		sigs.	
19·3	Dunton Green	33 14	37·1
		sigs.	
20·9	Sevenoaks	35 24	44·3
25·8	Hildenborough	42 02	44·3
28·4	TUNBRIDGE JUNC.	44 51	55·5
31·8	Southborough	51 26	31·0
33·2	TUNBRIDGE WELLS	54 23	28·5
35·5	Frant	57 54	39·3
38·2	Wadhurst	60 59	52·5
42·7	Ticehurst Road	65 55	55·0
46·3	Etchingham	69 45	56·4
48·5	Robertsbridge	72 14	53·3
54·4	Battle	80 27	43·1
59·6	WEST ST. LEONARDS	87 22	—

Net time 83 min.

TABLE VI
S.E.R.: 10.18 p.m. GRAVESEND–LONDON BRIDGE

Run No.	1	2
Engine No.	88	58
Engine Type	2-4-0	0-4-4 T
Load (coaches)	'9'	'9½'
Load tons full	120	125

Dist. Miles		Actual m. s.	Av. speed m.p.h.	Actual m. s.	Av. speed m.p.h.
0·0	GRAVESEND	0 00	—	0 00	—
2·1	Northfleet	4 02	—	4 10	—
4·1	Greenhithe	6 51	42·6	7 03	41·6
6·8	Dartford	10 13	48·6	10 47	43·3
8·6	Crayford	12 37	45·0	13 28	40·2
10·1	Bexley	14 34	46·5	15 29	45·0
12·0	Sidcup	17 39	36·9	18 31	37·7
13·6	New Eltham	19 58	41·5	20 34	46·8
14·5	Eltham	21 14	42·9	21 44	46·3
16·1	Lee	23 33	41·5	23 47	46·9
19·0	New Cross	27 13	47·4	27 43	44·3
21·1	Spa Road	29 57	46·0	30 29	45·6
22·0	LONDON BRIDGE	31 47	—	32 12	—

South Eastern and Chatham Railway

TABLE VII
L.C.D.R.: HERNE HILL–DOVER PIER

Run No. Train Engine, 'M3' 4-4-0 No. Load coaches Load tons (approx.)		1 9.14 p.m. 25 '10' 130		2 11.14 a.m. 13 '15½' 200		3 11.14 a.m. 17 '16½' 215	
Dist. **Miles**		*Actual* m. s.	*Speed** m.p.h.	*Actual* m. s.	*Speed** m.p.h.	*Actual* m. s.	*Speed** m.p.h.
0·0	HERNE HILL	0 00	—	0 00	—	0 00	—
1·0	Dulwich	2 32	—	2 36	—	2 32	—
1·8	Sydenham Hill	3 52	32·7	4 12	27·3	4 05	28·1
3·2	Penge	6 02	40·5	6 33	35·0	6 31	34·6
3·8	Kent House	6 44	53·5	7 17	51·0	7 16	50·0
4·7	Beckenham	7 39	56·5	8 10	58·5	8 12	55·3
6·0	Shortlands	9 17	48·7	9 49	48·5	9 57	45·3
6·9	BROMLEY	10 14	52·1	10 46	52·1	10 58	50·6
8·0	Bickley	11 37	47·7	12 13	45·5	12 36	40·4
10·8	St. Mary Cray	15 03	50·7	15 52	47·7	16 38	43·1
13·7	Swanley	18 10	54·7	19 01	54·0	20 02	50·2
16·5	Farningham Road	20 57	61·2	21 50	60·5	22 56	58·7
19·4	Fawkham	23 56	57·3	24 51	56·9	26 00	56·2
22·0	Meopham	27 11	47·8	28 19	44·7	29 38	43·0
22·9	Sole Street	28 24	45·5	29 39	42·5	31 00	39·5
29·0	Strood	34 21	61·2	35 49	59·1	37 19	58·0
29·8	Rochester	35 29	41·7	36 59	40·4	38 36	37·4
30·4	CHATHAM	36 14	50·0	37 47	46·8	39 29	42·2
32·0	New Brompton†	38 31	41·7	40 10	39·9	42 09	36·1
35·0	Rainham	42 06	50·3	43 53	48·6	46 01	46·7
37·6	Newington	44 53	57·1	46 50	54·0	49 02	52·9
40·8	SITTINGBOURNE	48 18	54·7	50 20	53·2	52 41	51·2
44·0	Teynham	52 10	50·3	53 54	54·6	56 48	48·5
48·0	FAVERSHAM	56 42	52·9	58 48	47·9	61 48	48·0
51·3	Selling	60 42	49·7	63 53	39·1	66 42	40·4
57·9	CANTERBURY	67 57	53·8	72 20	46·0	74 27	50·7
60·7	Bekesbourne	71 30	52·3	75 52	52·4	77 56	49·5
				sigs.			
63·8	Adisham	75 10	50·0	80 45	37·4	81 44	48·3
67·7	Shepherd's Well	80 21	45·1	90 21	24·1	87 44	39·0
71·1	Kearsney	83 56	57·6	94 05	55·3	91 17	57·8
73·3	Dover Priory	86 25	53·6	96 21	59·5	93 29	60·5
74·5	DOVER PIER	88 25	—	98 22	—	95 53	—
Schedule time		91		96		96	
Net time		87¾		93		95	
Minimum Speeds:							
Ensden Tunnel		—		28		32	
Shepherd's Well		—		—		36	

* Average speed from exact chainages
† Now Gillingham

TABLE VIII

L.C.D.R.: 5.45 p.m. DOVER HARBOUR–HERNE HILL

Run No. Engine 'M3' 4-4-0 No. Load coaches Load tons (approx.)	1 16 '15½' 200		2 20 '16½' 215		3 20 '18' 237	
Dist. Miles	Actual m. s.	Av. speed m.p.h.	Actual m. s.	Av. speed m.p.h.	Actual m. s.	Av. speed m.p.h.
0·0 DOVER HARBOUR .	0 00	—	0 00	—	0 00	—
0·7 Dover Priory . .	2 15	—	1 46	—	1 45	—
2·9 Kearsney . . .	—	—	6 39	27·0	6 38	27·0
6·3 Shepherd's Well .	13 20	29·9	12 38	34·1	13 08	32·3
10·2 Adisham . .	18 37	44·3	17 35	47·3	18 11	46·4
13·3 Bekesbourne . .	21 46	59·0	20 36	61·7	21 08	63·1
16·1 CANTERBURY .	35 00	51·9	23 39	55·1	24 05	56·9
22·7 Selling . .	34 24	42·1	33 06	41·9	32 57	44·7
26·0 FAVERSHAM .	37 29	64·2	36 16	60·7	36 08	62·2
30·0 Teynham . .	41 50	55·2	40 41	54·4	40 28	55·5
33·2 SITTINGBOURNE .	45 21	54·8	44 16	53·7	43 56	55·5
	p.w.s.		p.w.s.		p.w.s.	
36·4 Newington . .	50 26	37·7	49 24	37·4	49 06	37·2
39·0 Rainham . .	53 31	50·5	52 42	47·3	52 11	50·5
42·0 New Brompton .	56 55	52·9	56 09	52·3	55 29	54·5
43·6 CHATHAM . .	58 57	47·1	57 53	55·2	57 12	55·9
44·2 Rochester . .	59 42	50·0	58 32	57·7	57 55	52·3
45·0 Strood . .	60 53	40·2	59 31	48·2	59 11	37·9
51·1 Sole Street . .	71 11	35·5	68 59	38·7	69 45	34·5
52·0 Meopham . .	72 42	35·6	70 25	38·4	71 15	36·0
54·6 Fawkham . .	75 33	54·8	73 22	52·9	74 05	55·1
57·5 Farningham Road .	78 27	60·0	76 17	59·7	76 43	65·9
60·3 Swanley . .	81 57	48·0	79 38	50·2	80 00	51·2
63·2 St. Mary Cray .	85 11	53·5	82 48	54·9	83 15	53·5
					sigs.	
66·0 Bickley . . .	88 23	52·5	86 14	49·2	86 45	48·0
					sigs.	
67·1 BROMLEY . .	89 33	56·7	87 22	58·3	88 37	35·4
					sigs.	
68·0 Shortlands . .	90 22	60·6	88 12	59·5	89 55	—
69·3 Beckenham . .	91 51	53·4	89 45	51·1	92 34	—
70·2 Kent House . .	92 46	56·7	90 53	46·1	93 47	—
70·8 Penge . .	93 31	50·1	91 48	40·9	94 44	—
72·2 Sydenham Hill .	95 29	44·5	94 04	38·7	97 10	—
73·0 Dulwich . .	96 20	50·8	94 59	47·1	98 08	—
					sig. stop	
74·0 HERNE HILL . .	97 41		96 21		100 58	
Net times	96½		95		95	

Uphill Speeds:
  Lydden Tunnel . .
  (max.-attained)
  Ensden Tunnel (minimum) .
  Sole Street (minimum) .
	
	34
	
	33½
	32
			
			36
			
			33½
			32
					
					31
					
					36
					32	

TABLE IX

L.C.D.R.: 5.13 p.m. ST. PAUL'S–WESTGATE

Run No. Engine No. Engine Type Load coaches Load tons (approx.)		1 180 4-4-0 'M2' '10' 130		2 52 2-4-0 'L' '10' 130		3 183 4-4-0 'M2' '10' 130	
Dist. Miles		Actual m. s.	Speed* m.p.h.	Actual m. s.	Speed* m.p.h.	Actual m. s.	Speed* m.p.h.
0·0	ST. PAULS . . .	0 00	—	0 00	—	0 00	—
0·8	Borough Road .	2 02	—	1 58	—	1 41	—
1·2	Elephant & Castle .	2 41	39·2	2 39	37·4	2 16	41·5
1·9	Walworth Road .	3 41	39·8	3 41	38·7	3 10	44·2
2·7	Camberwell .	4 42	47·5	4 42	47·5	4 08	49·6
3·2	Loughborough Junc. .	5 25	46·0	5 21	50·8	4 49	48·2
4·1	HERNE HILL . .	6 40	43·2	6 33 sigs.	45·8	6 06 sigs.	42·5
5·1	Dulwich . . .	8 21 sig. stop	36·0	8 37 sigs.	28·3	7 58 sig. stop	32·4
5·9	Sydenham Hill . .	11 06	15·8	12 01	12·8	10 43	15·8
7·3	Penge . . .	14 00	30·2	15 00	29·3	13 38	30·0
7·9	Kent House . .	14 45	50·0	15 48	46·9	14 22	51·5
8·8	Beckenham . . .	15 38	58·4	16 50	50·4	15 18	55·5
10·1	Shortlands . .	17 17	48·0	18 39	43·6	17 05	44·3
11·0	BROMLEY . .	18 11	55·0	19 35	53·2	18 05	49·5
12·1	Bickley . . .	19 36	46·6	20 58	47·6	19 41	41·3
14·9	St. Mary Cray . .	23 05	48·2	24 27	47·7	23 31	43·9
17·8	Swanley . . .	26 08	57·1	27 39	54·4	26 50	52·5
20·6	Farningham Road . .	28 52	61·3	30 49	53·1	29 43	58·3
23·5	Fawkham . . .	31 46	60·0	34 03	53·6	32 53	55·0
26·1	Meopham . . .	35 00	48·2	37 33	44·6	36 24	44·3
27·0	Sole Street . .	36 15	44·4	38 53	41·5	37 42	43·0
33·1	Strood. . . .	42 36	57·6	45 57	51·8	44 02	57·8
33·9	Rochester . . .	43 57	35·5	47 13	38·0	45 10	42·8
34·5	CHATHAM . . .	44 50	42·4	48 06	42·4	45 58	47·0
36·1	New Brompton . .	47 25	37·2	50 39	37·6	48 33	37·2
39·1	Rainham . . .	51 02	49·8	54 13	50·5	52 17	48·2
41·7	Newington . . .	53 51	55·3	57 06	54·1	55 18	51·8
44·9	SITTINGBOURNE .	57 23	54·3	60 44	52·8	59 02	51·3
48·1	Teynham . . .	61 20	48·7	64 16	54·5	63 06	47·4
52·1	FAVERSHAM . .	66 11	49·5	68 53	52·0	68 18	46·1
58·8	Whitstable . . .	73 31	54·9	76 44	51·3	75 51	53·3
62·9	HERNE BAY . .	77 36	60·2	81 16	54·4	80 12	56·5
70·9	Birchington . . .	85 42	59·2	90 13	53·7	88 39	56·9
72·5	WESTGATE . .	88 02	—	92 21	—	90 41	—
Net time		85		88½		87½	

Note: Bridge slack on all runs at Sittingbourne

* Average speeds from exact chainages

'L'—'Enigma' Class, formerly *Lothair*

TABLE X

L.C.D.R.: MARGATE–HERNE HILL

Run No. Train Engine No. Engine Type Load coaches Load tons (approx.)		1 6.15 p.m. Margate 191 4-4-0 'M3' '13' 175		2 10.18 a.m. Westgate 54 2-4-0 'E' '17½' 230	
Dist. Miles		Actual m. s.	Speed* m.p.h.	Actual m. s.	Speed* m.p.h.
0·0	MARGATE . . .	0 00	—		
1·5	Westgate . . .	2 54	—	0 00	—
3·1	Birchington . . .	5 06	44·3	3 44	—
11·1	HERNE BAY . . .	14 08	53·3	14 11	45·8
15·2	Whitstable . . .	18 15	59·2	18 34	55·8
21·9	FAVERSHAM . . .	25 43	53·4	26 35 special stop	
25·9	Teynham . . .	31 24	42·2	38 34	—
29·1	SITTINGBOURNE. .	35 01 p.w.s.	53·9	42 18 p.w.s.	52·2
32·3	Newington . .	40 25	34·9	47 21	36·0
34·9	Rainham . . .	43 31	51·4	50 33	48·9
37·9	New Brompton . .	46 50	54·3	53 55	53·4
39·5	CHATHAM . . .	48 42	51·6	55 46	51·9
40·9	Strood . . .	50 32	45·8	57 28	49·4
47·0	Sole Street . .	60 33	36·7	68 47	32·4
50·5	Fawkham . . .	64 47	35·4	73 18	33·2
53·4	Farningham Road . .	67 30	64·2	75 58	65·2
56·2	Swanley . . .	71 10	45·9	79 20	49·9
59·1	St. Mary Cray . .	74 38	50·2	82 45	51·0
61·9	Bickley. . . .	78 04	50·2	86 05	52·3
63·9	Shortlands . .	80 01	58·5	87 59	60·0
65·2	Beckenham . . .	81 38	48·3	89 27	53·3
66·7	Penge . . .	83 29	48·7	91 12	51·5
68·1	Sydenham Hill . .	85 54	35·8	93 22	37·4
68·9	Dulwich . . .	86 52	49·8	94 17 sig. stop	52·3
69·9	HERNE HILL . . .	88 24		97 10	
Net times		86½		89¾	
Schedule time . . .		90		90	

'E'—'Europa' Class 2-4-0 formerly *Asia*
* Average speeds from exact chainages

X

"South Eastern & Chatham"

The Railway Times of 18th June, 1898 referred to talks of fusion between the South Eastern and the London, Chatham & Dover Railways. So often previously there had been talks that came to nothing, but since the retirement of Sir Edward Watkin things were much more hopeful, and with the South Eastern Chairmanship now in the very capable hands of H. Cosmo Bonsor any negotiations would be quite straightforward. He was a strong personality, but strong in a very different way from the 'Railway King'. A Member of Parliament, a Director of the Bank of England, a man associated with many charitable activities, he nevertheless found time to devote much detailed attention to the affairs of the South Eastern Railway, and it was he in particular who personified the new attitude of the Board towards the third-class traveller. In May, 1898, *The Railway Magazine* commented thus:

'The notion, once held in their board-room, that a person who, clad in respectable habiliments, ventured to travel in a third class compartment was guilty of something like an outrage upon the Company's revenue no longer finds encouragement, the present aim being to do everything that is possible to encourage this, the most profitable branch of traffic.'

Returning to *The Railway Times* of 18th June, that newspaper commented editorially:

'It was rumoured early in the week that Mr Forbes would retire at the end of this year, and "Chatham ordinary" promptly rose on the rumour. Probably the wish was father to the thought; but really Mr Forbes should recognize by this time that his retirement would be welcomed by those who have the future of the company at heart. He attempts too much for his years, with the inevitable result that the shareholders suffer.'

The newspaper was perhaps a little kind to Forbes in referring to his age, for there must have been many who had longed for his retirement for many years previously. Nevertheless it must be recognized that in its closing years of independent working the Chatham was a vastly improved railway. Much of this was due to William Forbes, the Traffic and Continental Manager; a nephew of the Chairman, he was a first-class railwayman, and later achieved great distinction, and a knighthood, as General Manager of the London Brighton & South Coast Railway.

On 29th June, 1898, a letter was sent from John Morgan, Secretary of the L.C.D.R., to the Stock Exchange Committee announcing the draft agreement between the two companies. It was not an amalgamation, but a working union. The two railways would operate as one in all matters concerning traffic and engineering but would remain financially distinct. The net receipts were to be divided in the proportion of 59 per cent to the South Eastern and 41 per cent to the Chatham. Cosmo Bonsor became Chairman of the Managing Committee, though J. S. Forbes was retained for 10 years as an adviser. On the engineering side both Stirling and Kirtley retired, and the post of Locomotive, Carriage & Wagon Superintendent went to Harry S. Wainwright, the former carriage superintendent of the South Eastern. R. R. Surtees of the Chatham became Chief Locomotive Draughtsman, and it was under his able guidance that the locomotive practice of the Managing Committee came to flourish so handsomely. The Chief Engineer was P. C. Tempest, formerly Permanent Way Engineer of the South Eastern. A Yorkshireman by birth his early training had been on the London & North Western Railway.

The fusion of the two companies from the operating point of view offered a wide variety of prospects; for economies in cutting out competitive and overlapping service; for the unification of locomotive, carriage and wagon design, and for maximum utilization of the numerous interconnecting routes. *The Railway Times* of 1898 stated the net saving was calculated at £100,000 per annum. In actual practice many concessions had to be made, so that the savings in operation were more than swallowed up, and the South Eastern shareholders, who had enjoyed no dividend less than 3¾ per cent up to the time of fusion and got 4½ per cent in 1898, now had to be content with 2 per cent in 1901, and a very slow and laborious climb back to 3½ per cent in 1910. The Chatham ordinary shareholders, as usual, got absolutely nothing right up to 1914. From the public point of view the whole railway situation in Kent underwent a complete metamorphosis, and the South Eastern & Chatham became one of the great railways of this country.

The working union could do nothing about one of the greatest traffic problems of the London area, that of Cannon Street. At the time of the 'union' there were four running lines from London Bridge into Cannon Street, and three from Cannon Street to Charing

Cross. The direct line avoiding the City terminus, and forming the base of the triangular layout was only double-tracked, and was used mainly by empty-stock trains proceeding to and from Bricklayers Arms sidings. The way in which the traffic was worked over Cannon Street bridge and through the maze of junctions on the Surrey side was really a marvel. In the summer service of 1899 there were, for example, 35 departures between 4 p.m. and 5 p.m., and of those trains only eight started from Cannon Street. That means there were twenty-seven passenger trains arriving during the same period, to reverse direction, and have fresh engines attached, and what was worse, to intersect the paths of other trains going in or out.

The signalling had been altered considerably since the original installation by Saxby & Farmer when the station was first opened in 1866. Instead of the old box with its two-way semaphores mounted on the roof there was the large No. 1 Box on a bridge spanning all the tracks entering the station. The interlocking frame had no less than 243 levers, but although there were larger frames, notably the 277 of Euston No. 2, L.N.W.R., the Cannon Street frame was the largest to have the levers all in one row. The frames at Euston and Waterloo, to take other examples, were in two halves, back to back, with the interlocking between them under the floor. In consequence of its arrangements the Cannon Street apparatus was 100 ft long. The signals themselves were grouped about the station and yard in picturesque groups of gantries and cantilever brackets. A characteristic feature of several of the gantries was to have bracket posts mounted on the main cross girder. This installation dated from 1893.

With so complicated a layout, and such a diversity of traffic and routes to be worked something more than a bell code for the classification of trains was needed, and C. V. Walker, the former South Eastern Railway Telegraph Engineer, had devised the earliest form of 'train describer', on a multiple scale, ever to be used. It had been considered essential to give the signalmen something more than an audible code. A visual indication was essential and Walker introduced the rotary form of train describer instrument that was standard on the South Eastern & Chatham Railway, and was adopted later by the Southern for the earliest installations of colour-light signalling in the London area. The accompanying sketch shows one of the Cannon Street indicators of 60 years ago. The needle was moved electrically to point to the class of train concerned. The description 'Tidal or Mail' for the Continental expresses will be particularly noted.

The installation handled the ever increasing traffic into and out

CANNON STREET – TRAIN DESCRIBER DIAGRAM

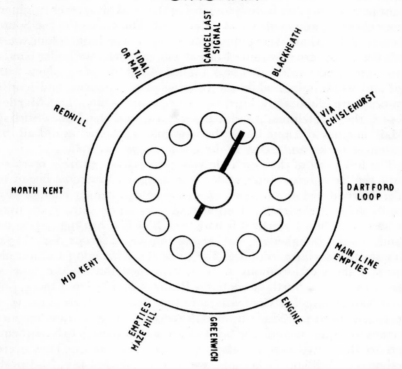

CANCEL LAST SIGNAL

TIDAL OR MAIL

BLACKHEATH

REDHILL

VIA CHISLEHURST

NORTH KENT

DARTFORD LOOP

MAIN LINE EMPTIES

MID KENT

EMPTIES MAZE HILL

GREENWICH

ENGINE

of Cannon Street until 1926, when the first phase of the South Eastern suburban electrification necessitated a complete remodelling of the approach tracks and of the station itself. Some of my earliest professional work as a signal engineer was on the preliminaries for this changeover, and I spent many a night in the new power signalbox that was built on the western side of the line near to the platform ends. I realized then for how brief a period in the middle of the night was this wholly-passenger station quiet, and we were free to move points at will. Some changes in interlocking were found desirable after the new layout had been in service for a few months. The alterations were not unduly extensive, but it took a month of nights to carry them out, working between the arrival of the up Dover mail at 1.20 a.m. and the first workmen's train in the early morning.

One of the most immediate and pleasing changes, following the fusion of the two companies, was the adoption of a new and highly

decorative engine livery. In their later years both the South Eastern
and the Chatham companies had used black, albeit smartly lined
out, and beautifully kept. But the Managing Committee struck the
right note at once, by having something that was altogether brighter,
more cheerful, and evidence of a new deal. The engines of the South
Eastern & Chatham were gorgeously arrayed. The basic colour was a
rich Brunswick green, with red-brown underframes; the boiler bands,
cab edges, and tender-sides had a band of lighter green edged with
red and white lining, while the running plate valances, and tender
frames were elaborately lined out in red and white. The Martley
2-4-0s, the 'Scotchmen', and Kirtley 'M's, and the James Stirling
'Mail' engines all came in for the new colour scheme, as did all the
passenger tanks, and many of the goods engines as well.

The full glory of the new style was even yet not entirely revealed
until the locomotives built under Wainwright's direction began to
take the road. Before that took place five new passenger engines of a
totally different design had commenced work on the line. At the time
of 'fusion' Ashford works still had five 'B' Class Stirling 4-4-0s on
hand, while Longhedge had an uncompleted order for 'M3's.
Despite this useful addition to the stock the Managing Committee
was still short of locomotives. It so happened that in the year of
fusion the Great North of Scotland Railway had ordered ten 4-4-0s
from Neilson, Reid & Company, and that before the end of the year
an urgent need to reduce train mileage made five of these engines
surplus to requirements. The S.E.C.R. was glad enough to have them,
and so these five very handsome 4-4-0s came south. They were
designed by William Pickersgill, who later succeeded J. F. McIntosh
as locomotive superintendent of the Caledonian Railway. On
the S.E.C.R. these Scottish 4-4-0s became Class 'G', and were readily
distinguishable by their side-windowed cabs, the graceful curve of
their splashers, and their elegantly shaped chimneys.

The first Wainwright engine was turned out at Ashford works in
June, 1900 – the 0-6-0 goods No. 255 – and was at once recognizable
as of Chatham rather than of South Eastern ancestry. It was a
simple, sturdy, straightforward design, having 5 ft 2 in. coupled
wheels, 18½ in. by 26 in. cylinders, and carrying a boiler pressure of
160 lb per sq in. It was finished in the brilliant new livery, with all
its elaborate lining out, and in addition had a polished brass dome,
and a brass seating to the safety valve column. A feature of South
Eastern practice retained was the Stirling steam reversing gear, from
my observation by far the best of any such device put on to British
locomotives. I need not disclose here how, when, and where it took

Above: Cannon Street. Tracks on the bridge as seen from the station roof.

Above right: Victoria: the S.E.C.R. frontage, which also includes, lower on the masonry, the inscription 'Great Western Railway'.

Lower right: Charing Cross: a view looking outwards from the platform end showing the old signalbox and a fine assortment of bracket signals.

Above: S.E.R. down stopping train entering Halstead (Knockholt) station, hauled by Class 'A' Stirling 4-4-0 locomotive.

Below: L.C.D.R. line express passing Swanley, headed by 4-4-0 locomotive No. 650, 'M3' class.

[*L.G.R.P. Nos. 21970 and 21327*

G.N.S.R. design 4-4-0, Neilson built, No. 680.   [*F. Moore*

Above: James Stirling's 'B' class 4-4-0 No. 446 in S.E.C.R. colours at the old S.E.R. sheds alongside Archcliffe Fort, Dover.

Below: a Wainwright Class 'E'.

   [*British Railways*

Left: The curious twin-hull steamer *Castalia*, built in 1874, in dock at Dover. This vessel had two half-hulls with a pair of paddle wheels in tandem between them.

Below: The turbine steamer *The Queen* loading mails from a boat train at Dover. The engine is Class 'D' 4-4-0 No. 730.

[*British Railways*

place, but in driving S.E.C.R. locomotives myself I found the Stirling reverser very easy to manipulate, and precise and dead-beat in its action.

But to revert to the Wainwright goods, 'Class C' as they became, their success was immediate, and in the years 1900–08 no fewer than 109 were built. It is interesting to recall that nine of them were built at Longhedge. In 1900 when engines were urgently needed two batches of them were built by contractors, fifteen each by Neilson, Reid and by Sharp, Stewart. The remaining seventy were built at Ashford. For their size no better 0-6-0 goods engines have ever worked in Great Britain. Massively built, in the finest traditions of Ashford, they have withstood the test of time, and no fewer than fifty-eight are still in service today in the Southern Region of British Railways. In a Region where the gradual superseding of steam had been in progress for many years before the Modernization Plan was launched this is certainly a tribute to their working efficiency and to their trouble-free service. As a later chapter of this book will show they had a fine turn of speed when requisitioned for express passenger duty in an emergency.

Then in 1901, came the first of the very celebrated 'D' Class 4-4-0s. The new era could not have been more perfectly epitomized than by these truly beautiful machines, and it is indeed fortunate that one of them has been preserved and restored to the original condition. In the gay colours of the S.E.C.R., of course, they looked a picture, but the grace and symmetry of their lines was never more apparent than at the end of World War II when most of them were running grimy and unkempt in unlined black. Despite this they still looked veritable aristocrats among locomotives. In 1946 I spent the best part of a day on the footplate of No. 733, working from Tonbridge shed on semi-fast duties, and though she had not seen a cleaner's rag for months, once the regulator was opened she became a real lady. Nor shall I forget the exclamations of delight and admiration at Shrewsbury, in 1956, when No. 75, or 31075 as she was then, backed down from Coleham sheds to head the Talyllyn Railway special for Towyn.

Hitherto the express locomotives of neither partner in the new alliance had been noted for their design style. There had been odd corners, angular projections and a general air of functionalism. But in the new 'D' Class the artistic hand of Wainwright was apparent, and a first-rate mechanical design was clothed in a unity of outward style and 'line' that made one of these engines a true *objet d'art*. They were capable of hard work on the road, and as their first

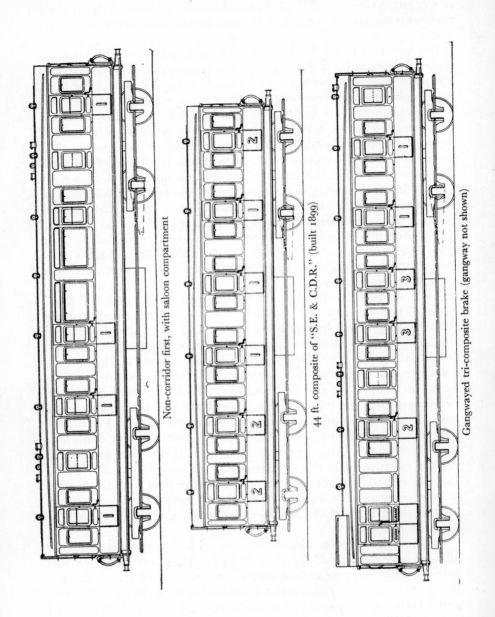

Non-corridor first, with saloon compartment

44 ft. composite of "S.E. & C.D.R." (built 1899)

Gangwayed tri-composite brake (gangway not shown)

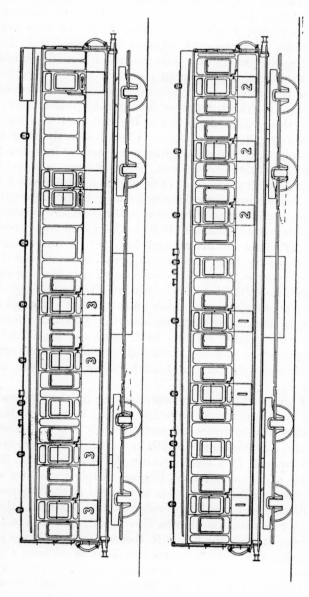

S.E. & C.R. boat train stock. The top drawing shows a third brake, the lower a semi-corridor first/second composite

[All drawings courtesy British Railways]

introduction coincided with the inauguration of the 'British Locomotive Practice and Performance' feature in *The Railway Magazine*
they quickly caught the eye of Charles Rous-Marten, who wrote of
them in warm praise. I doubt, however, if anyone who read his
glowing accounts of their work guessed that they were the *only*
express passenger engines of that time that would remain completely
unaltered in their design for over 50 years.

I am aware that twenty-one of them were extensively rebuilt by
R. E. L. Maunsell with superheater boilers and piston valves; but
the remaining thirty were unaltered to the end, and they outlasted
the larger Wainwright 4-4-0s of the 'E' Class. From the very beginning of their long career these engines were used on both the South
Eastern and the Chatham sections. Rous-Marten was evidently
unaware of the overall speed limit of 60 m.p.h. on the South Eastern
Railway, for in referring to earlier work with the Stirling engines he
commented on the slowness of the downhill running, in comparison
with the gay abandon of the L.C.D.R. engines, and their crews. By
this time the 'D' Class was introduced, however, Tempest had been
in charge sufficiently long to effect a great improvement in the
track, and speeds up to 75 m.p.h. were recorded with the new engines
on various sections of the South Eastern line. There was not at first
any acceleration of train times, either on the seaside expresses or the
Continentals. It was just at that time that the Northern Railway of
France was really getting into its stride with the De Glehn four-
cylinder compounds, and Rous-Marten drew many an unfavourable
comparison between British and French railway enterprise at that
time.

Today one can realize he was expecting too much, too soon. The
fusion of the two companies' staffs and rolling stock must have inevitably caused a great upheaval, and one feels that the locomotive
department did a remarkably fine job in a short time to get both the
'C' Class 0-6-0s and 'D' Class 4-4-0s on the road by 1901. Strange
though it may seem to us today, English people travelling abroad
in the early nineteen-hundreds were so assured of the superiority of
everything British over anything foreign as to compare the duration
of the railway ride from London to Dover with that from Calais to
Paris to the advantage of the S.E.C.R. Rous-Marten writes of passengers complaining that it took nearly *four hours* to go from Calais to
Paris whereas it took less than 2 hours to travel 'all that way from
London to Dover'! These critics, Rous-Marten added, seemed to
think Calais was no more than a northern suburb of Paris, and were
openly disbelieving when he tried to explain that the distance to be

run was roughly equal to that between London and Manchester. In face of such satisfaction the S.E.C.R. was not to be blamed for consolidating on other matters first, and letting acceleration of the Continental services come later.

The Managing Committee was not backward in providing excellent new stock for the boat trains, though in view of the relatively short journeys, to Folkestone Harbour, or Dover, it was not considered necessary to adopt corridor coaches. The principal services included one or more Pullman cars for those who were prepared to pay supplementary charges, and for the rest, the use of non-corridor stock helped to keep the train loads down. Before many years had passed many of the Continental boat expresses were loading to well over 300 tons. The bogie coaches built to Wainwright's design included the distinctive 'bird cage' ends to the brake thirds. The coach livery was a rich dark lake, as near as makes no matter to the colour used by the Great Western between the two 'chocolate and cream' periods. When new the S.E.C.R. coach roofs were white, and the striking effect was enhanced by use of scarlet roof boards on all the principal expresses.

The line drawings reproduced on pages 130 to 131 show some interesting examples of the Wainwright bogie main line stock of the early 1900s. The 44 ft composite is old enough to bear the legend 'S.E. & C.D.R.' on the original drawing. The body is entirely of wood, though carried on a steel underframe. The interiors of both first class, and second class compartments were beautifully finished, though with adornments that would nowadays probably be described as 'fussy Victoriana'. In view of the title on the drawing it is interesting to see that the elaborately cast brackets supporting the small luggage racks in the compartments had the initials 'S.E.C. & D.R.' woven scroll-fashion into the design. In the days immediately after the fusion of the two companies there seemed to be some doubt as to what the distinguishing initials should be. These carriages were electrically lighted, and a feature that remained standard S.E.C. practice was the relatively short bogie wheelbase of 8 ft, when even at that early date the Midland was using 10 ft and getting much better riding in consequence.

There are next three interesting examples of what might be termed 'boat train stock': a 'first', that included an open saloon portion; a composite, for first and second class passengers, and a third brake, including one of the picturesque 'birdcage' guard's compartments. All three vehicles were 50 ft long, yet because of the increased amenities in the form of lavatories the seating accommodation was considerably reduced compared with the 44 ft stock – 15 'firsts' and 19 'seconds', compared with 18 'firsts' and 24 'seconds' in the earlier stock. Having regard to the relatively short journeys involved on the S.E.C. these coaches were very well appointed. It is true that the absence of end-to-end corridor communication prevented any access, by ordinary passengers, to Pullman cars, where these were run; but as then operated these were treated as supplementary luxury vehicles in which patrons travelled the whole journey, rather than as refreshment cars generally available for the whole train. This remained the practice of both Brighton and South Eastern sections of the Southern Railway for many years.

The fifth drawing shows one of the tri-composite bogie brakes used on through-carriage services to other companies lines. One of them used to run on the 'Sunny South Special' express worked from the London & North Western Railway to various parts of the L.B.S.C. system. The S.E.C. through carriage was attached and detached from this train at Willesden. After World War I the S.E.C. and the L.N.W. introduced a complete train running between Liverpool, Manchester and the Kent Coast resorts, and this was composed of L.N.W. corridor stock with full restaurant facilities. Before the war, however, S.E.C. through carriages were also worked to Bradford and Manchester by the Midland route, and the tri-composite lavatory brakes, with their characteristic 'bird-cage' guard's compartments were used also on these services. At one time the Midland expresses concerned called at Kentish Town to attach the S.E.C. through carriages which had been worked up through Ludgate Hill and the City Widened Lines of the Metropolitan Railway. At another period the arrangement was far less favourable to through passengers from the S.E.C.R., as the through carriages having reached Kentish Town were then taken back into St Pancras to await the departure of the Midland express.

Even before the fusion the South Eastern had commenced a thorough transformation of the London suburban passenger stock, and in the nineties of last century a number of thirteen-coach train sets were introduced, accommodating first, second and third class passengers to the number of 478 per train. The tare weight of these trains was a modest 138 tons, and as they carried about 30 tons of passengers the locomotive department could scarcely complain that they had an excess of dead weight to carry about. The new suburban coaches were very neat, compact little things, close coupled, beautifully finished outside, and very comfortable within. The smart external finish was a welcome change from previous standards on both the South Eastern and the Chatham railways, and these suburban coaches had white roofs when new, like the main line bogies.

The change in style of coach painting on the South Eastern dates back to 1883. Until then the bodies had been a colour officially known as 'Wellington Brown', said to have been adopted in compliment to the Duke of Wellington who was Lord Warden of the Cinque Ports when the South Eastern first came to Dover. The upper panels were a pinkish cream. That, at any rate, was what they were intended to be, though in actual fact the majority of them did not always look so attractive. Ahrons's description is more picturesque: 'The colour of the upper portion was an unhealthy-looking flesh tint, with a brownish hue below by way of giving the impression that mortification had set in badly on the lower panels'! However, all that was changed when Wainwright got to work, and the London suburban trains thenceforth became uniform in style and finish, in place of the travelling caravans of all shapes and sizes of which Ahrons made so merry.

'The trains were always of considerable length', he wrote, 'probably longer on the average than any running out of the Southern London termini, and, formed of coaches of so many varying heights they seemed to give the impression of moving castellated walls. The vans, which were sprinkled up and down the train, as if they had been emptied into it from a pepper castor, put a finishing touch to the beauties of the 'coachscape', for they had the same style of raised roof boxes with attic windows above the guard's seats, that may still be seen in considerable numbers on the South Eastern.'

The first new suburban tank engine to be ordered by the Managing Committee was of a pure L.C.D.R. design, the 'R' Class 0-4-4 tank of 1891, slightly enlarged, and carrying 160 lb pressure instead of 150. An order for fifteen of these engines, Class 'R1', was placed with Sharp, Stewart, and delivery of them was taken in 1900. After the fusion a decision was taken to adopt the vacuum brake for the S.E.C.R., but to cope with the existing L.C.D.R. stock the new engines were originally fitted with both vacuum and Westinghouse. These engines formed the basis of an extensive programme of tank engine standardization, in which a boiler was designed for use in rebuilding the 'R' and 'R1' Classes, the Stirling 'Q' Class from the South Eastern, and the new 'H' Class, of which the first examples were built at Ashford in 1904. At one time there were 154 tank engines of the 0-4-4 type carrying the same design of boiler, although they were composed of three distinct classes, from the

L.C.D.R., from the S.E.R. and the S.E.C.R. These suburban tank engines, of whatever origin, were all decked in the gay and colourful livery of the express passenger engines, with the same profusion of polished brass and copper work.

While designs for new locomotives and rolling stock were being prepared, and while the older stock was being repainted in new and attractive styles, the Managing Committee was displaying its drive and enterprise in other directions as well. The construction of a new branch line in the year of grace 1901 might, in other circumstances, have seemed an enterprise foredoomed to failure, but the Chipstead Valley line was something quite out of the ordinary. Its ultimate goal was the racecourse on Epsom Downs, but in climbing to that altitude from its junction with the Caterham branch at Purley it passed through a beautiful countryside that offered high promise as a new residential district for London. There were stations at Chipstead, Kingswood and Tadworth, but it was in the layout of the terminus station that the South Eastern & Chatham Railway showed such acumen and foresight. This station was sited immediately adjacent to the racecourse, within a few hundred yards of the rails at Tattenham Corner.

Until the summer of 1901 Epsom race traffic had been shared by the London & South Western, and the Brighton Railways, and both stations lay some distance from the course. In carrying their new lines right to Tattenham Corner the S.E.C.R. at once secured an immense advantage over their rivals. Furthermore, the new station was specially laid out to cope with the tremendously heavy peak traffic of Derby Day. Some heavy climbing was involved between Chipstead and Tadworth, but the terminus was equipped with no fewer than seven platform roads, a spacious approach layout, and ample sidings for stabling the coaches of the race specials. The line was ready for the Derby of 1901, and the new arrangements worked without the slightest hitch.

The S.E.C.R. determined to make the utmost use of their advantage in position on the racecourse, and for Derby Day special through excursions to Tattenham Corner were run from Margate, Dover, Hastings, and the Reading line. These long-distance excursions brought a total of 2,283 passengers on the one day alone. Naturally, the heaviest traffic on Derby Day was from London, and race specials were run from Charing Cross, Cannon Street, St Pauls, London Bridge and East Croydon. On this very first Derby Day that the line was in use between 14,000 and 15,000 passengers travelled to Tattenham Corner station. In all more than fifty special

trains were run. It was not only the racegoers that were provided
for by the new line. The proximity of the terminus to the racecourse
led the Epsom Grand Stand Association to erect stables for 100
racehorses near the station, and a very large number of these horses
was conveyed from the inception of the branch line.

While the South Eastern and the Chatham companies were now
working in unison and to such excellent effect the keen competition
with the Brighton continued. Tattenham Corner was a masterstroke
in this particular contest, but the next S.E.C.R. venture did not have
such a lasting value. This was the Bexhill branch, opened on 1st June,
1902. The South Eastern had competed for the traffic to St Leonards
and Hastings, but as their line made a trailing junction with the
coast line of the Brighton at Bo Peep Junction, West St Leonards,
they were precluded from sharing any traffic from the popular resort
of Bexhill, 4 miles to the west of Bo Peep Junction. The South Eastern
Railway had obtained Parliamentary sanction for this line in 1897,
and although work was commenced in January, 1898, the hilly
nature of the country traversed, and the need for a long viaduct over
the Crowhurst valley resulted in the $4\frac{1}{2}$ miles of the new railway
taking nearly as many years to construct.

The new branch left the main line at a point about 2 miles south of
Battle; at this junction, a fine new station, Crowhurst, was built in
the style of the larger South Eastern stations. Between the main line
platforms there were four roads, providing for through running of
non-stopping trains. A common practice was to run through carriages
for Bexhill on the principal Hastings expresses, and these were
attached or detached at Crowhurst. From the time of opening the
line there was one purely Bexhill express in each direction, from
Charing Cross and Cannon Street, calling only at Tunbridge Wells,
and Sidley. The distance from Cannon Street was only 60·8 miles,
compared with 72 miles from Victoria (L.B.S.C.R.) to the Brighton
station in Bexhill. The S.E.C.R. not only cashed in on their reduced
distance, but carried the war into the heart of the rival camp by
running some of their through carriage services from Bexhill to
Victoria, L.C.D.R. route.

The latter service was one of the first developments that followed
the construction of the new interconnecting junctions between the
Chatham and the South Eastern lines at Chislehurst. The spurs
leading southwards from the Chatham line at Bickley Junction to the
South Eastern line at Orpington Junction, as it was then known,
were built in 1902. While use was made of them almost at once for
this new passenger service, and for numerous special workings the

principal object was to facilitate the freight workings from the South Eastern, to and from the London & South Western, and the West London Lines via Longhedge and Clapham Junctions. The northern spurs at Chislehurst, from the Chatham line at St Mary Cray Junction to Chislehurst Junction were completed 2 years later. Advantage was taken of the different levels of the Chatham and the South Eastern line south of Chislehurst to build all the new connections on the burrowing junction principle. The fact that the Chief Engineer of the Managing Committee, P. C. Tempest, was an old North Western man may have influenced this decision, for at that time no company had used the flying and burrowing junction principle to greater extent and effect than the North Western.

XI

The Years of Real Progress

DESPITE all the outward evidence of a 'new deal', and the attempts to smarten everything up, the S.E.C.R. continued to get a very bad 'press' for several years. The steady decline in the South Eastern dividend was a great disappointment to shareholders who had been fed for so long upon the prospects of a bumper harvest from amalgamation; but it is surprising to find how persistently hostile was the attitude of a journal like *The Railway Magazine*. G. A. Sekon lost no opportunity of taking a swipe at the Managing Committee, and it was noticeable that each year, in the usual review of summer train service facilities the South Eastern & Chatham was usually conspicuous only by its omission altogether from the review.

By an odd coincidence, on the very day I was beginning to write this chapter, what *The Times* called 'the latest transport fiasco' moved that newspaper to one of its inimitable fourth leaders, in which the early days of the Managing Committee are amusingly called:

'An air of comic opera, of invincible ineptitude, has enveloped the transport services of Britain from as long ago as the coming of railways. Our heartless ancestors dealt rough justice to the financiers, engineers, and executives who combined so romantically to bring up the 9.15. The little, overlapping companies were always good for a laugh, sometimes ribald; every now and then sardonic. The London Chatham and Dover became the Undone, Smash'em and Turn'em over. The South Eastern & Chatham main line was the scene of that fictitious tragedy in which a would-be suicide laid his neck on the line and died of starvation.'

My own childhood was spent in what sometimes became an aura of South Eastern & Chatham vagaries. We then lived at Reading, and it must be admitted that alongside the striding elegance of the Great Western the S.E.C.R. cut a very poor figure. That was not all. In the early years of this century railways and locomotives were common topics of conversation among people who could not in any circumstances be called railway fans. Just as today passers by will turn to look at a smart motorcar, and others will go sightseeing to an airport, so on a railway station of 60 years ago it was 'the done thing' to appraise and criticize the latest locomotives to be seen. My parents, and others in my family circle, would discuss things seen on a railway journey, and I well remember an uncle of mine, who lived in the north, describing to us his first sight of one of the then-new four cylinder 4-6-0s of the Lancashire & Yorkshire. And in the common talk of the day the South Eastern & Chatham was a Cinderella among railways.

Nevertheless, at one time we, as a family, were using it more than any other line. It took us on holiday expeditions to Margate, to Ramsgate, and to Folkestone, and on some of these trips the through trains off the Great Western system were obvious choices, otherwise there would have been changes of train at Redhill, and probably at Tonbridge as well. Those cross-country journeys seemed endless, with long waits at Aldershot, Guildford and Redhill. At one time I used to think that the slowness of those journeys was merely an impression of my boyhood until I came across the following passage in Ahrons:

'If anyone desired to sample the South Eastern in its palmiest state, I should have recommended him to try the Reading line. Reading to Redhill is 46¼ miles, and the fastest train appeared to average about 4 miles an hour, with occasional spurts to 5. I know that this is not far from the mark, because I once tried it myself, and decided to walk if ever I had to go that way again . . .'

At the time I used to journey over the line with my parents the schedule of the Birkenhead–Deal express was as follows:

Distance station to station, miles				Average speed m.p.h.
	Reading	.	dep. 2.50	
17·6	Aldershot	.	„ 3.22	35·0
8·3	Guildford	.	„ 3.38	36·0
12·4	Dorking	.	„ 4.3	33·0
7·9	Redhill	.	arr. 4.17	34·0
			dep. 4.21	
19·7	Tonbridge	.	arr. 4.43	53·7
			dep. 4.53	
26·6	Ashford	.	arr. 5.23	53·1
			dep. 5.26	
9·3	Sandling Junc.	.	arr. 5.39	43·0
3·8	Shorncliffe	.	„ 5.46	
0·7	Folkestone Central	.	„ 5.49	
7·4	Dover Harbour	.	„ 6.4	
10·0	Deal	.	„ 6.30	
4·1	Sandwich	.	„ 7.5	

The smart running east of Redhill is indeed a contrast to the speed on the Reading branch, though things had improved since the days of Ahrons's adventures in the nineteenth century.

I remember one occasion most vividly. The train came in from the north, and to the accompaniment of the usual 'flap' that surrounded most family expeditions in Edwardian times we all piled in. After all the anxiety over the loading of our mountains of luggage had subsided, and my father was beginning to relax the train started, with a shattering crash that nearly put us all through the partition into the next compartment. Amid the resulting disorder I remember very well my mother remarking: 'What can you expect from a South Eastern engine!'

In the meantime, important developments were in hand. Prior to the union of 1899 the South Eastern Railway had put in extensive alterations and extensions at Folkestone Harbour. The 'new pier', built in 1863 and the enlargement of 1883, had not proved adequate for handling the increased traffic, and a decision was taken in 1897 to extend the harbour pier somewhat on the lines of the Admiralty Pier at Dover. The pier station was much too small for handling boat expresses of bogie stock, while the harbour station was still used for local passengers who found a station in the lower and most crowded part of the town a convenience, and were prepared to spend the time travelling to the junction station, and travelling down the branch rather than alighting at Radnor Park, or the junction station itself. In extending the harbour pier, however, the South Eastern Railway took full advantage of the experience obtained in handling cross-Channel traffic at Dover, and instead of embarking passengers from a narrow, and exposed platform on the pier Folkestone was provided with a fully equipped and well-sheltered station alongside the steamer berths.

This important work was completed in 1905. From that time onwards the boat trains ran through the old harbour and pier stations right alongside the steamers. The reclaimed land immediately west of the pier, which had built up naturally by the eastward drift of the shingle was used for laying in the carriage sidings for stabling stock, while the steamer berths were such that the largest packets of the day could berth alongside at any state of the tide. This facility had existed for many years at Folkestone; but the ships were always getting larger to meet the demands for increasing accommodation and increased luxury, and in 1903 the South Eastern & Chatham Railway decided to have no more paddle steamers. Owing to their size the new turbine steamers could not use Folkestone as a port until the improvements were completed in 1905. On the Folkestone Harbour branch the locomotives employed were the Stirling 'R' Class 0-6-0 tanks. Some of these engines, still retaining their dome-less boilers, were engaged on this duty until the mid-1930s.

The close of 1905 was marked by an event that, had it happened 2 hours later, might have been a catastrophe without equal in the history of British railways; this was the collapse of part of the roof at Charing Cross station. Despite many ribald jests at their expense both the Chatham and the South Eastern railways had a good record of immunity from accident. But the Charing Cross affair might have been ghastly if it had happened in the suburban rush hour. A tie rod in one of the roof trusses broke, owing to a flaw in welding during the original manufacture. The flaw was internal, and could not have been detected save by X-ray photography. During the life of the roof the flaw had gradually opened out until it finally caused the rod to break altogether. The fracture occurred at 3.40 p.m. and it brought down 70 ft of the roof. Although the stock for the 3.50 p.m. Hastings express was at the platform loading up there were relatively few people about, and the only casualties were three workmen who were engaged on the roof at the time. The station was put completely out of action for a time, and the S.E.C.R. was fortunate in having three other London termini, in Victoria, St Pauls, and Cannon Street at which, variously, the Charing Cross traffic could be handled.

Returning now to normal happenings, the improvements at Folkestone made possible an interesting development in the Continental services run by the Managing Committee. In conjunction with the Zeeland Steamship Company the L.C.D.R. had participated in the working of a service to Holland, plying between Queenborough Pier, Sheerness, to Flushing. This route, it was claimed, had many advantages over the short sea routes across the Straits of Dover. There was a very long sail, in sheltered waters, giving plenty of time for passengers to get off to sleep before the open sea was reached. The sea passage was 111 miles in length, and when the Great Eastern began to speed up and generally improve the service from Harwich to the Hook of Holland the length of the sea passage from Queenborough to Flushing was a crippling handicap. Accordingly the service was transferred from Queenborough to Folkestone in 1911, and with some fine new turbine steamers on the job the Flushing route was once more highly competitive. Like that from Harwich the new service via Folkestone was by night.

While the extension and modernization of the railway-owned port at Folkestone was being completed developments on a vast scale were in progress at Dover. I have told earlier how the Dover Harbour Board decided upon the construction of a commercial pier, as the first stage in the development of a large commercial harbour. Towards the end of the nineteenth century, however, international relations in Europe, which had been quiet since the dramatic and humiliating defeat of France in the war of 1870–1, began to grow less friendly. Public opinion in France in the 1890s was definitely anti-British, and the German Emperor was already regarded in this country as a dangerous man. A heavy programme of naval construction was therefore commenced, and the Government decided upon a great scheme for a strongly fortified harbour enclosing the whole of Dover Bay. This would provide an eastern base and anchorage for the Royal Navy, and an outpost of the great naval bases of Portsmouth, Portland and Plymouth farther down the Channel.

This large scheme was entirely naval in its origin and underlying purpose, but it had the effect of causing the South Eastern & Chatham Railway to change its own plans completely. To obviate the inconveniences and hardships in changing from train to boat on the Admiralty Pier it had been proposed to build a series of steamer berths out from the shore, apron-wise, much in the style of the present Car Ferry Terminal, but on a site near to the Train Ferry Dock. These new berths would have been adjacent to the old Harbour and Town stations, and would have been convenient for trains taking either the Chatham or the South Eastern route to London. When the Government scheme was launched, however, both railway and Harbour Board found their own plans surrounded and encompassed by the naval establishments, and the next step was to use the Prince of Wales pier for both Continental and Ocean traffic. From the railway point of view this arrangement might just pass in connection with an occasional liner. The trains had a very awkward and roundabout run, making a sharp curve away from Hawkesbury Street, crossing the bridge beside the Wellington and Granville Docks and the Tidal Harbour, and finally running out very slowly on to the narrow pier. For regular packet services the difficulties would be intolerable.

Making a quick survey of the other major packet stations in Great Britain, and noting the magnificent facilities available at Holyhead for example, at Fishguard, and Parkeston Quay one could not fail to be struck unfavourably by the conditions at Dover. The enterprising management of the South Eastern & Chatham Railway therefore decided to embark upon a scheme that would place Dover second to none, with a Marine station that would be worthy of the Gateway to England. Allied to this enterprise and drive in management it is important to take note of some very significant changes in personnel that were taking place about this time. It was referred to in *The Railway Magazine* as the 'North-Westernizing' of the S.E.C.R. Tempest had already come to the South Eastern in 1895, and the track was sufficiently improved for the new Wainwright 4-4-0s to run up to 75 m.p.h. soon after they were introduced. Then, in 1907 the post of Goods Manager fell vacant, following the death of Mr George Wallis. Another North Western man in the person of Francis H. Dent secured the post. Dent was the second son of Admiral Dent, for many years Marine Superintendent of the L.N.W.R., and he was no more than 40 years of age on his appointment to the S.E.C.R.

Francis Dent joined the L.N.W.R. at the age of 17, and within 9 years he was appointed Assistant Superintendent of the Chester & Holyhead Division. In view of the importance of the Irish traffic, any appointment on that division was considered a 'key' post, and a strong pointer that the man concerned was on the way up; and sure enough within 6 years Dent was made Divisional Superintendent at Chester. In 1902 he had moved to London, as District Goods Traffic Superintendent, and five years later he went to the S.E.C.R. Two years later, in 1909, his old chief, Sir Frederick Harrison, General Manager of the L.N.W.R., retired. Within a very short time Sir Frederick had joined the Board of the South Eastern Railway, soon becoming Deputy Chairman, and his services were almost immediately requisitioned as a member of the Managing Committee. His vast experience in the management of the L.N.W.R. must have been invaluable in the councils of the S.E.C.R., especially in alliance with the Parliamentary and business experience of the Chairman, Cosmo Bonsor. The South Eastern & Chatham was now fairly poised 'to go places'.

The Dover Marine station, on which work was commenced in 1910, was a magnificent piece of work. In broad outline the plan was to build a new quay wall running in a straight line from the fort that marked the extremity of the original Admiralty pier to a point where the pier joined the foreshore. This enclosed a triangular area which was to be reclaimed by tipping chalk cut from the cliffs between Dover Castle and the South Foreland. The large 'slice' cut from the cliffs is still clearly apparent today. The S.E.C.R. financed the reclamation, and the job was done by the Harbour Board. The work of building the quay wall and filling in behind took three years, and while it was in progress the cross-Channel steamers sailed from the

The up Hastings Pullman Car train near Grove Park, hauled by a 'B' class
Stirling 4-4-0.

[L.G.R.P. No. 21258

Above: Up Folkestone and Dover express near Grove Park, hauled by 'L' class
4-4-0 No. 771.

[F. E. Mackay

Below: The 9 a.m. Continental Mail near Grove Park, hauled by 'E' class 4-4-0
No. 165. Note the mail vans.

[H. Gordon Tidey

Steam rail motor car No. 1, used on the Sheppey Light Railway.

[British Railways

Above: Push and pull auto-train on the Greenwich Park branch.

[F. Moore

Below, left: L.C.D.R. Crystal Palace train at Honor Oak.

[N. Wakeman

Below, right: Train from L.C.D.R. at Harringay G.N.R., hauled by Kirtley 0-4-4 tank No. 80, Class 'A2'.

[H. Gordon Tidey

Above: Up Continental Mail passing Folkestone Junction. This photograph is of historical interest as it shows one of the very few instances of an 'L' class 4-4-0 recorded in service in the original colours – plain lined green and lettered 'S.E. & C.R.' on the tender. The engine, No. 773, is one of the batch built by Borsig.

[*British Railways*

Below: Horsebox special for Tattenham Corner, passing Honor Oak Park, L.B.S.C.R., hauled by the pioneer 2-6-4 tank engine No. 790.

[*H. Gordon Tidey*

The Great Landslip in Folkestone Warren, showing the train that was carried away by the subsidence and the east end of Martello Tunnel in the background.

[British Railways

Admiralty Pier extension. The boat trains had to run right out beyond the fort, and during that period the transfer from train to boat was often made in the most uncomfortably exposed conditions.

As a boy I was taken to Dover at this time. We chartered a rowing boat and made our way out towards the Prince of Wales Pier. There was a fairly strong wind going, and my chief recollection of that particular trip was of the clouds of chalky dust flying from the tipping work in progress behind the quay wall. It was a relief to get back again, and walk down the breezy promenade of the Admiralty Pier, almost to the end of the newest extension. There we saw the 2.20 p.m. from Charing Cross, the Ostend boat express arrive, and I remember clearly the very brisk speed at which the train ran along the pier, and at which the engine negotiated the sharp curve in the line round the fort. With a glittering Wainwright 4-4-0 on the job it was indeed a thrilling sight compared with the strictly restrained running of the Stirling 0-6-0 tanks at Folkestone Harbour, to which I was then more accustomed. The work of building the Marine Station began in 1913, but it was not finished when war broke out in August, 1914.

Mention of the Wainwright 4-4-0s brings me to the later locomotive developments in pre-war years. The success of the 'D' Class was followed by the rebuilding of the Stirling 'F' Class 4-4-0s, with domes boilers as the originals needed renewal. Beginning with engine No. 140, in 1903, no fewer than seventy-six of this class, out the original total of eighty-eight, were so treated and in this condition sixteen of them were still in service in January, 1947. All but two of the larger Stirling 4-4-0s of the 'B' Class were similarly rebuilt, and nineteen of them were running in January, 1947. The second new Wainwright 4-4-0 design, Class 'E', came out in 1905, and from the prominent external difference of having Belpaire fireboxes the proportions were slightly larger all round. Nevertheless construction of both classes continued. In 1906 Ashford Works turned out five 'D' Class, and four 'E's', and in 1907 the Works built six 'D's' and ten 'E's'. Of this latter class No. 516 was for some years the pride of the line, and was used for Royal trains and other special occasions.

Wainwright followed the fashion of the day by building steam rail motor cars for light branch duty. The need for something new was forced upon the locomotive department when it was agreed that the S.E.C.R. should take over the working of the Isle of Sheppey Light Railway. The steam rail motor cars were handsome little things, finished in the standard carriage 'lake', and this colour was continued forward to include the cab sides and tank sides of the locomotive unit. The domes were of polished brass, as in the ordinary locomotives. Two cars were built in 1905, for the Sheppey and Hundred of Hoo branches, and six more followed in 1906. One of these latter went to the Hayes branch, another to Westerham and the remainder worked down on the coast, some running to Dungeness and New Romney, while the others worked on the Sandling–Sandgate branch, and on the Elham Valley line. They had a maximum speed of about 35 m.p.h. on the level.

By the year 1910 business on the S.E.C.R. was much on the increase; the loading of the principal express trains was often topping the 300-ton mark, while the development of the Kentish coalfield was building up a useful westbound freight traffic. The smart running of passenger trains was becoming a reality instead of a pious hope, and the use of larger locomotives for both passenger and goods traffic was being seriously considered. As long previously as 1907 a design had been prepared in the Ashford drawing office for an inside-cylinder 4-6-0. From the accompanying drawing it would have looked something like a six-coupled version of Class 'E'; but although the maximum axle load did not exceed 18 tons the Civil Engineer would not accept the engine. In 1911 Wainwright had another go, this time with the very handsome outside cylinder 4-6-0 shown herewith; at about the same time a design for an 0-8-0 goods engine was also worked out. Both 4-6-0 and 0-8-0 designs were non-superheated, but while they were under consideration two 4-4-0s of the 'E' Class, Nos. 36 and 275 were experimentally equipped with superheaters, the former with the Robinson apparatus, and the latter with the Schmidt. This rebuilding took place in 1912.

Although the cylinder diameter was increased from $19\frac{1}{4}$ in. to $20\frac{1}{2}$ in. the nominal tractive effort remained the same, as boiler pressure was lowered from 180 to 160 lb per sq in. The total weight was slightly increased, by just enough to preclude the use of these two engines over any part of the Chatham system. The maximum axle load was increased from $17\frac{1}{2}$ to $18\frac{1}{2}$ tons. This restriction was to have an interesting sequel in later years. Route restrictions apart, however, engines 36 and 275 were two of the finest the South Eastern & Chatham ever had. The ordinary engines of Class 'E' were excellent machines, but while they had strength and abundant steaming power they had not the freedom in running of the superheater variants. I shall never forget a footplate journey I made on No. 275 in 1947. She was then something of a veteran, but even then she was a Rolls-Royce of a locomotive, silent in her action, amazing in the almost contemptuous ease with which she lifted a 250-ton train

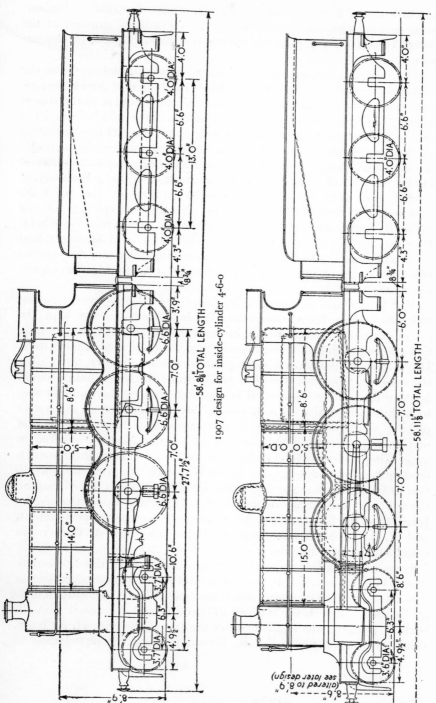

1907 design for inside-cylinder 4-6-0

1911 design for outside-cylinder 4-6-0

out of London Bridge and up to Knockholt. At that time enthusiasts were making eloquent speeches over the continuing prowess of the South Western 'T9' 4-4-0s; but old 275 had got any 'T9' of those years stone cold!

The second 4-6-0 project was turned down as definitely as the earlier design of 1907 had been, and so the best that could be done was to have more superheater 4-4-0s, generally similar to the superheater 'E' Class, but with the largest boilers that could be permitted on the South Eastern section. On the basis of nominal tractive effort the new engines were to be the same as Nos. 36 and 275, but actually the design did not go through quite as it had been originally planned in the Ashford drawing office. In the autumn of 1913 Wainwright retired, and with his going locomotive affairs on the S.E.C.R. underwent a profound change. The 'North-Westernizing' of the S.E.C.R. had been carried a stage further in 1911 when Francis H. Dent was appointed to succeed V. W. Hill as General Manager, and there was more than a faint resemblance to North Western managerial efficiency in the changes that were wrought at Ashford in the ensuing two years.

The last years of Wainwright's superintendency were less distinguished than the earlier ones. While Robert Surtees kept the job of locomotive design firmly in hand the administration generally was allowed to drift, till one found it was the dour Scots Chief Clerk, Hugh McColl, who was wielding almost absolute power, and ruling the running department with a rod of iron! Such a situation could become intolerable, and when Wainwright retired the management took this opportunity for a thorough 'clean up', to use an expressive piece of modern slang. They decided upon one major change that savoured more of the Midland than of the North Western, in appointing an independent officer as Locomotive Running Superintendent, and in changing the title of Wainwright's previous office to that of Chief Mechanical Engineer. To fill these posts the Managing Committee went right outside the S.E.C.R., and appointed A. D. Jones, from the Lancashire & Yorkshire, as Running Superintendent, and R. E. L. Maunsell, from the Great Southern & Western as Chief Mechanical Engineer.

Even in this latter appointment the affinity with the London & North Western was continued, for at that time Inchicore Works was noted for its partiality for Crewe methods. Three successive chiefs at Inchicore had been trained at Crewe, and Maunsell himself, born in Ireland, was trained under the last of the trio, H. A. Ivatt. When he came to the S.E.C.R. Maunsell was given *carte blanche* to reorganize the whole department, and his first task was to get new express locomotives ordered for the summer services of 1914. The Surtees superheater 4-4-0 design was available, but Maunsell was reluctant to accept it as it stood, and he took the unusual step of consulting his former chief draughtsman at Inchicore, W. Joynt, on the details of the valve setting. At the suggestion of the latter engineer some amendments to the Ashford design were made, and authority was then given for twenty-two engines of the class to be ordered, straight off the drawing board. The British locomotive building firms were all exceptionally busy at the time; Ashford could not take on the work, so an order for ten was placed with Borsig, of Berlin. The contract for the remaining twelve was awarded to Beyer, Peacock & Company.

With these engines on order Maunsell set about the reorganization of the department, and he built up an entirely new team from outside the S.E.C.R. as follows:

Assistant Chief Mechanical Engineer and Works Manager, Ashford	G. H. Pearson (G.W.R.)
Assistant Works Manager	C. J. Hicks (G.S. & W.R.)
Chief Locomotive Draughtsman	J. Clayton (Midland)
Chief Draughtsman (Carriage & Wagon)	L. Lynes (G.W.R.)
Cost Accountant	H. J. Tonkin (G.W.R.)
Works Assistant	H. Holcroft (G.W.R.)

The new organization thus savoured strongly of Swindon, rather than of Crewe, while James Clayton, though at first strongly indoctrinated with Midland practice, had experienced the thrill of working with Cecil Paget in the design of the famous, though unfortunate 2-6-2 experimental sleeve-valve locomotive No. 2299. The skill with which Maunsell welded these diverse individuals into a strongly-integrated team is evident from events at the time of the grouping of the railways in 1923. Then it was the men of the S.E.C.R. who took virtual control of all locomotive affairs on the newly formed Southern Railway.

In the meantime the growth of traffic and the enterprise of the management had exceeded the available motive power, and as a temporary expedient locomotives were borrowed from the Great Northern and from the Hull & Barnsley. It so happened that these hirelings were all of Stirling design, 2-4-0 and 0-6-0 respectively, so that engines of Patrick Stirling's and Matthew Stirling's design joined those of James Stirling, in serving the S.E.C.R. – a remarkable 'family party'. The Great Northern engines, to the number of fifteen, were transferred early in 1914, and had the initials 'S.E. & C.R.' painted on their tenders; but the Hull & Barnsley 0-6-0s came a year later, as a result of war conditions. Trade through the port of Hull was much restricted, and some goods locomotives were surplus to needs, while at the same time the South Eastern and Chatham was exceedingly hard pressed. The Matthew Stirling 0-6-0s retained the initials 'H. & B.R.' on their tenders, and *The Railway Magazine* of the day records some of the amusing guesses made by passengers at what the initials stood for. 'Highland and Brecon' was perhaps widest of the mark!

The new express engines, 'made in Germany', were shipped to England in parts, landed at Dover, and erected at Ashford Works. Borsig sent over about twenty skilled erectors, and these men were engaged on the job to within a few weeks of the outbreak of war, in August, 1914. The ten German-built engines of the 'L' Class, as they were known, were beautifully finished; it was indeed a unique occurrence for a British railway to buy express locomotives from Germany, and the firm saw to it that a superb job was made of the contract. But in another respect they marked the beginning of a great change in the appearance of S.E.C.R. locomotives. The polished brass domes and copper capped chimneys were absent, and although the basic colour was still brunswick green, with light brown underframes, the lining-out was far less elaborate than on the Wainwright engines, and consisted of a single scheme of black and yellow. At the same time the older engines, as they passed through the shops, had their brass domes painted over green, and their copper tops painted black. This was merely a mild foretaste of the austerity that was to descend on the S.E.C.R. in the war years.

Before closing down completely upon the pre-war scene, a note on the principal train services will be of interest. The outward-bound Continental expresses were:

Time of Departure	London Terminus	Packet Station	Description
9 a.m.	Charing Cross	Dover	Morning Mail
10 a.m.	Charing Cross	Folkestone	Paris
11 a.m.	Victoria	Dover (via Chatham)	Calais Boat Express
2.20 p.m.	Charing Cross	Folkestone	Paris in 6 hr. 50 min.
2.20 p.m.	Charing Cross	Dover	Ostend Boat Express
9 p.m.	Charing Cross	Dover	Night Mail

Inward bound the 5.20 p.m. up from Dover may be specially mentioned. This was described in the public timetables as 'Royal Mail

Express', and was, so far as I can trace, the only train in either direction to have the pre-fix 'royal'. It was booked to run non-stop to Herne Hill in 100 minutes; after dividing there the two portions reached Victoria and Holborn Viaduct at 7.10 and 7.15 p.m. respectively.

On the Chatham line the down Granville Express, at 3.25 p.m. from Victoria took 110 minutes to Margate in 1910, calling at Herne Hill and Westgate intermediately, while 'The City Fast Train', leaving St Pauls at 5.12 p.m. ran non-stop to Faversham, and thence to Margate. The fast afternoon excursions to the Kent Coast that were such a feature of earlier Chatham days were advertised in the timetables, but at the time of which I am now writing they were run from Charing Cross, calling at London Bridge, and New Cross, and switching over to the Chatham line at Chislehurst. In the summer of 1910 this train made a non-stop run over the 53 miles from New Cross to Whitstable in 99 minutes, while the total time from Charing Cross to Margate was 2½ hours. Another notable service was the 'Fast Midnight', on Saturdays only, or rather early Sunday morning, running non-stop from London Bridge to Whitstable in 78 minutes; this latter gave the quite creditable average speed of 43 m.p.h. at that bewitching time of the week.

In the last years before the war some new, and very smart timings were introduced including a 90-minute run from Victoria to Margate, and a new Continental boat express with a 90-minute run from Charing Cross to Dover. This latter was much the fastest boat express ever regularly scheduled by the S.E.C.R., and its working was made all the more difficult because of the constructional works in progress at Dover Harbour. The train had, on arrival, to run right out to the very end of the Admiralty Pier extension, to a point three-quarters of a mile beyond Dover Town station and 77¼ miles from Charing Cross. The load of the train was not usually a heavy one, under 200 tons, but the Wainwright 4-4-0s made light of it, and on one occasion when Mr Cecil J. Allen was a passenger the net time was 86 minutes, though the actual arrival on the pier was 1½ minutes late due to a signal stop in Folkestone Warren.

XII

The S.E.C.R. at War

FROM the very day that the war with Germany began the South Eastern & Chatham Railway was in it up to the hilt. Other railways had to organize rapidly the running of troop trains, and upon the London & South Western fell the brunt of the work in getting the British Expeditionary Force to Southampton. But they did have a few days notice. On the S.E.C.R. there were emergencies to be faced at once. The headlong advance of the German armies through Belgium, the destruction of towns, sent refugees in their thousands fleeing to the Channel ports, and the packet steamers sailing for England were called upon to convey enormous crowds. Many of these unfortunate people stepped ashore at Folkestone with little more than the clothes they wore, and upon the railway fell the task not only of getting them away from the coast but of finding food and accommodation for them.

Dover was immediately taken over by the Government for use for naval and military traffic exclusively, and three S.E.C.R. steamers, the *Empress*, the *Riviera* and the *Engadine* were requisitioned for service with the Royal Navy. Folkestone remained open for civilian traffic, yet such was the flood of refugees from Belgium that for some little time the service was virtually suspended. The Admiralty one day requested that every available boat should be sent to Ostend, and on one day alone S.E.C.R. steamers landed 6,000 refugees at Folkestone. The war had not been raging for long before the steamers were involved in some exciting episodes. The *Invicta* rescued some of the survivors from H.M.S. *Hermes*, which had struck a mine, and when the Belgian ship *Amiral Ganteaume* was torpedoed, *The Queen* went to the rescue. Although this S.E.C.R. steamer was in deadly danger of being sunk by the same submarine she stood by, and picked up 2,200 panic-stricken refugees – a marvellous feat of seamanship and humanity. Dover Marine station, although unfinished, was immediately brought into use as a landing stage for the wounded.

Although the heaviest traffic in the weeks immediately following the outbreak of war, in sheer numbers of troops conveyed, fell upon the South Western, military traffic on the S.E.C.R. was very intense, and the connections to the northern lines, through the Thames Tunnel, and via Ludgate Hill were worked to the limit of their capacity. Such was the pressure at one time that it was thought that the passenger service would have to be completely suspended. Fortunately this was not necessary, and with the Expeditionary Force safely in France train workings on the S.E.C.R. returned to something a little nearer to normal except, of course, for the Continental traffic. Even so, it was still possible for civilians to travel to France, via Folkestone and Boulogne; in the meantime ambulance trains were brought into Charing Cross, and leave trains to Victoria.

While the traffic department and the steamers were coping with the very unusual and exceptional conditions, a totally unexpected task befell the locomotive department at Ashford. Despite the speed of the German advance a large proportion of the working stock of the Belgian railways, and of the French lines overrun had been withdrawn to comparative safety in France, but all supplies, spare parts and servicing facilities for these locomotives had been lost. To use them effectively consumable spares needed to be available, and Maunsell undertook to provide these parts. It was a tremendous task. The existing parts had to be checked, measured up, and drawings made at Ashford Works; in some cases special tools were necessary to produce parts different from anything used on British railways. Although Ashford was perhaps most favourably situated to undertake such a task there was another reason for it. On the outbreak of war the Railway Executive Committee was formed, consisting of the General Managers of ten leading railways, and from the outset Maunsell acted as Chief Mechanical Engineer to the R.E.C.

Before continuing with the more serious aspects of the war as they came to affect the S.E.C.R. there is one last comedy to relate, a comedy savouring more of the days before the fusion of the two old companies than of the businesslike methods of the Managing Committee. Maunsell, though Irish to his fingertips, was the very reverse of the old English idea of a typical Irishman, who was expected to do and say funny things, and to be generally a bit mad! As one of his senior assistants at Inchicore once bewailed after an 'irregularity' had been uncovered: 'Mr Maunsell is a terrible sthraight man . . .' Well, one day early in the war when he was reviewing the general shortage of locomotives on the S.E.C.R. he came across the fact that while sixty-six of the 'H' Class 0-4-4 tank engines had been authorized only sixty-four had actually been built. The last had been completed at Ashford as long ago as 1910.

Investigation revealed that the parts for the remaining two had been 'lost' in the Works, used for repairs of other engines, and so on. The story goes that Maunsell just about turned the place upside down to get the missing parts found, or replacements made, with the result that two new 'H' Class tanks appeared from Ashford, Nos. 16 and 184, in the early months of 1915.

In the worst competitive days of the L.C.D.R. and the South Eastern, when disillusioned shareholders and wiseacres of all kinds were frequently bemoaning the wastefulness of having two competing routes from London to Dover the South Eastern Board always seemed to take the attitude that the Chatham was an unwarranted intrusion. They were, however, glad enough to accept the hospitality of the Chatham line in 1877, when a landslip occurred in the Folkestone Warren, and blocked the line for a short distance east of the Martello Tunnel. This occurrence came perhaps as a warning, and the minor slips that came in 1881, 1885, 1886 and 1896 were all very promptly dealt with. But for the existence of the one-time competitive line to Dover, however, the 'incident' of December, 1915, might have been a national, rather than a railway tragedy. In the earlier part of that month rainfall in the Folkestone and Dover area had been exceptionally heavy, and a slight slip of the chalk had taken place in one of the cuttings between the Martello and Abbotscliff Tunnels. It was not serious, but in view of the continuing bad weather a sharp look-out was kept, and watchmen specially posted.

Then, on the evening of 19th December, at about 6.50 p.m. a watchman stationed in the Warren heard the noise of a fall of chalk, just as a down passenger train was leaving Folkestone Junction. With the utmost promptitude in the use of detonators and his red lamp he succeeded in stopping the train just after it emerged from the Martello Tunnel. Already the whole area, and the permanent way with it was subsiding, and the engine and the first four coaches of the train were borne some distance towards the sea. The actual slip took place quite gradually, and thanks to the alertness of the watchman there were no casualties; but the engine, a Class 'D' 4-4-0, and the coaches could not get back, and they were eventually dragged away by hawsers. The section where this train was caught was only the beginning of the trouble, and the full extent of this tremendous blocking of the line was not revealed until daylight next morning.

From a line of cleavage in the deep chalk cutting 180 yards from the eastern end of the Martello Tunnel the line was distorted and pushed out of alignment for a distance of nearly two miles. One could say that roughly the whole length between Martello and Abbotscliff Tunnels was affected, though fortunately neither of the tunnels themselves suffered any damage. One of the worst features of the 1877 slip was the damage it caused to the east end of the Martello Tunnel. Apart from this, however, the engineers of the S.E.C.R. were faced with a task of such seriousness that the abandonment of the line, permanently, was considered. Since its construction in 1844 danger from the steady encroaching of the sea had increased. Some defence works had been erected, and drainage headings put in, but the action of the sea on the base of the chalk cliffs had rendered them unstable, and the great landslip affected not merely the Warren, but the whole area extending to the high cliffs inshore of the railway. At its greatest width the disturbed ground covered a width of nearly half a mile, and at the Warren Halt the line of the railway had been pushed 53 yards towards the sea.

For security reasons during the war this great misfortune was kept out of the newspapers and technical journals, and it was not until 1919 that the full story was revealed. In the meantime all traffic to Dover had to use the Chatham route, and the twin bores of Shakespeare's Cliff Tunnel were used for the storage of ammunition trains. The extent of the slip, and the vast amount of cutting and filling that would have been necessary to restore the alignment of the railway led to the decision to abandon the line for the duration of the war. It was not merely a case of earth-moving, and the man power that it would need. The slip was generally thought to be due to geological reasons that would need careful and extensive surveys, and during the war time could not be spared for such work. The existence of the Chatham line proved a godsend, so much so that after the war it was seriously proposed to abandon the line through the Warren altogether.

From the Warren we must, for the time being, transfer attention to Dover itself, where the new Marine Station was approaching completion at the outbreak of war. To save time, and to minimize the discomforts of a sea passage it was immediately arranged to use Dover as the landing place for sick and wounded from the battle areas, but with the Marine Station uncompleted only the Admiralty Pier extension could be used. Even with ordinary passengers that exposed landing stage had been anything but ideal, and for ambulance work, particularly as the storms of autumn and winter were experienced it became almost impossible, and the traffic was transferred to Southampton. In those early months there were hopes in some uninformed quarters that the war might be a short one; whatever facile hopes there may have been the casualty rate in France in the late autumn of 1914 was so high that already the facilities at South-ampton were proving inadequate, and orders were given therefore for the Marine Station at Dover to be completed in the quickest possible time. By a wonderful effort on the part of all concerned it was possible to begin handling ambulance traffic there on 2nd January, 1915.

The station layout was conceived on the most generous lines. There are two island platforms each 700 ft long and 60 ft wide, the platforms affording ample space for all the usual amenities, in the most modern and attractive style. The old tracks on the Admiralty pier are used for locomotives of arrived trains proceeding to the running sheds, and for empty stock drawn ahead from the station on to the pier extension when necessary to clear the station platforms for immediately following traffic. During the war the old locomotive depots at Dover Town and Dover Priory had to be used. It was not until Southern Railway days that the large modern depot on the seashore was available. Although completed in such haste as a wartime measure the Marine Station project was a joint enterprise of the Dover Harbour Board and the S.E.C.R.; the respective contributions to the cost were £400,000 by the Harbour Board on the reclamation work, and the construction of the new quay wall, and £300,000 by the Managing Committee. The Government, the armed services and the country as a whole could feel vastly indebted to the initiators of this great enterprise.

Between the opening of the station for military traffic and the end of February, 1919, no fewer than 4,000 ambulance steamers were received – an average of nearly three per day – and in connection with each boat there were usually at least two trains. The number of patients just exceeded 1¼ million, but in addition to the ambulance traffic there passed through Dover Marine Station 1¾ million overseas leave and draft men in the four years of war. It is perhaps significant of the part the station played in the war effort of the South Eastern & Chatham Railway that when the time came for a war memorial to be erected by the Managing Committee, it was placed at Dover Marine, rather than at one of the many London terminal stations. When public service was resumed, to Ostend, in January, 1919, the handsome stone facings of the station became familiar to many travellers on peaceful and pleasurable errands, and the shelter afforded, as compared with the rigours of the old Admiralty Pier landings, were much appreciated.

At Ashford locomotive works once the upheaval caused by the

sudden transition to war conditions had been surmounted, Maunsell and his newly-recruited staff were able to give some consideration to new locomotive design. In evolving a policy for the future standardization was to be the watchword, with interchangeability of parts as between one class and another, and the ultimate ideal of working the traffic of the railway with the fewest number of different locomotive classes. Not for nothing had Maunsell recruited so many of his new staff from Swindon, and in the early days the influence of G. H. Pearson, his principal assistant and locomotive works manager at Ashford, was continuous and strong. The growth of the freight traffic on the S.E.C.R., quite apart from war conditions, had been giving some concern, and the rapid advance in the quality of the coal mined in Kent gave some distinct pointers to the development of future business. An early decision was that one of the new designs should be of the 2-6-0 type, and while Pearson strongly favoured the use of tank engines on medium-distance passenger trains the possibility of standardization, as between the proposed 2-6-0 and a 2-6-4 tank, was hopeful.

The prototype S.E.C.R. 2-6-0, No. 810, was completed at Ashford in the summer of 1917, but its rather gaunt lines and utilitarian appearance were not likely to rouse very much enthusiasm among those who had delighted in locomotives of the Wainwright era. Recalling the past associations of the men mainly concerned in its detail design one could recognize the Great Western influence in the taper boiler, and the top feed apparatus, and the Midland associations of Clayton in the shape of the chimney, the cab, and the tender. The top feed was a pure Ashford design, though achieving the same object as Churchward's well-known arrangement on the Great Western. The trays through which the water cascaded down were helical in form, and arranged in a casing shaped like a steam dome. In the works this device became known as the 'helter-skelter lighthouse'.

The superheater was relatively small in heating surface, as in Great Western practice, but Maunsell was not content to take one of the existing proprietary types and use it as it stood. The *dictum* that he impressed upon his design staff was 'make everything get-at-able', and neither the Schmidt nor the Robinson superheater came up to his requirements in this respect. In the Swindon superheater any element could be withdrawn without interfering with any other element, though Churchward's arrangement was applicable to no more than two rows of elements. Maunsell produced a design that was just as accessible as Churchward's but was

capable of being built in much larger sizes. In the pioneer 2-6-0
engine there were three rows of elements. At Pearson's insistence
the valves were given long laps and long travel, though this feature
was at variance with the previous experience of James Clayton,
and of Maunsell himself. Before the war was over, however, Clayton
had become closely associated with Churchward, in a connection
to be mentioned later, and he came to need no further persuasion to
include items of Great Western practice in future S.E.C.R. and
Southern Railway locomotive design.

Despite the conditions of wartime opportunities were found to
carry out a full series of trials with the 2-6-0 engine No. 810, taking
indicator diagrams. It was, of course, no more than a moderate
powered engine, with a nominal tractive effort of 26,040 lb at 85
per cent working pressure, and the optimum output took place at a
speed of about 50 m.p.h. at which the indicated horsepower was
about 1,000. Although the maximum occurred at about 50 m.p.h.
the power output was sustained between 900 and 1,000 over the
speed range from 25 to 60 m.p.h. In other words No. 810 was an
ideal mixed-traffic locomotive. The 2-6-4 tank engine No. 790 was
identical to No. 810 in every respect save in the coupled wheel
diameter, which was 6 ft against 5 ft 6 in. on the 2-6-0. The 2-6-4
tank, Class 'K', was intended for express passenger working on all
trains on the S.E.C.R. system, up to, but not including, the boat
trains.

Pearson's experience of fast tank engine working on the Great
Western had its influence here, and there was also the spectacle of
many fast trains on the London Brighton & South Coast Railway
worked by the Marsh Class 'I3' 4-4-2 tanks. If the Brighton could
run non-stop from Clapham Junction to Fratton with an 'I3',
certainly a 'K' Class 2-6-4 of the S.E.C.R. ought to be able to run
non-stop to Folkestone, or Margate. While the war was still on an
interesting test was carried out with engine No. 790 on the 1.40
p.m. boat train to Folkestone Junction, running non-stop over the
70·9 miles from Charing Cross. The load consisted of four Pullman
cars, six non-corridor bogie coaches and a six-wheeled van, weighing
310 tons tare. With the non-corridor part of the train very full
the gross load was probably around 340 tons. The schedule was
then quite an easy one – 102 minutes start to stop – but the main
object and concern of the test was the water consumption. It turned
out to be a very close thing, for although the tanks were full at
Charing Cross they finished with only 150 gallons. This showed a
total consumption of 1,850, and although this was equivalent to

no more than 26 gallons per mile it was far too tight for regular working. When the 2-6-4 tank class was multiplied in Southern Railway days the new engines were used on shorter runs.

Towards the end of the war there was a good deal of talk in Government circles about the future of the railways, and many politicians were in favour of nationalization. A good deal of leeway in locomotive construction would have to be made up when the fighting actually ceased, and the Government asked the Association of Railway Locomotive Engineers to put forward proposals for some new standard designs. The A.R.L.E. was a rather exclusive 'club' to which only the Chief Mechancial Engineers of the various railways and their senior assistants belonged, and within that circle the idea of 'standard' designs was not generally welcome. Four railways only showed any active interest; these were the Great Western, Midland, Great Northern and Lancashire & Yorkshire. Churchward, Fowler, Gresley and Hughes formed an informal committee, and Maunsell as Chief Mechanical Engineer of the wartime Railway Executive Committee was asked if he would make the drawings. Thus James Clayton came into the picture, and for a time worked in close co-operation with Churchward. The project of 'standard' locomotives came to nothing, but it was an experience that was to exert a profound influence on future S.E.C.R. designs.

One reaction from the volume of war traffic flowing over the South Eastern & Chatham Railway was the disruption of some of the staple civilian traffic. Passenger business was strictly curtailed, but goods was at first handled in the old go-as-you-please way that characterized much freight train operating in this country. Goods was accepted at the stations and the trains were despatched as and when they were ready. In wartime this quickly led to hopeless congestion on the S.E.C.R. and it was then that a system of traffic control was instituted, very similar to that already yielding such excellent results on the Midland Railway. During the war years the S.E.C.R. was fortunate in having in the vital office of Superintendent of the Line a very able railwayman in Edwin C. Cox, who had joined the South Eastern as long ago as 1883, at the age of fifteen. In 1911 he had been selected to succeed William Thompson as Superintendent of the Line, and then, at the age of 43, he was the youngest railway Superintendent in Great Britain. National recognition of the great part the S.E.C.R. was playing in the war came early, when in the New Year Honours of January, 1916, the dignity of a Knighthood was conferred upon the General Manager, Francis H. Dent.

Regulation of the civilian goods traffic of the line was a relatively small part of Cox's vast responsibilities. To make the utmost use of the line timetable paths from London to the Channel Ports were laid down for the entire 24 hours of each day. Troop, ambulance and other special trains were run in the first available path, and in the case of traffic to and from Dover and Folkestone the utmost use was made of the many alternative routes. Trains might start from Charing Cross, for example, switch to the Chatham line at Chisle-hurst, run via Maidstone, and re-join the South Eastern line at Ashford. Freight train movement was controlled with the very minimum of paperwork. A telegram was all that was necessary to allocate a train to a particular timetable path; engines were avail-able on a 'round-the-clock' basis, and the volume of special traffic handled was prodigious. Much of the heavier equipment and supplies went to the ferry port of Richborough, between Sandwich and Ramsgate. These trains were mostly routed via Tonbridge, Ashford and Canterbury.

Special mention must be made of the gun-powder specials run from Woolwich Arsenal to Richborough. These were marshalled at Hither Green, and when they were ready to start all traffic on the down line was stopped at Charlton. Their explosive freight was carried for the most part in wooden box trucks, and everything else was kept clear until they were through the succession of long tunnels. Seeing their engines pounding up the heavy banks, throwing showers of sparks, there must have been many whose hearts were in their mouths; but it was all taken as one of the hazards of war, and fortunately no accident occurred with any of these gunpowder specials. In all this work the various S.E.C.R. 0-6-0 goods engines performed prodigies of work. It would be interesting to know what records of utilization they attained, but by working the traffic with the minimum of paperwork the number of accurate records left are scanty. We do know, however, that between 5th August, 1914 and 31st December, 1918 the total number of special trains, excluding empties, was 101,872, or an average of 66 special trains per day!

The new Maunsell engines came upon the scene relatively late in the war, and there were, in any case, only the two prototype machines available at first; thus the brunt of it all was borne by the Wainwrights, reinforced, of course, by the 'L' Class 4-4-0s of 1914. There was irony in full measure surrounding the batch built by Borsig's in that they were just finished in time to take a major part in the war effort of the S.E.C.R. Towards the end of the war, in October, 1918, the London *Evening News* had occasion to refer to

CRYSTAL PALACE HIGH LEVEL STATION

Above: Entrance to this imposing terminus of the L.C.D.R. branch line, as it existed in 1954.

Below: The lavish platform accommodation and grandiose interior architecture – another 1954 picture.

[*R. C. Riley*

L.C.D.R. 'M3' class No. 647 in austerity livery.

The first three-cylinder 2-6-0, No. 822.

'E1' class rebuilt 4-4-0 No. 165.

Above: Kent Coast portion of the 'Sunny South Express' (L.N.W.R. stock) leaving Margate, hauled by 'D1' class rebuilt 4-4-0 No. 494.

Below: The 9.05 a.m. through express to Cannon Street leaving Bexhill, hauled by 'L' class 4-4-0 No. 776.

Above: Oxted line train near Upper Warlingham, hauled by 'F' class 4-4-0 No. 198.

Below: Down train on the L.B.S.C.R. line near Purley, hauled by rebuilt Stirling 4-4-0 No. 94.

[The late C. Laundy

these engines thus: 'One can feel a sort of unholy joy at the thought that the engines had helped to move millions of troops to the battle-field, and helped to bring over tens of thousands of Hun prisoners.' In addition to regular draft, leave and ambulance trains, the S.E.C.R. kept a small stud of 4-4-0 express engines, maintained in first class condition and ready for immediate use on the 'Imperial Specials'. These trains were liable to be chartered at little more than a moment's notice to convey dispatches, couriers, or high-ranking officers or civilians. Those taking the South Eastern route were designated 'Imperial Special A', and those by the Chatham route 'Imperial Special B'. It is pleasing to record that four of the old L.C.D.R. 'M3' Class 4-4-os were set aside to run the 'B' specials.

In running the wartime traffic on the S.E.C.R. Cox and his staff had, for the most part, to make do with what they had in 1914, in the way of motive power, carriages, wagons and truck facilities. Authority was given, however, for the resignalling of Victoria station. By 1916 the traffic in military personnel was enormous, and to give some assistance a scheme of all-electric signalling was worked out. Having regard to contemporary practice in the U.S.A. the specification called for three-position upper quadrant semaphore signals. As no British manufacturer was then in a position to supply these, although the contract was awarded to the British Power Railway Signal Company, the signals, the electric point machines and certain other equipment were obtained from the General Railway Signal Company, of Rochester, New York. The installation was quite a large one by the standards then prevailing. The locking frame, having a total of 200 levers, was of the standard G.R.S. pattern, with horizontal pull-out slides instead of miniature levers. Of the total of 200 levers, 107 were for signals, indicators, and releases, and 47 were for points.

The locking frame was duly manufactured in America, and shipped to England. But it never arrived. The vessel conveying it was tor-pedoed and sunk, and another locking frame had to be made. As a result the work at Victoria was barely finished when the war ended. The second frame is still in service today, though when both the Brighton and the Chatham sides of Victoria were resignalled with modern colourlight signals in 1939 the old frame was modified to have miniature levers of the latest type. The S.E.C.R. installation at Victoria attracted a good deal of attention in railway engineering circles at the time of its completion, as it was the first of any size on a main line railway in this country to break away from the traditional two-position lower quadrant signal. It is perhaps fitting that this breakaway should have been pioneered on a railway with a notable record of signalling development, and to the honour of installing the first sections of Sykes 'Lock and Block' was added, in the stress of war conditions, the first three-position upper quadrant signalling.

When the Armistice came in November, 1918, the South Eastern & Chatham Railway had a fine record of war service to its credit, and this chapter may be fitly closed by quoting a letter from Sir Douglas Haig, (afterwards Earl Haig), the Commander in Chief of the British Army in France, to Cosmo Bonsor, Chairman of the S.E.C.R. Managing Committee:

'The Army in France owes much to all connected with the control of our railway companies in the United Kingdom, and indeed in the Empire. They have at all times shown the greatest willingness to help us in every possible way in their power. Track has been torn up to give us rails; engines, trucks, men, capable engineers, operations staff, &c., all have been sent abroad to us, regardless of their own special needs and demands of the people at home, and without a moment's hesitation.

'But we have been more closely associated with the South Eastern & Chatham Railway than any other. The bulk of our ammunition and stores required for the maintenance of our armies, as well as several millions of men as reinforcements and on leave, have passed over their system. Their sphere of duty, too, has been nearest to the shores of France and Belgium, and consequently more open to hostile attacks by air and fears of invasion by sea. Undisturbed by any alarms the traffic for the Armies in France has never ceased to flow. This reflects the greatest credit on all concerned with the Company.'

XIII

Post-War Developments

THE end of the war found the South Eastern & Chatham Railway in good form for the period of reconstruction and development. Despite the burden of the wartime responsibilities they had carried so well the leading officers were quick to change over to normal activities, and the four years between the Armistice and the grouping of the railways in January, 1923, were remarkably productive of new developments of major importance. An early decision was to concentrate the whole of the Continental traffic at Victoria. The growing intensity of the suburban business at Cannon Street and Charing Cross, with electrification under active consideration, and some interesting traffic-movement studies in hand suggested this move; in addition, with the electric signalling referred to in the previous chapter Victoria station was well equipped to take more traffic than in pre-war years.

This decision created an immediate locomotive problem. At that time the civil engineer was not prepared to allow the 'L' Class 4-4-0 locomotives on any part of the old Chatham line, due to underline bridge weight restrictions. Neither would he accept the two Wainwright superheater 'E' Class 4-4-0s Nos. 36 and 275. At first the line through the Folkestone Warren was still closed, but even when this was cleared the boat trains would still have to use some part of the Chatham line to reach Victoria, and this made it necessary to use the non-superheater Wainwright 'D' and 'E' Class engines. New trains of corridor stock were proposed, and when these were in service the minimum loads of the principal boat expresses would be more than the old non-superheater engines could comfortably handle. The task was to run boat trains of 300 tons tare over the 78 miles from Victoria to Dover Marine, via Tonbridge, in 100 minutes.

The problem was met by the celebrated rebuilding of the 'E' Class 4-4-0 No. 179 with a superheater. It could not be done on similar lines to the existing superheater 'E' Class engines, as those two engines had a maximum axle load of 18 ton 10 cwt against 17 ton 12 cwt of the non-superheater 'E' 4-4-0s. The basic principles of the reconstruction were to provide a larger grate, and greater capacity for burning coal, high-degree superheat, and to replace the original slide valves by larger diameter piston valves having ample port openings and long laps. The addition of the superheater and the use of a larger firebox was going to mean extra weight, and so the weight was cut down in every other respect. The large, gracefully-curved splashers were replaced by some narrow, attenuated ones; the running plate was cut away over the coupled wheels, and the heavy cast iron drag box was replaced by a fabricated steel one.

In outward appearance the rebuilt engine bore a striking resemblance to the Midland Class '2' 4-4-0s of the '483' rebuilt, and superheated variety, but this likeness was in superficial points only. The S.E.C.R. engine No. 179 was a true rebuild, in that the original boiler was used – even up to the dome cover, which was suitably cut down – and much of the original motion parts were used. The design was a blend of 'E' Class and 'N' Class practice, so much so that no additional spares had to be carried for the 'E1', as No. 179 was classified. The increased weight on the bogie was compensated for by reduced weight at the rear end, and the adhesion weight of No. 179 was only 33½ tons, as against 34 tons 18 cwt on the original 'E' Class. The total weight was 52½ tons, against 52¼ tons in the original. So rapidly was the work of rebuilding done at Ashford that No. 179 took the road in April, 1919. She was an immediate success, and ten other engines of the 'E' Class were sent to Beyer, Peacock for alteration on similar lines.

The 'E1' Class engines were splendid runners. At first there was a certain amount of trouble with steaming, while the men got used to the relatively long sloping firegrates. The natural vibration of the engine at speed tended to shake the fire down into a heap at the front, but with careful attention throughout the journey keeping a thick fire under the door, and tapering to a thin layer under the brick arch they steamed very freely, and were very fast and exceptionally powerful engines in relation to their nominal tractive effort. The well-designed cylinders and valves had a capacity for using large volumes of steam, so that these engines were capable of sustained outputs of 900 to 1,000 indicated horsepower at 60 m.p.h. – at least equal to the capacity of the 'N' Class 'Moguls' at this speed. Although details of their performance will be discussed more fully in the next chapter I cannot forebear to mention one run with engine No. 19, and a load of 294 tons tare when the average speed with a down boat train was 59 m.p.h. between Paddock Wood and Sandling

Junction, and speed at no time fell below 50 m.p.h. on the long rise to Westenhanger.

Mention of Westenhanger leads me to a story of boat train running, which although it carries us forward several years beyond the immediate post-war period is worth telling at this stage. One day in October, 1923, the engine of the 11 a.m. down Continental boat express broke a crank axle at Westenhanger. When the immediate 'flap' was over, and the engine had been towed back to Ashford Works, the Chief Mechanical Engineer's department were surprised to find that the engine was not one of the rebuilt 'E1's' but a Wainwright superheater 4-4-0 No. 275. Inquest on the failure proceeded as usual, but Ashford were as curious to know what No. 275 was doing on that train at all. At the time the design of the 'E1's' was prepared this engine and her sister 4-4-0 No. 36 were banned over the Chatham line between Orpington loop and Victoria. Enquiries brought the news that following upon certain bridge strengthenings the maximum axle-load limit had been raised. Apparently the Locomotive Running Superintendent had been told, but the C.M.E. had not!

Oddly enough the relaxation must have taken place at least *two years before* the mishap to engine No. 275 at Westenhanger. In the late summer of 1921 the fine new corridor stock was introduced on to the principal boat express trains, and a photograph of one of them about to leave Victoria was published in *The Railway Magazine* for November, 1921. And heading that train, for all the world to see, was the Wainwright superheater 4-4-0 No. 275. Evidently no one in the C.M.E's department at Ashford spotted it! As a result of the enquiries made following the Westenhanger incident of 1923, Maunsell was permitted to increase the adhesion weight of the 'E1' engines. This was done very simply by reinstating the old cast iron drag boxes of the 'E' Class, which had fortunately not been scrapped. This increased the weight on the rear pair of coupled wheels by about one ton. This change did not take place until after Grouping.

The corridor stock introduced on the boat trains in the autumn of 1921 represented something quite new in S.E.C.R. carriage design. For the first time ordinary passengers, other than those paying Pullman supplements were provided with something other than non-corridor carriages. Even so, the new stock included only first and second class accommodation. There were four different types of vehicle: first, second, first brake, and second brake, so that the full boat train still contained a mixture of vehicles, including Pullman cars, and the picturesque third brakes, with the 'bird-cage' roof over the guard's compartment. In passing I should add that the standard 'Pullman' colours were not used for the cars running on the S.E.C.R.; they were painted in the crimson lake of the ordinary carriage stock. The new corridor coaches were 64 ft long over the gangway connections, and had a tare weight varying, as between the different types, from $30\frac{1}{2}$ to $31\frac{3}{4}$ tons.

In many respects the design was a most distinctive one. All the four varieties were fitted with end vestibule doors only, and having regard to the working in conjunction with Pullman cars they were all fitted with Pullman type gangway connections, and Buckeye automatic couplings. Adjustable side buffers were also fitted for working in conjunction with ordinary stock. Internally the coaches, first class and second alike, were handsomely finished, the 'firsts' with green upholstery and the 'seconds' in red. Every compartment was fitted with removable tables, so that meals could be served from the Pullman cars to any compartment in the corridor part of the train. Outwardly, in their plain, almost streamlined bodies, without any panelling, and their absence of doors except at the ends, they represented quite a departure, not only for the S.E.C.R. itself, but for British railways in general. Only the London & North Western, in its American boat train stock, and on the famous afternoon 'West Coast Corridor' train had made any appreciable use of end door carriages. So far as I know, the new S.E.C.R. stock was the only type of carriage to carry the coat-of-arms of the Managing Committee.

Even before the war had ended the S.E.C.R. was giving urgent consideration to the suburban traffic problem. During the war Cannon Street station had been extensively used for goods traffic, and between 5th August, 1914, and 31st December, 1918, a total of 5,803 goods trains, conveying 175,000 wagons, had been dealt with. One thing was certain: the old practice of using Cannon Street as an intermediate station between Charing Cross and London Bridge was as good as dead, and the post-war services were planned on the basis of trains using either Charing Cross or Cannon Street as the terminal point. So far as the S.E.C.R. was concerned electrification of the suburban lines was no vague idea of the future, and in March, 1918, an interesting and significant appointment was made, of A. Raworth, as Electrical Engineer.

At that time the S.E.C.R. was the only remaining line south of the Thames not to have commenced electrification of the suburban lines, though until the outbreak of war all the activities of the Managing Committee were dictated by considerations of financial stringency remaining from the days before the fusion of the two companies. Mr Raworth came to the S.E.C.R. with a wide experience of electric railway traction both as a contractor, and later on the London & South Western Railway. Following war service in the R.N.A.S. he did not return to the South Western, but immediately took up the S.E.C.R. appointment. The war was not ended a month before the Managing Committee had sent him to the United States to study and report upon electrification developments there. He came so rapidly to the fore that following his evidence for the S.E.C.R. before the Government-appointed 'Electrification of Railways Advisory Committee,' he was appointed Chairman of the General Managers' Committee on Suburban Traffic Operation. Thus through the personality of Mr Raworth the S.E.C.R. was in the very forefront of this important matter of post-war development.

Recalling the low esteem in which all the Southern lines were held little more than twenty years earlier one can appreciate the tremendous drive and energy put into the management of the S.E.C.R. in particular during the intervening years, and the appointment of Raworth strengthened an already strong and well-integrated team of officers. Early in 1920 Sir Francis Dent retired from the General Managership, after holding the office for nine eventful years. He was succeeded by P. C. Tempest who combined with it his previous office of Chief Engineer. Tempest was one of the very few railway engineers who succeeded to the General Managership of their own railway. One can recall Sir James Inglis, of the Great Western, Mathieson, of the Caledonian, and a mechanical engineer in Sir John Aspinall of the Lancashire & Yorkshire; but none of these men retained their previous full responsibilities as an engineer. Naturally his chief assistant Mr George Ellson, a future Chief Engineer of the Southern Railway, began to come to the fore, and it was he who gave details of an important piece of reconstruction work at Cannon Street in the course of a paper to the Institution of Civil Engineers, in 1921.

Cannon Street was built in 1865–6, yet during the First World War the axle-loadings accepted were some three times as great as those prevailing when the structure was originally put into service. With electrification in prospect, and the need to provide for the use of still heavier steam locomotives the question of strengthening the bridge was investigated. This investigation was carried down to the very foundations, estimating the increased loads that would be imposed on the London Clay beneath the river on which the piers were founded. Fortunately the original foundation and main supports were exceedingly massive, and needed no attention; but the whole

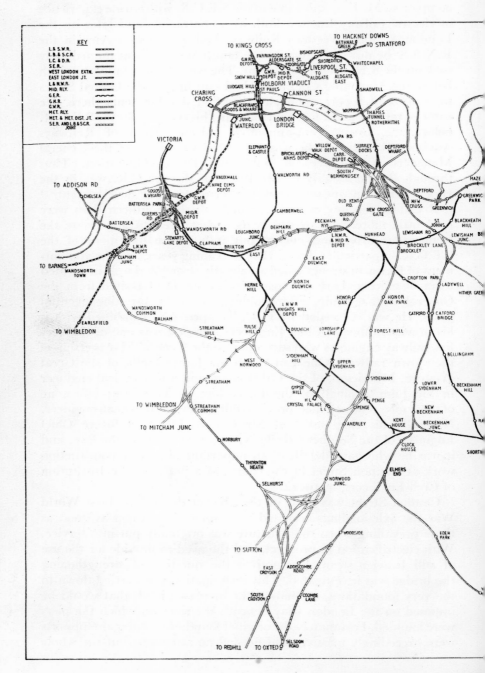

The suburban system of the S.E. &

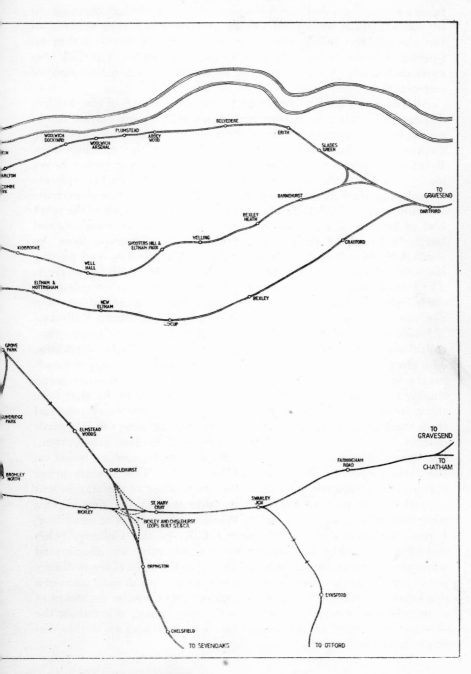

superstructure needed strengthening. With a bridge carrying so intense a traffic it was a matter of the greatest importance to avoid all but the slightest interference; but it was equally essential that no interference should be caused to river-borne traffic. The task was carried through by what can only be described as a masterpiece of organization.

All the work had to be done below the surface of the bridge. Temporary stagings were constructed in the river, and certain tracks on the bridge closed to traffic for short periods while additional main girders were threaded into position between the existing ones. Reinforcing plates were added to the main girders carrying heavy loads, and this work was done overnight after traffic had completely ceased. The time available was all too short, however, and extreme difficulties arose from the restricted space in which much of the work had to be carried out. The new main girders, six in number, and having a length of 443 ft, were 'launched' into position from the south side, threading them between the existing girders, and passing them over rollers placed on the temporary stagings built in the river. The completion of the work paved the way for the complete re-modelling of the track lay out on the bridge, which was carried out when electrification was eventually undertaken by the Southern Railway.

While the strengthening of Cannon Street bridge was in progress, consideration was being given to improvements at Charing Cross. The electric signalling at Victoria, with three-position upper quadrant semaphores, had proved so successful that a scheme using similar equipment was worked out for Charing Cross. By that time there would have been no need to import the necessary material from the U.S.A., and I have among my own drawing office records designs for the gantries that were prepared in December, 1920. These new structures were to straddle the tracks, and be based on the main girders of the Charing Cross bridge. This scheme never materialized, however, and when the resignalling of the station was carried out as part of the electrification project the new signals were four-indication colour lights. While on the subject of signalling, I must mention the use by the S.E.C.R. of the Coligny-Welch distinguishing lamp for distant signals, whereby an illuminated white chevron was displayed immediately to the right of the ordinary signal lamp. This was used at a time when the caution indication of a distant signal at night was red, and there was otherwise no means of distinguishing between a distant and a stop signal, other than the driver's knowledge of the road. The Brighton also used this distinguishing lamp.

In pre-war years the express train services to the Kent Coast resorts were very much the 'poor relations' of the Continental boat trains. I have already referred, in Chapter XI, to the designation 'fast train', applied to the best of the Folkestone, Dover and Ramsgate services, in contrast to the term 'express' for all the boat trains. So far as timings were concerned there was a great improvement after E. C. Cox became Superintendent of the Line, yet as soon after the war as the summer of 1921 the South Eastern & Chatham had at least one service that was faster than in the summer of 1914, namely that to Folkestone. In the latter year the fastest service from Charing Cross took 91 minutes for the run of 70 miles, whereas in 1921 an acceleration to 85 minutes took place. In that same summer also full pre-war speed was restored to Margate, 74 miles in 90 minutes, by the Sundays only 'Thanet Pullman Limited'. In the winter of 1921 Hastings also joined this favoured band of resorts. So far as speed was concerned there was actually a slight improvement, as the overall time of 90 minutes scheduled in 1921 was from Charing Cross whereas the pre-war time was from Cannon Street, $1\frac{1}{4}$ miles less in distance.

That the South Eastern & Chatham Railway was bent upon casting off for ever the old stigma of sloth and inefficiency was shown in the last summer of its independent existence, when the Folkestone expresses were accelerated to run non-stop between Charing Cross and Folkestone Central, in 80 minutes, and when among the fastest runs on the leading British railways the S.E.C.R. was sixth from the top. At the time of the Grouping, in January, 1923, it was the only railway in Great Britain to have any services from London to a provincial town that were faster than those of 1914. Recalling the tremendous burden of traffic carried during the war this was a most remarkable achievement, and of lasting credit to the team of officers so ably led by Sir Francis Dent. So far as the actual running of the trains was concerned the accelerated expresses to Folkestone and Hastings were mostly worked by the 'L' Class 4-4-0s, and except for the Pullman cars these were made up of old non-corridor stock. For the Margate expresses reliance had to be placed mainly upon the Wainwright non-superheater 4-4-0s, since the eleven rebuilt 4-4-0s of Class 'E1', all stationed at Stewarts Lane, were fully occupied on the boat trains.

The question of more locomotives for the Kent Coast trains over the Chatham line came to the fore with the reintroduction of pre-war speed. The 'Thanet Pullman' was a relatively light train, and on Sundays an 'E1' could usually be spared for the job; but the 3.15

p.m. ex-Victoria, allowed 92 minutes to Margate was a different proposition, and details of a number of runs suggest that while the Wainwright engines had plenty of power to do the job there was difficulty in making the water supply last out. Accordingly authority was given for ten more engines to be rebuilt with superheaters. The actual locomotives taken for conversion this time were from the 'D' Class. There were actually thirteen non-superheater 'E' Class 4-4-0 remaining, but these were all in excellent condition, and at Ashford it was felt that the capacity of the express stud as a whole would be best improved by converting ten 'Ds' into 'D1's' rather than taking a similar number of 'E's'. As with the 'E1' rebuildings, the work was done by Beyer, Peacock in 1921, but although the tractive effort of the new 'D1's' was slightly less than that of the 'E1s' because of the larger wheel diameter of 6 ft 8 in., against 6 ft 6 in. there was little to choose between the performance of the two classes. The 'D1' Class quite apart from their numbers, could readily be distinguished from the 'E1' Class by the absence of top feed apparatus on the dome.

The final locomotive development on the S.E.C.R., the three-cylinder 2-6-0 No. 822, was completed at Ashford in December, 1922, but was actually the sequel to a chain of events extending back to 1918. In that year the first Gresley three-cylinder locomotive, the 2-8-0 No. 461 was completed at Doncaster; it aroused much interest, and not a small amount of criticism on account of the rather complicated conjugated valve gear, to enable three sets of valves to be actuated by only two sets of gear. H. Holcroft was one of the critics, and in correspondence in the technical press of the time he described a form of conjugated gear he had invented while in the drawing office at Swindon, and which had been patented on the instruction of Churchward. As a result of this correspondence, and a subsequent paper read before the Institution of Locomotive Engineers, Gresley took the unusual step of consulting Holcroft on the design of the valve gear for a new three-cylinder locomotive he was working on. At that time Holcroft was away from Ashford, in charge of a Railway Executive Committee Depot at Purfleet, and it was largely on the strength of his suggestions that the simplified form of the 2 : 1 conjugated motion was applied to the Great Northern 2-6-0 locomotive No. 1000, and subsequently to the whole range of Gresley Pacifics.

Long before any of these famous engines had appeared Holcroft was recalled from Purfleet, and given the task of designing the valve gear for a three-cylinder version of the 'N' Class 2-6-0; this engine was eventually interposed in the regular series of two-cylinder 2-6-0s under construction at Ashford in 1922. The Great Northern three-cylinder 'Mogul' No. 1000 was completed at Doncaster in 1920, and when the S.E.C.R. engine No. 822 appeared roughly eighteen months later its construction was attributed to the success of the Gresley design. Actually it was the invention of a S.E.C.R. man, and his suggestions, that paved the way for the Great Northern No. 1000, though circumstances did not permit using the idea at Ashford until some time after the Great Northern engine had appeared. No. 822 was an excellent job. She differed from the Doncaster design in that the valve chests were set inwards, thus providing clearance for the links to the conjugated gear which were attached to the rear end of the outside cylinder valve rockers. By so doing, instead of attaching to the front as in the Gresley design, the factor of expansion of the valve spindles was eliminated. No. 822 was the forerunner of several classes of three-cylinder locomotives on the Southern Railway, though the principle of the conjugated valve gear was not used on the most famous of them all, the 'Schools' Class 4-4-0s, and on the later 2-6-0s of Class 'U1'.

Notwithstanding the preparation of plans for the electrification of the suburban lines the S.E.C.R. was faced with an urgent demand for increased 'rush-hour' services into and out of Cannon Street and Charing Cross. The old practice of having trains serving both termini had been abandoned for some years, but the great majority of suburban trains called at London Bridge, and that station was used as an exchange point for passengers wishing to interchange between Cannon Street and Charing Cross trains. At the beginning of 1922 there were 36 up trains booked to pass through London Bridge between 9 a.m. and 10 a.m., a remarkable achievement in itself with steam haulage and mechanical signalling, but not nearly enough to satisfy the needs of an ever-increasing traffic. Improvement was effected by a scientific re-study of track and signalling facilities, and a complete replanning of timetables to make the utmost use of the layout and equipment available.

One of the great troubles of a system like that existing between London Bridge, Charing Cross and Cannon Street lies in the delays that can occur at the conflicting junctions. In designing a new series of timetable paths arrangements were made for parallel moves to take place simultaneously. For example, at Borough Market Junction the time to bring trains out of Cannon Street on the two down lines was when there was other traffic coming in, and a case that can be quoted is that of the 8.22 a.m. from Beckenham which was booked to pass Borough Market Junction at exactly the same time as the 8.48 a.m. empty stock Cannon Street to Bromley (North), and the 8.48 a.m. Cannon Street to Erith were travelling parallel to each other over the junction on the two down roads. In addition, there was the 6.55 a.m. Hastings–Cannon Street express passing at the same time. At that moment the junction was being used to its utmost capacity with no question of conflicting movements.

The whole London suburban service on the old South Eastern lines was re-planned to include parallel moves over junctions wherever possible. Prior to this re-arrangement the service was being worked practically to its limit, with the result that unpunctuality, once started, grows snowball fashion and cannot be recovered until the service has thinned out. This is most unsatisfactory for the daily business travellers. With the parallel system there was a handsome margin in reserve. The 'parallels' at Borough Market Junction were designed so that it was possible to despatch six trains every four minutes from London Bridge: three up, and three down. In the up direction two Cannon Street trains leave simultaneously, followed two minutes later by one for Charing Cross. The two for Cannon Street were paralleled by two coming out at Borough Market Junction. This timetabling provided for a maximum of 30 trains an hour into Cannon Street, and 15 into Charing Cross, but in the service as first introduced only 25 of the thirty possible 'paths' into Cannon Street were actually used.

Strict punctuality was the keynote of success of this system, and those who had wept either in sorrow or in anger over the muddles or ineptitude of the old S.E.R. would have rubbed their eyes in wonder had they been able to stand for an hour in Borough Market Junction box in that last year of the S.E.C.R., and seen the suburban trains coming through 'as punctual as chronometers', or to see the way Cannon Street, Charing Cross and London Bridge handled the evening rush-hour traffic, all with steam, and all with semaphore signals. The whole service, including light engines and empty stock movements, was planned to the last detail. Standing places for light engines were specified, also the exact columns where they had to take water. Trains were made up to the maximum length possible in the terminal platforms. Express engines working tender first were used to take empty stock of long-distance residential trains out to the stabling grounds, and every endeavour was made to keep to the minimum the number of engines standing idle outside Charing Cross and Cannon Street, and so to plan platform working as to minimize light engine and shunting movements.

The traffic department of the S.E.C.R. did not attempt too much at once in this timetable reorganization, and it was applied only to the morning rush-hour. When it had been well-tried and the staff were accustomed to it the evening rush-hour service was tackled. From 5.15 p.m., until 6.57 p.m. there was an arrival every two minutes at London Bridge, while between 5.23 p.m. and 6.31 p.m. fifteen of the arrivals from Cannon Street were 'parallels'. There were thus 50 down trains through London Bridge in 68 minutes – 33 from Cannon Street, and 17 from Charing Cross. To say this was a masterpiece of traffic organization is an understatement. One can only echo the words of a leading railway journal, which in describing the system said that the South Eastern & Chatham had, in it, advanced very materially the science of railroading.

XIV

Locomotive Performance : 1900-22

THERE is no doubt that in the field of express train running the achievements of the Managing Committee for many years fell far short of expectations. Despite its shaky financial history, despite the stigma attached to its local rolling stock and train services, the Chatham probably put up the highest express train speeds run regularly south of the Thames, at any rate until the turn of the century. With the influence of Longhedge in locomotive design prevailing over that of Ashford there were many, no doubt, who hoped to see the Chatham hustling the South Eastern into better things, and the production of the 'D' Class 4-4-0s raised the highest expectations. The management took a more prudent course, preferring to concentrate upon all-round punctuality rather than a programme of spectacular main line acceleration. The travelling public was grateful enough of the great improvement in punctuality, and so far as Continental journeys were concerned the comfort and smoothness of travel on the S.E.C.R. blinded the majority of English travellers to the shortcomings in pure speed.

On the Northern Railway of France the Du Bousquet–De Glehn era was blossoming into its full maturity. Magnificent locomotive work was being done daily by four-cylinder compound locomotives of both the 4-4-0 and the 4-4-2 type, and experienced observers of locomotive performance, such as Charles Rous-Marten, were quick enough to point out the disparity between the work done on the English and the French side of the Channel. In the early months of 1901 *The Railway Magazine* published two cartoons by H. W. Hartnell. The first was entitled 'Railway Speed', and showed Father Time admonishing Britannia thus: 'Madam, how is it that your two friends have outpaced you? I hope to see you at the head of the list again, for I well know what you can do.' In the background, behind a pensive and somewhat crestfallen Britannia were France and America. The second cartoon was entitled 'What does "ONWARD" mean?' In this Father Time was shown in his workroom, and on the bench were models of a Nord Compound 4-4-2 and an L.C.D.R. 'M3' 4-4-0. An exasperated Father Time was exclaiming:

'Why you can't – or won't – go, when the Frenchman gives you a lead, I'm sure I don't know!' Underneath *The Railway Magazine* commented editorially: 'Wait till Mr Wainwright's new engines are allowed to show their powers.'

Rous-Marten's earliest recordings with the new engines showed consistently good work, though he has left us with little in the way of detailed logs. On the 9 a.m. down Continental Mail engine No. 730 had a load of nine postal vans and six bogie coaches, about 220 tons behind the tender, and ran the 75½ miles from Cannon Street to the steamer berth on the Admiralty Pier in 96½ minutes despite 6½ minutes lost by adverse signals on the London side of Chislehurst. From there the remaining 66 miles to the pier were covered in 76½ minutes without anywhere exceeding a maximum speed of 66 m.p.h. An abbreviated log of the return journey, on the first portion of the 5.15 p.m. up boat train is given in Table I herewith, and was remarkable in that not a single check of any kind was experienced.

TABLE I

5.15 p.m. DOVER–VICTORIA

Engine: Class 'D' 4-4-0 No. 730
Load: Eight 8-wheel and two 6-wheel, 210 tons

Dist. Miles		Actual m. s.	Av. speed m.p.h.
0·0	DOVER	0 00	—
3·3	Kearsney	6 07	32·4
6·8	Shepherdswell	12 36	32·4
16·6	CANTERBURY	22 40	58·3
27·4	Faversham	33 38	59·0
33·7	Sittingbourne	39 43	62·1
44·1	CHATHAM	50 21	58·6
51·6	Sole Street	64 07	32·8
60·8	Swanley	74 00	55·8
67·6	Bromley	81 12	56·6
74·5	Herne Hill	88 45	54·8
78·4	VICTORIA	95 05	

On this trip the work as far as Sole Street was certainly excellent. Nothing exceptionally vigorous was attempted at the start, up the long ascent at 1 in 132 to Lydden Tunnel, but to average all but 60 m.p.h. between Canterbury and Faversham must have involved a very fast climb of the 4½-mile bank at 1 in 132 from Canterbury to Ensden Tunnel, and a fast run down through Faversham. The average speed of 32·8 m.p.h. from Chatham up Sole Street bank, with its five miles of almost continuous 1 in 100 following the severe reduction of speed round the Rochester curves, was also quite good. Such restrictions were apt to be interpreted rather more liberally in the old days than is essential with the heavy locomotives of today, and it is probable that the train went over Rochester Bridge Junction at nearer 40 m.p.h. than 30. Being an advance section of the main train no stop was made at Herne Hill, where portions for the City were usually detached from Chatham line trains.

On a later trip with the same train Rous-Marten had engine No. 737, the member of that beautiful class that has now been restored to her original condition, and is housed in the B.T.C. Museum at Triangle Place, Clapham. The load was 220 tons, but unfortunately Rous-Marten gives only the sketchiest of detail. The minimum speeds were 34½ m.p.h. climbing to Shepherdswell and 30 m.p.h. on Sole Street bank, while a maximum of 82 m.p.h. was attained downhill. Rous-Marten does not say where the latter feat took place, but from general standards of running on the Chatham line I would guess it was on the descent from Ensden Tunnel to Faversham. In any case No. 737, on this fine run, was running a good four minutes ahead of the times of No. 730, as shown in Table I, by the time the outer suburbs of London were reached, and she entered Penge Tunnel, 72 miles from the start in 81 minutes. An arrival at Herne Hill in 85 minutes was then easily possible, but unfortunately the train was stopped at Sydenham Hill, for 6¼ minutes. The net time of 85 minutes showed an excellent average of 52·6 m.p.h. from start to stop.

Boat trains apart, the so-called 'Folkestone Special Express', leaving Cannon Street at 4.36 p.m. provides an interesting example of the early work of the 'D' Class locomotives, and another of Rous-Marten's recordings is shown in Table II. Speed did not fall below 30 m.p.h. up the 1 in 120 past Grove Park to Elmstead Tunnel, and the downhill running from Knockholt was checked by the relaying slack near Sevenoaks. But seeing that the train was then running late the work from Tonbridge onwards was not energetic, and it was not until the Canterbury portion had been slipped at Ashford that any determination was shown to get in on time. The driver may have been a little apprehensive of his water supply holding out, and therefore may not have been 'pushing' the engine unduly from Tonbridge.

Table III provides an interesting comparison between the work of the last Stirling class of 4-4-0 and the Wainwright Class 'D' on the up Folkestone Pullman car train, again non-stop from Folkestone Central to Cannon Street, in 90 minutes start to stop. The Stirling engine did work as good, if not slightly better than the Wainwright on the uphill sections. It was particularly notable to see the recovery of speed inside Sevenoaks Tunnel. It is true that the gradient eases considerably through the tunnel itself, to 1 in 144, as compared with the long grind at 1 in 122 from a mile out of Tonbridge. Usually, the easing in the gradient is neutralized by the tendency of locomotives to slip on the chronically wet rails inside the tunnel, and the driver of No. 453 was evidently doing well on this occasion. On the other hand the Wainwright engine made by far the faster running between Ashford and Tonbridge, and her average of 66·6 m.p.h. from Pluckley to Paddock Wood included a maximum speed of 74 m.p.h. at Headcorn, against the average of 63·5 and the maximum of 70 m.p.h. by the Stirling engine. The permanent way slacks were worth about 4 minutes total on each run, so that the net times of 76 and 74¼ minutes to passing New Cross represented very good work for this period on the S.E.C.R.

If the schedules themselves were not accelerated, certainly the work of the locomotives became progressively harder. In the years 1901–6 the loads of the Continental boat expresses lay in the range of 200 to 250 tons, but in the last years before the outbreak of World War I it was not unusual for the more popular trains to load up to 300 and even 350 tons on the same schedules, and with the same engines as in earlier days. The work set before the Wainwright non-superheater 4-4-0s of Classes 'D' and 'E' in the years 1911, 1912 and 1913 was little below that of the widely-praised 'Precursors' of the L.N.W.R., and of the Great Eastern 'Claud Hamilton' Class 4-4-0s. Unfortunately the very nature of the Continental services, with the frequent necessity of relief portions and the fitting in of conditional 'paths' when the arrival of the steamers at Folkestone or Dover was behind time rendered the boat trains liable to delay en route, so that the locomotives did not get the same opportunity for consistently showing off their capabilities as did their contemporaries on the closely-regulated services of the L.N.W.R. and of the Great Eastern.

In Table IV I have set out details of three journeys up from Folkestone, on all of which very fine work was done by 'E' Class 4-4-0 locomotives. These runs were clocked by Mr Cecil J. Allen. The 9.05 p.m. up from Folkestone Harbour was in some respects the most important train of the day, and with a load of 325 tons behind the tender No. 176 certainly began well. Although this crack express was running on time, traffic regulation in the Tonbridge area was adrift on this occasion, and signal delays costing a full 10 minutes were experienced. Taking the second and third runs to this point

before proceeding further with the first, engine No. 179 started rather
slowly up from Westenhanger with her 350-ton train, and speed
did not exceed 65 m.p.h. at Headcorn; but on this trip a clear road
was obtained until after London Bridge had been passed. The third
run gave promise of being the best of all. This was made on the up
Ostend boat express leaving the Admiralty Pier at 7.55 p.m.; on
this service passenger stops were made at Dover Town and Folkestone Central, and the log tabulated begins at the latter point. The
start was much more vigorous, with speed rising to 44 m.p.h. up the
1 in 266 to Westenhanger, and touching 68 m.p.h. at Ashford; then
came a whole succession of checks, so that the 26·6 miles from
Ashford to Tonbridge took 34 minutes 25 seconds.

From Tonbridge all three engines got a clear run up to Knockholt,
and the hill-climbing was very similar on each run. On the 9.05 p.m.
engine No. 176 was handicapped at the start from the very slow
speed at which Tonbridge station was passed, and although accelerat-
ing to 28 m.p.h. on the 1 in 122 gradient, there was some falling off
inside Sevenoaks Tunnel, Engine No. 179 did well with her 350-ton
train, while on the Ostend train the acceleration during the passage
of the tunnel confirmed the impression that there was a most expert
hand at the regulator, on this trip. The rapid recoveries in speed on
the brief favourable stretch from Sevenoaks to Dunton Green will
be noted, and the minimum speeds at Knockholt were all excellent
with such relatively heavy loads. Collectively these three runs form a
fine tribute to the capacity of the Wainwright Class 'E' engines. I am
only sorry that I have no record of the superheater engines 36 and
275; the only reference to the latter exists in details of a run on the
relief portion of the 9 a.m. down Continental Mail, which was so
delayed by checks from the first portion as to be of little interest.

After the war the day of the Wainwrights, as first-line express
passenger engines was over, but until the stud of Maunsell superheater rebuilds was increased by the addition of the 'D1's' to the
eleven 'E1's', the non-superheater engines, and particularly the
'E' Class were called upon for work on some of the boat trains,
and an excellent example of their post-war work is detailed in Table
V. Quite apart from the locomotive work the merest glance at the
log reveals the vastly better traffic regulation, that became typical of
the S.E.C.R., and of the Southern, under the superintendency of
E. C. Cox. Apart from that welcome feature the running was very
similar to that shown in the pre-war runs in Table IV. The schedule
was no doubt a relatively easy one; but it provided for slow running
through the Folkestone Warren over the site of the great landslip

of 1915. Even the crack 11 a.m. down was at first allowed 103 minutes from Victoria to Dover Marine, though this was sub-sequently quickened to 100 minutes when the new alignment through the Warren had consolidated, and no further signs of trouble were apparent.

Although so clever a rebuild and so potentially excellent an engine, the 'E1' Class was not at first an unqualified success. They demanded considerably more skill in both driving and firing than the Wainwrights. I have already referred to the technique needed in firing. On the driver's side of the footplate they needed a light rein, for two reasons: the large steam ports admitted such a 'gulp' of steam at each stroke that any attempt to work with a wide open regulator, and long cut-off would run them out of steam in no time, and secondly they were prone to slipping. This latter trait was not altogether surprising seeing that they had 1½ tons *less* adhesion weight than the non-superheater 'E' Class. The increased weight at the leading end was compensated for by the reduction on the rear pair of coupled wheels. They were rostered to work trains of up to 300 tons tare without assistance on the fastest boat trains timings, and generally speaking there was not much margin in reserve.

I have details of 36 runs on the 11 a.m. down from Victoria, in which every one of the ten Beyer-Peacock rebuilds is concerned; the loads varied between 288 and 301 tons tare, and the general im-pression one gains is that while some particularly expert crews could get brilliant work out of the engines, in the majority of instances there was not more than two or three minutes in hand on the 100-minutes timing. The slack through Tonbridge was then down to 20 m.p.h., and from this the 41·4 miles to Folkestone Junction had to be run in 46 minutes. On one occasion this was cut to 41¾ minutes with an average speed of 59 m.p.h. over the generally rising length from Paddock Wood to Sandling Junction. This was with engine No. 19, and a load of 294 tons tare. Mr Holcroft, who was on the footplate, calculates that the engine was developing 950 indicated horsepower for 42 minutes on end, but from details he has given me of the actual working conditions it is clear that the engine was being run at the very limit of its capacity.

The cut-off was 30 per cent throughout, and the regulator partly open. Boiler pressure was maintained very steadily at 175 lb per sq in. from Tonbridge until nearing Ashford, but all the time the cylinders were very gradually beating the boiler, and water level was falling steadily. From a full glass at Tonbridge the level had fallen by 3 in. at Pluckley; but a brief closing of the regulator due to Ash-

ford West distant being sighted at caution, and a couple of minutes
with both injectors on, restored the water level. This procedure,
however, set the boiler pressure on the downward path, though after
Smeeth, with the end of the hard work in sight, the firing was being
eased. This was a classic example of the way a steam locomotive
can be run for an appreciable period beyond its maximum sustained
capacity, by a careful and systematic mortgaging of the boiler.
The speeds during this fine spell of running were 65 m.p.h. at
Paddock Wood; 69 at Staplehurst; a minimum of 57 at the top of
the long, gradual rise from Headcorn towards Ashford; 60 through
Ashford, and a final minimum of 50 m.p.h. at Westenhanger.

Table VI includes details of a run clocked by Mr Cecil J. Allen
on the same train, with No. 497, on which the performance east of
Tonbridge was little inferior to that of engine No. 19, just described.
In the early stages there was a bad signal check at Dulwich that
handicapped the ascent of the Sydenham Hill bank; but the timing
evidently provided for some recovery margin through the outer
suburbs, since the train was practically on time at Bickley Junction,
and some excellent climbing from Orpington made it nearly 2
minutes early at Knockholt. The sustained speed of $32\frac{1}{2}$ m.p.h. on
the 1 in 120 here was quite a notable effort. But so gently was the
descent to Tonbridge taken that a minute was lost here, though no
doubt preparations were in hand on the footplate for the fine effort
that was to be made on the fast-running section of the line. Although
the maximum speed did not exceed 66 m.p.h., against 69 by engine
No. 19, the minimum speed at Westenhanger was higher – 51
m.p.h. against 50 – and Sandling Junction was passed $2\frac{1}{2}$ minutes
early. There was a permanent way check through the Warren on
this occasion, but the train came into the Marine station dead on
time.

The combination of 300-ton loads, and the type of locomotive
auailable precluded any acceleration of the Continental expresses,
and so, for the first time in S.E.C.R. history the seaside expresses,
from 1921 onwards, began to steal the thunder of the boat trains.
In that summer the time of the best trains, non-stop between Charing
Cross and Folkestone Central, was quickened to 85 minutes, and in
the following year to the really excellent overall time of 80 minutes.
It was on these trains that the 'L' Class 4-4-0s came into the lime-
light. Although by the summer of 1921 these handsome engines had
put in eight years of hard work little was known of them by locomotive enthusiasts in general. During the war years those who might
have a spare afternoon in which to do a little 'stop-watching' were

not likely to choose the S.E.C.R. for their expeditions, and the locomotive authorities at Ashford were engulfed in wartime activities so quickly after the first arrival of the 'L' Class locomotives, that the usual testing and observation concerned with a new design went mostly by the board. To connoisseurs of locomotive performance the 'L' Class were an unknown quantity at the end of the war.

From talks I have had with Ashford men one rather gains the impression that they were 'nobody's baby'. They were ordered and built at a time when everything was in a state of flux. There was upheaval enough with a stranger like Maunsell being appointed to succeed Wainwright; but one can well imagine the sense of pique felt in the drawing office when the new design was not accepted as it stood. It would not have been so bad if Maunsell had altered it 'off his own bat' as it were, but to send it to Inchicore for criticism was a bitter pill for Ashford to swallow. Anyway, there were probably many on the S.E.C.R. who could not work up much enthusiasm about the new engines, and I have heard it said that they were not bad engines on a bank, but were hamstrung at the front-end, and lacked the freedom and speed not only of the new rebuilds, but of the old Wainwrights. This criticism arose no doubt from the change in the valve setting which was made at the suggestion of the drawing office. Whatever the Ashford drawing office may have thought, or whatever hard feelings they may have retained the Running Department were not likely to hold any such inhibitions, and when the Folkestone flyers were put on it was the 'L' Class engines that were used.

Looking through the various published records of the years 1920 to 1923 it is evident that the 'L' Class fairly stole the show so far as speed was concerned. Far from appearing hamstrung they claimed all the highest maximum speeds published in those years. It is true that the 80-minute Folkestone expresses were not normally as heavy as the boat trains. It was not until after Grouping that any new passenger stock was available for the ordinary trains, and except for the Pullman cars the accelerated services were worked entirely with old S.E.C.R. non-corridor carriages. The Flushing and Ostend boat trains had much the same timings between Orpington and Folkestone, but these trains were limited to a maximum unpiloted load of 175 tons tare with the Maunsell rebuilt engines. On the 80-minute Folkestone trains the 'L' Class 4-4-0s took trains of over 300 tons tare at holiday times, though timekeeping could not be relied upon in such conditions. A tare load of about 250 tons seemed about the practical maximum. With loads of about 200 tons tare the 'L' Class engines fairly romped away with it, as the run detailed in Table VII clearly shows. On another trip with the same engine, despite the reputedly sluggish characteristics of the class, the 21 miles from Smeeth to Marden were covered at an average speed of 67·3 m.p.h. with a sustained speed of 72 m.p.h. on the level at Staplehurst.

The 'L' Class engines also did excellent work on the heavily-graded Hastings line, and Table VIII shows the running of No. 765 on the 3.40 p.m. down, non-stop from Charing Cross to Crowhurst. There was a bad check right at the start, causing a loss of nearly 3 minutes to New Cross; but after that the performance to Tonbridge was fully up to the 80-minute Folkestone standard. Following the double slack at Tonbridge, for the Hastings trains have the second sharply curved junction to negotiate, No. 765 did splendidly up the 1 in 95–100 to Tunbridge Wells, not falling below 33 m.p.h. The latter station was passed on time, and the gentlest of downhill running from Wadhurst was enough to take the train through Battle nearly 3 minutes early. The hill-climbing capacity of the same engines is well displayed on another run over this route in which No. 764 passed Wadhurst, 18·3 miles from the Crowhurst start, in 26 minutes having sustained 34 m.p.h. up the long 1 in 132–100 bank – 6½ miles of it – with a load of 310 tons.

In the post-war years reliance had to be placed mainly upon the Wainwright 'D' 4-4-os for express train running over the Chatham main line to the Thanet resorts, and with heavy weekend loads rising frequently to over 300 tons timekeeping was not always to be relied upon on trains like the 3.15 p.m. Margate non-stop from Victoria, allowed 92 minutes for the run of 73·9 miles. Even after the introduction of the 'D1' rebuilt 4-4-os things were often little better, and one reluctantly forms the impression that the schedule was too severe with the maximum loads permitted to the 'D' and 'D1' Class locomotives unpiloted. Two of the best runs on record with this train were made after the Grouping, both, significantly with the same engine, No. 502, and a very competent driver. On neither journey was strict overall time kept. The actual times were 92½ minutes with 259 tons tare, and 94¼ minutes with 291 tons tare; but both journeys included some slight checks, and the net time was about 2 minutes inside the actual in each case.

On of the most interesting runs that any recorder was fortunate enough to clock on the Chatham line came to Mr Cecil J. Allen in 1923 when travelling on the 5.20 p.m. up express from Margate to Victoria. The trip began well, with a 'D1' 4-4-o obviously in good form. But after Faversham something went amiss, and after giving the 'two crows', for assistance, as Sittingbourne was passed, the train stopped at Newington, the driver having spotted a 'C' Class 0-6-0 goods in the siding there, headed towards London. There was no question of telephoning Control and waiting instructions. The men on the spot took things into their own hands. In the remarkably short time of 6¾ minutes the trains had exchanged engines, and the 5.20 p.m. ex-Margate was away again hauled by engine No. 581. The driver then achieved the remarkable feat of keeping, to within 10 seconds, the sectional times of this express, as between Chatham and Victoria. It was not as though the 'C' Class are very large or powerful 0-6-0s. The grate area is only 17 sq ft, the boiler pressure 160 lb per sq in. and the cylinders 18½ by 26 in. Yet Driver Ovenden coaxed out of this relatively small engine an effort as good as many contemporary runs with 4-4-0 express locomotives.

The log is detailed in Table IX. Time was lost in climbing Sole Street bank, and it was not surprising that further time was lost on the fast running stretch between Sole Street station and Bickley Junction. Yet here the engine was taken along in remarkable style considering its size and the diameter of its coupled wheels, 5 ft 2 in. Speeds were attained of 64 m.p.h. at Farningham Road, 60 at St Mary Cray, and 57 between Bickley and Bromley. With skilful and resolute handling of the engine through the suburban area the small amount of lost time was regained, and Victoria was reached in 53 minutes 10 seconds from passing Chatham. As a result of this excellent locomotive work, and the promptitude with which the driver seized his opportunity to get a substitute engine the train was only 14 minutes late into Victoria. This indeed is a praiseworthy note on which to end this brief account of twentieth-century locomotive work on the South Eastern & Chatham Railway.

TABLE II

4.36 p.m. CANNON STREET– FOLKESTONE

Engine: Class 'D' 4-4-0 No. 734
Load: Eight 8-wheel, three 6-wheel, 250 tons*

Dist. Miles		Actual m. s.	Av. speed m.p.h.
0·0	CANNON STREET .	0 00	—
3·7	New Cross . .	6 45	—
6·0	Hither Green . .	10 06	41·2
7·8	Grove Park . .	13 10	35·2
		p.w.s.	
10·1	Chislehurst . .	17 56	29·0
12·6	Orpington . . .	22 10	35·4
14·1	Chelsfield . . .	24 48	34·1
15·4	Knockholt . .	26 45	40·0
19·4	Dunton Green . .	31 18	52·8
		p.w.s.	
20·9	SEVENOAKS . .	33 09	48·7
25·8	Hildenborough . .	38 07	59·2
28·3	TONBRIDGE (slack) .	40 39	59·2
33·6	Paddock Wood .	47 03	49·7
38·2	Marden . . .	51 57	56·3
40·7	Staplehurst . .	54 48	52·7
44·0	Headcorn . .	58 10	58·7
49·2	Pluckley . . .	63 58	53·8
54·9	ASHFORD . .	70 14	54·7
63·0	Westenhanger .	79 00	55·5
64·2	Sandling Junction .	80 30	48·1
68·0	Shorncliffe . .	83 58	65·7
68·7	FOLKESTONE . .	85 04	—

* Three vehicles slipped at Ashford
Net time about 83 minutes

TABLE III

8.30 a.m. FOLKESTONE–CANNON STREET

Run No. Engine No. Engine Class Load tons gross		I 453 4-4-0 'B' 200		I 745 4-4-0 'D' 200	
Dist. Miles		Actual m. s.	Av. speed m.p.h.	Actual m. s.	Av. speed m.p.h.
0·0	FOLKESTONE . .	0 00	—	0 00	—
5·7	Westenhanger . .	9 17	—	9 20	—
		p.w.s.		p.w.s.	
13·8	ASHFORD . .	18 24	—	18 44	—
19·5	Pluckley . .	24 12	59·0	24 26	60·0
24·7	Headcorn . .	29 09	63·1	29 08	66·4
28·0	Staplehurst . .	32 09	66·0	31 58	69·9
30·5	Marden . .	34 35	60·8	34 22	62·5
35·1	Paddock Wood .	38 58	62·9	38 30	66·7
40·4	TONBRIDGE .	44 40	55·7	44 00	57·8
42·9	Hildenborough .	48 40	37·5	48 03	37·1
45·2	*Sevenoaks Tunnel* IN .	53 14	30·3	52 24	31·7
47·2	*Sevenoaks Tunnel* OUT .	56 45	34·0	56 14	31·4
47·8	SEVENOAKS .	57 39	—	57 03	—
49·3	Dunton Green .	59 32	47·8	58 53	49·1
53·3	Knockholt . .	64 58	44·2	64 24	43·6
		p.w.s.		p.w.s.	
56·1	Orpington . .	68 03	54·4	67 31	54·0
		p.w.s.		p.w.s.	
58·6	Chislehurst . .	71 30	43·5	70 58	43·5
60·9	Grove Park . .	74 44	42·5	73 49	48·4
62·7	Hither Green . .	76 41	55·4	75 45	55·8
65·0	New Cross . .	79 57	42·3	79 20	38·5
		sigs.			
68·7	CANNON STREET .	86 24	—	84 11*	

'B'—Stirling design   'D'—Wainwright design
* Stop at Cannon Street home signals, ¼ mile short of the station

TABLE IV

UP CONTINENTAL BOAT EXPRESSES

Run No. Train Engine 'E' class 4-4-0 Load tons gross	1 9.5 p.m. Folkestone Har. 176 325			2 1.40 p.m. Folkestone Har. 179 350			3 7.55 p.m. Dover Pier 179 320		
Dist. Miles	m.	s.	m.p.h.*	m.	s.	m.p.h.*	m.	s.	m.p.h.*
0·0 Folkestone Junc. Sdgs.†	0	00		0	00				
1·2 FOLKESTONE CEN.	—			3	45		0	00	
6·9 Westenhanger	12	35	41	13	35	37	10	00	44
15·0 ASHFORD	20	50	66½	22	05	—	17	55	68
25·9 Headcorn	—		70	—		65	38	40	—
31·7 Marden	36	50	—	—		—			sigs.
36·3 Paddock Wood	sig. stop			43	25	—			sigs.
41·6 TONBRIDGE	55	10	—	49	25	—	52	20	—
— Hildenborough	—		25½	—		27	—		28
— Tunnel IN	—		28	—		26½	—		30
— Tunnel OUT	—		26½	—		—	—		—
49·0 SEVENOAKS	72	45	—	64	40	54	—		55
— Dunton Green	—		58½	—		32	—		33
54·5 Knockholt	80	05	35	72	25	68	74	30	—
— Hither Green	—		71½	—		—			sigs.
66·2 New Cross	91	20	—	84	35	—			sigs.
69·2 LONDON BRIDGE	—		—	88	45	—	96	45	
71·1 CHARING CROSS	99	05	—	96	15	—			
Net time	89			91½			84		

* Max. and min. speeds by stop watch
† Sidings: 0·2 miles nearer Dover than Junction Station

TABLE V
DOVER MARINE–VICTORIA
Load: 300 tons tare 315 tons full
Engine: Wainwright 'E' class 4-4-0 No. 315

Dist. Miles		Sch. min.	Actual m. s.	Av. speeds m.p.h.
0·0	DOVER MARINE . . .	0	0 00	—
6·0	Folkestone Junc. . . .	14	12 55	—
12·8	Westenhanger . . .		24 05	36·4
16·6	Smeeth . . .		28 20	53·6
20·8	ASHFORD . . .	33	32 35	59·3
26·5	Pluckley . . .		38 35	57·0
31·7	Headcorn . . .	44	43 30	63·5
35·0	Staplehurst . . .		46 35	64·2
37·5	Marden . . .		49 10	58·0
42·1	Paddock Wood . . .	54	54 05	56·3
47·4	TONBRIDGE . . .	62	60 20	50·8
49·9	Hildenborough . . .		65 00	32·2
54·8	SEVENOAKS . . .	76	75 55	26·9
56·3	Dunton Green . . .		77 50	47·0
60·3	Knockholt . . .	83	83 50	40·0
63·1	Orpington . . .	86	86 55	54·4
65·4	*Bickley Junc.* . . .	90	89 45	48·7
69·3	Beckenham . . .	95	95 05	44·0
			p.w.s.	
72·3	Sydenham Hill . . .		101 20	28·8
74·0	HERNE HILL . . .	103	103 55	39·4
76·7	Battersea Park Road . .		108 05	38·9
78·0	VICTORIA	110	110 30	

Net time 106½ minutes

TABLE VI
11 a.m. VICTORIA–DOVER MARINE
Load: 299 tons tare, 315 tons full
Engine: Rebuilt 'E1' class 4-4-0 No. 497

Dist. Miles		Sch. min.	Actual m. s.	Speeds† m.p.h.
0·0	VICTORIA . . .	0	0 00	—
4·0	Herne Hill . . .	8½	8 15	—
			sigs.	
5·7	Sydenham Hill . .		12 15	—
8·7	Beckenham Junction .	16½	17 20	—
12·6	*Bickley Junction* .	22½	22 45	—
14·9	Orpington . .	27½	26 20	—
17·7	Knockholt . .	31½	29 40	32½
21·7	Dunton Green . .		35 35	60
23·2	SEVENOAKS . .	38½	37 15	
30·6	TONBRIDGE . .	46½	45 40	20*
35·9	Paddock Wood . .	53	52 20	
46·3	Headcorn . .	63	62 25	66
56·2	ASHFORD . .	75	73 40	
66·5	Sandling Junction .	86½	84 05	51 (min.)
71·0	FOLKESTONE CEN. .		88 40	66
			p.w.s.	
78·0	DOVER MARINE . .	100	99 25	

† Max. and min. by stop watch   * Speed restriction
Net time 96 minutes

TABLE VII
4.5. p.m. CHARING CROSS–FOLKESTONE
Load: 200 tons tare, 220 tons full   Engine: 'L' class 4-4-0 No. 761

Dist. Miles		Sch. min.	Actual m. s.	Speeds* m.p.h.
0·0	CHARING CROSS . .	0	0 00	—
1·9	LONDON BRIDGE .	5	4 25	
4·9	New Cross . . .	9	8 25	—
7·2	Hither Green . .	12	11 15	45
11·3	Chislehurst . . .	18	17 20	37½
13·8	Orpington . . .	21	20 45	48
16·6	Knockholt . . .		24 20	41
20·6	Dunton Green. . .		28 30	69
22·1	SEVENOAKS . . .	31	29 55	53
27·0	Hildenborough . .		34 45	76½
29·5	TONBRIDGE . . .	38½	37 05	(slack)
34·8	Paddock Wood . .	44½	42 45	65
			p.w.s.	
39·4	Marden . . .		47 25	—
41·9	Staplehurst . . .		50 35	—
45·2	Headcorn . . .	54	53 45	65
50·4	Pluckley . . .		59 10	55
56·1	ASHFORD . . .	65	64 45	65
60·4	Smeeth . . .		69 20	—
64·2	Westenhanger . .		73 30	53
65·4	Sandling Junction .	75	74 55	—
69·2	Shorncliffe . . .		78 35	65
69·9	FOLKESTONE CEN. .	80	79 40	

* Max. and min. by stop watch   Net time 78 minutes

TABLE VIII
3.40 p.m. CHARING CROSS–CROWHURST
Load: 217 tons tare, 235 tons full   Engine: 'L' class 4-4-0 No. 765

Dist. Miles		Sch. min.	Actual m. s.	Speeds* m.p.h.
0·0	CHARING CROSS . .	0	0 00	—
			sigs.	
1·9	LONDON BRIDGE .	5	7 25	—
4·9	New Cross . . .	9	11 45	49
7·2	Hither Green . .	12	14 45	46
10·3	Elmstead Woods .		19 15	39
11·3	Chislehurst . . .	18½	20 35	—
13·8	Orpington . . .	22	24 00	49
16·6	Knockholt . . .	26	27 45	43
20·6	Dunton Green. . .		32 00	64½
22·1	SEVENOAKS . . .	32½	33 40	47
27·0	Hildenborough . .		38 40	70½
29·5	TONBRIDGE . . .	40½	41 25	(slack)
34·4	TUNBRIDGE WELLS .	49½	49 15	33
36·7	Frant . . .	53½	52 50	50/64
39·3	Wadhurst . . .		55 45	52½
43·8	Ticehurst Road .		60 20	63
47·4	Etchingham . .	66	64 00	64
49·6	Robertsbridge . .		66 10	64/45
55·6	Battle . . .	76	73 15	59
			sigs.	
57·6	CROWHURST . .	80	77 50	—

* Max. and min. by stop watch   Net time 74 minutes

TABLE IX

SOUTHERN (S.E. & C.) RAILWAY: NEWINGTON–VICTORIA

Load: 241 tons tare, 265 tons full
Engine: 'C' class 0-6-0 No. 581

Dist. Miles					Sch. min.	Actual m. s.		Speeds† m.p.h.
0·0	Newington	.	.	.	0	0	00	—
2·7	Rainham	.	.	.		5	50	—
5·7	Gillingham	.	.	.		10	00	47
7·3	CHATHAM	.	.	.	12	12	00	20*
7·9	Rochester	.	.	.		13	20	—
10·7	*Cuxton Road Box*	.	.		19	00	$34\frac{1}{2}$
14·7	Sole Street	.	.	.	27	27	45	$25\frac{1}{2}$
18·2	Fawkham	.	.	.		32	40	
21·1	Farningham Road	.	.		35	45	64
23·9	SWANLEY JUNC.	.	.	37	39	20	41
26·8	St. Mary Cray	.	.	.		42	40	60
29·0	*Bickley Junction*	.	.	44	45	30	$42\frac{1}{2}$ (min.)
29·6	Bickley	.	.	.		46	30	57
31·6	Shortlands	.	.	.		48	40	41
32·9	Beckenham	.	.	.	50	50	35	51
35·9	Sydenham Hill	.	.		54	45	$36\frac{1}{2}$
37·6	HERNE HILL	.	.	58	57	25	(slack) 30
						p.w.s.		
41·6	VICTORIA	.	.	.	65	65	10	

Max. and min. by stop watch
* Speed restriction

Epilogue

THE South Eastern & Chatham Railway entered the Grouping era with a fine record of achievement. In summing up the events of the twenty-three years of the Managing Committee, Cosmo Bonsor, who had been Chairman throughout this period, referred to the state of affairs prevailing in 1899:

'I do not think I am exaggerating when I say that when the South Eastern and the Chatham companies came together they were both singularly unpopular. Their services were bad. The complaints, both public and private, as to the unpunctuality of the trains were very numerous and I think I might almost add that they were a standing joke with the clown of the pantomime and with the comic gentlemen in the Music Halls.'

How things had changed in the intervening years I have endeavoured to show, and under Bonsor's leadership the S.E.C.R. had a fine team of officers, headed by Tempest, Cox, Maunsell, Raworth and A. D. Jones, the last four of whom were to play a very important part in Southern Railway affairs. At first there was no immediate change in organization and Tempest, like his brother General Managers on the Brighton and on the South Western continued to hold office. When the re-organization did come in the late summer of 1922 it is no exaggeration to say that S.E.C.R. men took most of the 'key' positions under the ex-L.S.W.R. General Manager, Sir Herbert Walker. Three men were appointed to 'chief officer' positions at once, in R. E. L. Maunsell, Chief Mechanical Engineer, E. C. Cox, Operating Superintendent, and A. D. Jones, Locomotive Running Superintendent. A. W. Szlumper, of the South Western, became Chief Engineer, but he retired in 1927, and an S.E.C.R. man, G. Ellson, took his place. Again Raworth was appointed to the 'key' position of Assistant to the General Manager for Electrification, and it was he who planned the electrification of the former S.E.C.R. suburban services.

In the Chief Mechanical Engineer's department S.E.C.R. men virtually swept the board. Maunsell set up his headquarters at Waterloo, where Clayton and Holcroft continued as his assistants. There a central design section was set up, and the leading draughtsman chosen for the job was W. G. Hooley, another Ashford man.

It was on his board that the preliminary design for such locomotives as the 'Lord Nelsons' and the 'Schools' was worked out. Pearson was appointed Assistant Chief Mechanical Engineer of the Southern Railway, and continued in charge at Ashford, so that practically all positions of importance in the new re-organization fell to members of Maunsell's team.

Naturally the men of the Brighton and the South Western were not so enthusiastic about the new organization, and not every feature of S.E.C.R. practice proved suitable for perpetuation in the changed conditions and vastly heavier traffic of the late 'twenties'. The decision to build additional engines of the 'K' Class 2-6-4 tank design would have been admirable had the track been suitable for carrying such heavy locomotives. The South Eastern, and the Brighton had used shingle ballast, laid on a foundation of ash, and the inadequacy of this in modern running conditions was unfortunately high-lighted by the disaster near Sevenoaks in August, 1927 when one of the new 2-6-4 tanks left the road, and part of the train smashed into the central pier of Shoreham Lane bridge.

Taken all in all, however, the South Eastern & Chatham contribution to the railways of Britain in the Grouping era was a massive one, far greater than anyone could have foreseen twenty years earlier. The complicated series of competitive lines in the Isle of Thanet was rationalized, by the closing of the old L.C.D.R. terminus at Ramsgate Harbour, by closing the South Eastern line to Margate, and providing a continuous run around Thanet from Margate (L.C.D.R.) through Ramsgate to fork at the Minster triangle, one line continuing to Sandwich and Dover, and the other following the old S.E.R. route to Canterbury. This layout was used later for the Saturdays only 'rounders' – trains going outward from Victoria, via Chatham, to Ramsgate, and continuing, without uncoupling engine from coaches to provide a return train to London via Dover and Folkestone.

The shades of J. S. Forbes must have chuckled when his route was the first to be electrified throughout to Dover, and some of the crack Continental expresses, including the 'Night Ferry', were transferred to it in consequence. From several recent runs in the cabs it has been borne home to me particularly what a fine road the Chatham is, whether tearing pellmell down the straight to Farningham Road, or in the hilly country east of Faversham where T. R. Crampton was so often at variance with the old Chatham Board. But it is above all in Dover and Folkestone that one's own memories, and the thoughts cf far earlier days well up almost to overflowing. In this country railways are often chided for their inefficiency and contentment with archaic methods, and the operation of the boat trains from Folkestone Harbour could be quoted as a classic example. But today, as one listens to the Great Western pannier tanks blasting their way up the steep gradients of the Harbour branch, and the laborious reversal of heavy trains takes place in Folkestone Junction sidings one thinks not of railway inefficiency but of the implacable attitude of the residents of Folkestone who persistently blocked each and every attempt of the South Eastern Railway to improve things.

At Dover, on the foreshore, only Shakespeare's Cliff Tunnel remains as a reminder of the old days, and to many travellers those tall Gothic-shaped, single-line bores must have been almost as symbolic of an English homecoming as the White Cliffs themselves. The Town and Harbour stations have vanished without trace, and only the tracks on the Admiralty Pier remain as a reminder of the time just before World War I when the boat trains ran right out on to the extension. Today the tenders of locomotives shedded and serviced at the fine depot on the shore are loaded with Kentish coal. It is the same at Ramsgate. Today also, interest in the great project that led to the discovery of the Kentish coalfield – the Channel Tunnel – is as great, and as full of controversy as it was in Sir Edward Watkin's day. There was controversy to be sure over any project with which Watkin was associated. He was one of those men who seem to generate enthusiasm and opposition in about equal quantities. One just wonders if the citizens of Folkestone might have been less intractable had the great scheme for the Harbour station been piloted by another hand!

Railways in the pre-Grouping era were no greater and no less than the men who owned them and ran them, and to those of us who delight in things historical the story would have been lost most of its charm if all lines had been ruled with the cold, ruthless efficiency of a Richard Moon, or all locomotive departments with the scientific precision of a Churchward, or the traffic regulation controlled by the master organization of a Paget. The South Eastern, and the Chatham had, between them, a goodly share of railway characters, and queer though their idiosyncrasies appear to us at times they certainly provided the foundation on which the able railwaymen of the twentieth century were to build an organization in which the old South Eastern Railway motto 'Onward' meant something more than a vague hope.

Index